ROY ORBISON

Sound Matters

a series edited by Michael Jarrett

ROY ORBISON

THE INVENTION OF

AN ALTERNATIVE

ROCK MASCULINITY

Peter Lehman

Temple University Press
PHILADELPHIA

Temple University Press, Philadelphia 19122
Copyright © 2003 by Temple University
All rights reserved
Published 2003
Printed in the United States of America

Library of Congress Cataloging-in-Publication Data

Lehman, Peter.
  Roy Orbison : the invention of an alternative rock masculinity /
Peter Lehman.
    p.   cm. — (Sound matters)
  Includes bibliographical references and index.
  ISBN 1-59213-036-4 (cloth : alk. paper) — ISBN 1-59213-037-2
(pbk. : alk. paper)
    1. Orbison, Roy—Criticism and interpretation.   2. Rock music—
United States—History and criticism.   I. Title.   II. Series.

ML420.O78 L44 2003
782.42166092–dc21   2002043555

2   4   6   8   9   7   5   3   1

For William Luhr

And music played in the Penny Arcade
Yes, it played and it played, played all the time

Contents

Acknowledgments

ince my love of Roy Orbison's music began in 1960, there is no way I can adequately acknowledge everyone who has contributed to my love and understanding of his music. Over the years so many good friends and family members have gone to Roy's concerts with me, Melanie Magisos, Bill Luhr, Susan Hunt, Russell Merritt, and Steve Lehman foremost among them. My daughter Eleanor, Melanie, Russell, Gary Keller, and Joe Sheehan have also accompanied me at various tribute concerts. Without sharing that music with these people and others, it would mean so much less to me. And the same goes for the recorded music. While Orbison fans frequently take particular delight in listening to his records alone in the dark (and I am no exception), I have also immensely enjoyed sharing them with others. This book is dedicated to William Luhr, my lifelong friend and coauthor. When we met in 1968, Roy's music held no special significance for Bill. Needless to say, that is no longer the case.

Mary Beth Haralovich, Bill Luhr, Hans Braendlin, Bonnie Braendlin, Hubert Niogret, and Joe Sheehan have brought relevant material to my attention during the writing of this book and I thank them for it. Marjorie Heins generously commented on a draft of Chapter 7. As I was completing the manuscript, Jean Lauer, a graduate student at Arizona State University, supplied valuable research assistance, and Justine Kleiback, my graduate research assistant, prepared the index and helped read the page proofs. Special thanks are due to Brandt Sleeper, my former student at the University of Arizona, who served as a music consultant for the Appendix. If ever a teacher learned from a student, I learned from Brandt. He is generous, articulate, well informed, and most of all clear—in every way an outstanding teacher. This book has benefited immensely from responses by Krin Gabbard and Mike Jarrett to the original proposal. Lest Krin's reputation be tarnished by association, let the record show that he has never for a moment reconsidered his low regard for Roy's music, all the while contributing from his wealth of knowledge of jazz. Mike Jarrett is quite simply the most knowledgeable person about music I have ever met. He has been an inspiration to me throughout, as well as a great reader of the finished manuscript. Special thanks go to David Lynch for taking time from a busy schedule to talk with me about Roy's music, and to Bob Jenkis, my former Ohio University student, for arranging that interview.

The fans also deserve special mention. Ab Roos of Holland has shared his astonishing knowledge and resources with me, going to a lot of trouble for an American friend he has never met. I thank him for his passion, knowledge, generosity, and shared resources; they have been truly invaluable. Over the years, Orbison lovers have benefited from fan club newsletters and web sites. I gained much more than knowledge of what Roy thought about cheeseburgers from these sources, including his tour schedule, reprints of articles and interviews, information about hard-to-find recordings and the like. Mick Perry (whom I never met) and Burt Kaufman (whom I met briefly in a hotel in Odessa while attending the first Wink tribute concert) have been of great service to me and to all Roy's fans, worldwide, through their hard work for Orbison fan clubs. Along with Ab Roos, they have made a historic contribution to our knowledge of the music of one of the great popular singers of our time.

The assistance of Janet Francendese, my editor at Temple University Press, has been instrumental. No sooner had I finished *Running Scared: Masculinity and the Representation of the Male Body* than she expressed interest in this book, the groundwork for which was laid in the final chapter of *Running Scared*. Janet is a true hands-on editor (I have a heavily marked-up copy of the manuscript to prove it) and having her interest and support enabled me to feel confident about writing a book that marked a new direction for me. Remarkably, she continued to inspire that confidence even as I digressed and completed two other books. She told me bluntly that I was too obsessed with Orbison not to complete this book. She was right, of course, and I hope the results justify her commitment. Suzanne Wolk, the copyeditor, brought a wealth of knowledge about music and a passionate love of it to bear on this project, and my book is much improved as a result of her work. Special thanks go to Don Staples for the paperback back cover photograph of me standing in front of the rooming house on Fry Street in Denton where Roy Orbison lived while attending North Texas State.

Finally, I owe a great debt to Melanie Magisos for her invaluable suggestions about how to make the book better. Over the years she has good-naturedly put up with my obsessive passion for Roy's music and concerts, accompanying me to countless of the latter, listening to me rave about them, the recordings, and anything and everything even remotely connected to the master. If Roy had the voice of an angel, she has the temperament of one. I cannot thank her enough.

ROY ORBISON

1

There Are Many Roy Orbisons

n 1960 rock 'n' roll and pop music were quite rightly perceived as diminished by two watershed events: Elvis Presley's enlistment in the army and Buddy Holly's death. I was fifteen years old at the time and, like many others, I felt a void that it seemed would never be filled. No one was positioned to carry on what those greats had begun, or so it seemed. Suddenly, as if out of nowhere, Roy Orbison appeared—a man who, unbeknownst to most rock 'n' roll fans (myself included), had close personal ties with both Presley and Holly. Yet one would not have guessed this listening to "Only the Lonely," Orbison's first smash hit in 1960. Where had this rich voice, with its startling falsetto, come from? Who was this mysterious figure who sang such a strange song—which sounded more like two songs than one—so beautifully?

Orbison not only seemed to come from nowhere; he seemed to stay there. As much as I loved his music (and I loved it more than any other music I had known), I knew virtually nothing about him. I did not know what he looked like, how old he was, whether he was married—and I didn't care. Although I bought all his records and listened to the radio in rapt anticipation of the next one, it was years before I learned anything about him beyond what his music told me. When I finally saw his picture, it meant nothing to me—he looked like a grown man to whom I could not relate in any way. And once again, I did not care. When I went to dances

1

where local bands or records played, Orbison's music was rarely included because amateur teen bands could not cover him, and his songs were difficult to dance to, anyway. This too meant nothing to me.

Finally, during my first year in college (1963–64), I heard Roy Orbison live. Nothing could prepare me for the experience; it caught me as much by surprise, and had as strong an effect on me, as first hearing "Only the Lonely" had done nearly four years earlier. I was startled by his appearance; he was dressed all in black and wore dark glasses, though it was a nighttime concert. I was prepared to be disappointed in his singing, aware of the cliché that rock 'n' roll singers were the product of studio magic and couldn't really sing. But Orbison sang in such a magnificent, powerful voice that I couldn't believe my ears. And those were the days before sound boards and elaborate mixing systems; basically the microphone was turned on and that was it. The speaker system was nothing to brag about, nor was the venue, the "Youth Building" of the Dane Country fairgrounds in Madison, Wisconsin. We sat on folding chairs!

The musical success of this odd figure continued for four years, for all practical purposes ending in 1964 with "Oh, Pretty Woman" as quickly as it had begun in 1960 with "Only the Lonely." Since it was never clear where he had come from, no one seemed to pay much attention to where he had gone; he was just gone. He continued to make music but no one seemed to care, or even know. I was living in New York between 1968 and 1971, and even in Manhattan I could not find a record store that bothered to stock one copy of a newly released Orbison album; I had to special order them. There was never an Orbison section; many of the clerks did not even know who he was. When I told people about his music, the ones who recognized his name often thought he was dead.

He was totally forgotten, or so it seemed. When he died unexpectedly in 1988, Bono, the lead singer of the immensely popular band U2, proclaimed him the greatest singer of his time. How could that be? Why was he dismissed as just another cog in the pop music industry teen-machine during his lifetime, but acclaimed as a great artist in his death? What had happened between 1964 and 1988? This book will attempt to answer that question, bringing to bear much of what film

studies has taught us about authorship as well as formal and ideological analysis of media within popular culture. Although popular music is
different from movies, there are obvious parallels between the film studios and the record companies, between film directors and music producers, between movie stars and rock stars, between form and narrative
in popular film and music, and between the representation of gender
and sexuality in both art forms. Unlike popular music, film studies has
a longstanding tradition of analyzing in detail both individual films and
complete *oeuvres* of important directors. I hope that this book will mark
the beginning of such work in rock 'n' roll.

Had Roy Orbison died in the 1970s, his death would have received
minor attention in the media, perhaps a one-paragraph obituary in the
larger city newspapers. It is unlikely that network radio or television
would have paid attention. In 1988, however, his death was a media
event. A major network radio news program began with an excerpt from
one of his songs; *USA Today* featured a cover story on him in the entertainment section; the talk shows, including *Good Morning America*, featured segments about him; the covers of *People Magazine* and various
tabloids advertised the stories within; and *Rolling Stone* put him on the
cover and published his first *Rolling Stone* interview. Within a short
period two biographies appeared, *Only the Lonely*, by Alan Clayson, and
Dark Star: The Roy Orbison Story, by Ellis Amburn. Orbison's star power
in death eclipsed anything he had ever experienced in life. Yet Orbison had released little new music in the final years before his death.
Indeed, "Not Alone Anymore," his one solo song on *The Traveling
Wilburys, Vol. 1*, was the most significant addition to his *oeuvre*. Despite
the success of the supergroup, much of the sudden attention he was getting was based not on his recent work (his CD *Mystery Girl* would not
be released for a few months), but on the rediscovery and reassessment
of his past accomplishments. He could have, and should have, received
much of this attention years earlier. The origins of this book lie in those
years of neglect, when it was beyond my wildest dream that by the
time I wrote this book, Orbison would be widely recognized, both pop-
ularly and critically, as a major figure of rock 'n' roll.

In his *Newsweek* obituary, David Gates claimed that, along with Elvis
Presley, "Orbison . . . elevated a bastard form of regional music into

something approaching art song" (Gates 1988, 73). This assessment is at once boldly perceptive and deeply troubling. Gates is undoubtedly right that Orbison was worthy of the sort of praise reserved for serious artists. But the reference to "a bastard form of regional music" smacks of class and racial assumptions that identify the music of poor, uneducated, rural whites, and the blacks from whom they appropriated it, as illegitimate and of little value.

In his history of Sun Records and the birth of rock 'n' roll, Colin Escott similarly claims that "Hillbilly and rockabilly were essentially southern musics; the hits Orbison scored in the 1960s were timeless and placeless. Like Elvis Presley, but unlike Jerry Lee Lewis and Carl Perkins, Roy Orbison transcended his roots" (Escott 2001, 145). Like Escott, I have long been struck by the timeless quality of Orbison's music. With a few trivial exceptions, most of his Monument hits between 1960 and 1964 in no way sound like early sixties pop or rock. It is precisely because he was never really of his time that Orbison's music sounds as fresh today as when it was recorded. Orbison's songs do not invoke nostalgia for a bygone era, and therefore they stand out when played on oldies stations. But Escott also emphasizes place, and he is right: the "placelessness" of Orbison's music has some connection with Gates's sense of its transcending regional music. Strangely enough, Orbison's music has no regional roots or character, a point of great significance when considering it in the context of race.

Finally, Gates and Escott point to a paradox in critical discourse on Orbison: on the one hand, he is treated as a unique and sometimes even bizarrely eccentric figure in rock 'n' roll, while on the other hand he is linked to Elvis Presley, the figure who best epitomizes rock 'n' roll in terms of masculinity and sexuality. Both Presley and Orbison contributed to this perception through public statements about their friendship and their high regard for each other's music.

But if Orbison transcended the norm and was somehow exceptional, how do we resolve the question raised by Gates's judgment? Isn't popular music, by definition, tied to place and time? Isn't that essential to its popularity? Standard histories of rock 'n' roll certainly presume this as they jump from Presley as a figure of fifties rebellion to the Beatles as figures of sixties countercultural revolution. And if pop music is of its time, why should a "test" of timelessness be applied to it? Doesn't that reek of "high art" criticism and of the misapplication of the criteria of classical music to popular music? Much academic criticism—influenced by cultural studies, a desire to rid the academy of a canon, and anti-*auteurist* sentiment—avoids this question by approaching popular culture in a way that examines how different works or genres become meaningful to different audiences in different places at different times; claims for the greatness of individuals are studiously avoided.

Yet this is also a serious error. If Gates makes the mistake of unintentionally insulting and devaluing an entire class of music, cultural studies makes the mistake of devaluing the accomplishments of particular works and *oeuvres*. Nearly everything is of some value to someone at some point in time (for example, teenage boys and heavy metal, or the relationship of rock 'n' roll to dancing and romance), and while it is important to respect and understand that value, it is also incumbent upon students of popular culture to make value judgments. The idea of a canon is both inevitable and desirable. What is important is that we constantly revise our canons and include as many voices as possible in their creation.

In their effort to transcend the traditional high art/low art dichotomy, practitioners of cultural studies have been guilty of a serious omission. It was and remains important to understand the function of popular art in relation to age (for example, teenagers and rock), class (for example, working class and country), race (for example, rap and African Americans), and gender (for example, Madonna and women).

But this is only part of our obligation. For lovers of all kinds of music, it is particularly offensive when classical music is referred to as "serious" music, as it commonly is. What could be more serious to certain working-class whites in the late sixties and early seventies than the music of Merle Haggard? In this usage, "serious" connotes the privileges of economic class and higher education. But even within the world of classical music, not everyone is a Beethoven or a Mozart. Indeed, many of the contemporaries of these two composers have long since been forgotten and many, for good reason, will never be rediscovered. Just as it has been important for classical musicians and scholars to understand the accomplishments of a Beethoven or a Mozart, it is equally important for scholars of popular culture to understand the accomplishments of a Merle Haggard or a Roy Orbison. We cannot simply assert that rock and country music are worthy of serious attention as genres without making the case for the accomplishments of the figures working within those forms. Yet that is close to what is currently happening.

Gaining respect for popular culture is not enough. It is easy to argue that there is no significant aesthetic distinction between what can be accomplished in popular fiction and what in "literature," but such claims are useless without careful analysis of individual works and *oeuvres* that supply convincing evidence. I have argued that the treatment of the theme of sexuality and war wounds in *The Nothing Man*, a pulp novel by Jim Thompson, is important and daring in a manner that makes it impressive when considered alongside the work of Ernest Hemingway, a "serious" writer (Lehman 1993). It is precisely because film studies analyzes specific Westerns, such as those of John Ford, that Westerns can be regarded as a "serious" art form. Not all pulp novels are artistic accomplishments worthy of inclusion in a canon, nor are all Westerns—but some of them are.

While it is certainly true that we can learn something by studying the value of country music in general to many working-class whites, it is also true that we can learn something by studying how the works of the greatest country musicians—Hank Williams, Merle Haggard, George Jones, Johnny Cash, to name a few—rise above that their peers and achieve distinction. To argue this is not to devalue country music as a whole any more than to argue for Beethoven's greatness over his peers devalues classical music. The old-fashioned notion of the timeless genius who transcends his place, culture, and history to discover universals truths is, thank heavens, long gone. But there are other ways to recognize the importance of individual artists within history, culture, and ideology and to study both what distinguishes their work from that of others and why it has outlasted that of their peers.

In any generation there are a handful of musicians, whether they make classical or popular music, who achieve that status, and it is important for us to know why. Roy Orbison was one of those artists and, with full appreciation and respect for the rock 'n' roll of his time, I will never-

theless argue that Orbison did indeed reach far above and beyond it in
something of the way Gates indicates. The analogy with the art song,
however, to which I shall return in the next chapter, presents a problem. Arguing by analogy is notoriously difficult since we must keep in
mind the differences as well as the similarities. The *auteurs* of the art
song were the composers, and their compositions can be separated from
the various performers of those songs in a way that is not the case with
Orbison. Precisely because of the manner in which rock 'n' roll is inextricably tied to *recorded* music, Orbison is part of a different tradition.
He may be a great composer, but that does not mean he is analogous
to Schubert. And this remains true even if Orbison's songs become standards that will be reinterpreted by others for years to come. If his aesthetic accomplishment approaches that of someone like Schubert, it
does so in a different way.

A project like mine is limited because the unique quality of the
voice, "the grain of the voice," in Roland Barthes's memorable phrase,
escapes the language of analysis. It is so much easier to talk about the
aesthetics and ideology of lyrics than to characterize the accomplishments of the voice. We have critical tools with which to trace formal features such as motif and narrative style (though we must avoid falling
into the trap of evaluating them on a literary or poetic model). When,
in a song like "Windsurfer," we hear the language in which a young
woman rejects her lover's plea to go away with him ("No, no, never no"),
it achieves a heightened, somewhat poetic function, though it would not
have such a function in a Shakespeare play or sonnet. Similarly, it is
easier to trace the patterns of masochism in the Orbison persona's sexual behavior than it is to characterize the moaning, groaning sounds of
pain/pleasure in which Orbison sings of those behaviors.

Nevertheless, it is important to attempt to capture these things in
words. In Chapter 3 and the Appendix I will at least sketch in the features of the voice and the music that everything else in this book circles
around. And although most of this book analyzes the aesthetics and ideology of Orbison's lyrics; his image, persona, and performance style; the
use of his music in film narratives; the cultural discourses of race and gender that have sprung up around him; and the discourses of critics and
musicians who have written and spoken about Orbison, none of these

things, nor all of them taken together, make the music worthwhile. It is the music as sung and recorded or performed by Orbison that makes all the other forms of analysis worthwhile. And it is only the beauty of the music that makes it important to understand, for example, its unusual embodiment of gender and sexuality. That Orbison did not adhere to the norms of masculinity of his time does not make his hits important; that he sang in an eerie falsetto in songs that defied all expectations is what makes the gender and sexual components of his music and persona so important. If this book succeeds, it will do so by giving the reader a guide by which to hear the recordings in a new and richer context.

Some artists achieve greatness by mastering the norms of their form and some by departing from those norms. Orbison belongs to the latter group. For that reason, probably, he receives no attention in James Miller's *Flowers in the Dustbin: The Rise of Rock and Roll, 1947–1977*. As an intellectual and cultural historian, Miller is interested in tracing the important moments that determined the shape and evolution of rock 'n' roll. That story can quite rightly be told without mention of Orbison. Miller notes, "By the Spring of 1957, rock and roll in many respects had achieved its definitive form ... the key cultural values, glorifying rebellion, delinquency, youthful disorder" (Miller 1999, 138). A little later he observes, "the music and its idols offered a focus for fantasies of youthful revolt and sexual mastery—a ritual representation of potentially unruly impulses" (143). Orbison's music and persona are not really about any of these things. Indeed, much of his music revels in the opposite of sexual mastery. Even the "driving beat" and "teen-oriented lyrics" Miller describes as characteristic of rock 'n' roll are absent from many of Orbison's greatest hits.

Apart from the running time of his songs, which strictly followed the AM radio Top 40 format, virtually nothing about Orbison's music conformed to the norms of his time. The songs he wrote, the way he sang them, the manner in which they were produced, the style of his live concert performances, the development of and circulation of his persona in the media—all departed drastically from the norm. Though Orbison's accomplishment lies in understanding that departure, this is not, of course, to say that there weren't many important rock singers from the period who embody those norms.

This points to yet another paradox about Orbison—his relationship to many of the recognized giants who do embody the rock 'n' roll norm. Again, Miller's book sheds light on this point in two ways. He mentions Orbison only twice, both times in relation to the oft-mentioned fact that the Beatles intended "Please Please Me" as a tribute to Orbison. The Beatles, of course, are central to the mainstream rock 'n' roll tradition that Miller traces, and he devotes chapters to them. In his preface, he notes some highlights of his career as a professional music critic, among them seeing Bruce Springsteen in concert as he was poised for fame, and having "the chance to meet and talk with a great many of my musical heroes, old and new, from Sam Phillips and Paul McCartney to David Bowie and Elvis Costello and Bono of U2" (Miller 1999, 17). All of these musicians have gone on record about their extraordinary respect for Orbison. How is it that Orbison quite rightly has no place in Miller's history and yet is a hero to so many of his musical heroes?

This book is about one of the strangest, oddest figures in the history of rock 'n' roll. In the late 1980s, *Playboy* magazine ran a picture of Orbison and Frank Zappa. It caught my attention not only because I thought the accompanying article would be in part about Orbison, but because I wondered what connection the writer would make between these two figures. The answer was an aesthetic of "weirdness." The article mentioned only one other singer: Tiny Tim. The writer's observation about the shared "weirdness" of these figures indicated that by the late eighties Orbison's strangeness was becoming more widely recognized. The inclusion of Tiny Tim served another very valuable function: it showed that however much one departs from the norms of one's time, there is no necessary connection between that departure and artistic accomplishment. Frank Zappa, like Orbison, is a figure for whom a serious case for artistic greatness can be made; Tiny Tim is not. Just as there are great artists who embody norms, there are very bad artists who depart from them. Like it or not, such value judgments are vital to understanding our field. In this book I will make the case not just for Orbison's uniqueness, but also for his greatness.

Although my parallel work in film studies led me in the 1990s to develop the view of popular culture I have described above, in 1996 Simon Frith similarly argued that cultural studies had avoided what he called the "value problem." In the effort to collapse the high art/low art distinction, Frith noted that many defenders of popular culture "draw the wrong conclusion from this: what needs challenging is not the notion of the superior, but the claim that it is the exclusive property of the 'high'" (Frith 1996, 16). Unfortunately, in the years since Frith made this perceptive observation, no significant change has occurred.

Like lovers of any art form, Frith notes that fans of popular music make judgments and assess differences: "There is no reason to believe a priori that such judgments work differently in different cultural spheres. There are obvious differences between operas and soap operas, between classical and country music, but the fact that the objects of judgment are different doesn't mean that the processes of judgment are" (17). Frith's insight here is crucial to understanding why it is possible to experience no serious disjunction between loving Orbison's music and loving Mozart's. Although such pluralism sometimes bewilders people, the love of radically different genres of music involves the exact same processes of judgment and discrimination in each case. Listening to Orbison is not a form of "slumming," a lapse in taste, or a case of arrested adolescent development; it is much like listening to Mozart.

Orbison is, as I have noted, best known for a string of hits he recorded for Monument Records between 1960 ("Only the Lonely") and 1964 ("Oh, Pretty Woman"). As amazing as his accomplishments were during those four years, they comprise only a small part of his total output. He began in the 1950s with Sam Phillips at Sun Records. Although he had only one minor hit with "Ooby Dooby," he recorded sixteen songs, including the somewhat bizarre "Chicken Hearted," the earliest work to question conventional notions of masculinity, which became such a prominent theme in Orbison's work.

This first phase of Orbison's career includes a series of recordings he made at the Jim Beck Studio in Dallas and at Norman Petty's studio in Clovis, New Mexico. Orbison in fact first recorded "Ooby Dooby" in 1955 at the Beck Studio and then in 1956 in Clovis, and then again later in 1956 he rerecorded it in Memphis at Sun Records after signing with that label.[1] Orbison was dissatisfied with Sam Phillips's strong control at Sun, however, and he recorded a number of other songs at Clovis while under contract to Sun.[2] In the mid-fifties, the Teen Kings, the group to which Orbison belonged, performed weekly on live television in Odessa, Texas. Orbison sang lead vocals, played lead guitar, and cowrote the original songs with the other members of the group. Most of the group's material was never recorded for or released on Sun Records.

After leaving Sun, Orbison's career took a little-known turn. He did not go directly to Monument but instead, following the lead of Elvis Presley, signed with RCA, recording six songs produced by Chet Atkins.[3] These songs supply an important link between Orbison's rockabilly period and the later Monument ballads. Once again, none of the songs is major but some, such as "Paper Boy," reveal a growing poetic awareness in the lyrics and introduce motifs Orbison would later develop much more fully. Orbison sings in a somewhat delicate, fragile style that is far removed from the powerful voice he would develop at Monument. As with the switch from Clovis to Sun, however, the move from RCA to Monument was bridged by a common song: the first song Orbison released at Monument was the previously unreleased "Paper Boy" from the RCA sessions.

Shortly thereafter, "Only the Lonely" (1960) marked Orbison's first major breakthrough in both vocal style and songwriting. He sang in a richly nuanced voice with a startling range, while the song itself had a complex structure, perhaps the result of its combining what had been two separate songs. The following year, with "Running Scared," he added an equally startling new dimension to his vocal style, this time revealing a vocal power, in the song's conclusion, not heard before. Structurally, "Running Scared" abandoned the verse-chorus-verse sequence typical of the time. All the major elements of Orbison's style were now in place, and they would provide him with a stunning succession of hits, culminating with "Oh, Pretty Woman" in 1964. Then his fortunes were reversed.

Orbison signed with MGM in 1965, and over the next nine years the studio released eleven albums of new material. The MGM period has been almost entirely overlooked, usually considered one big wasteland in Orbison's career. And while there is no question that the general quality of his work fell off dramatically, the picture is more complex than that. Orbison recorded some very good songs, and even some experimental numbers, during this period. But he lost control over the production style he had developed with Fred Foster at Monument Records, a small, independent label. MGM was a major label at the time, and Orbison's music moved stylistically more into the mainstream. His hits ceased in the United States, though they continued in England and Australia.

The way critics generally respond to Orbison's MGM period bears an interesting analogy to a common perception of Elvis Presley's career. Daniel Wolff criticizes the manner in which Peter Guralnick's two-volume biography of Presley opposes the pre-1960 Presley to the Presley who resumed recording after his stint in the army. The first volume celebrates "'a sense of daring, high-flying good times almost in defiance of societal norms' while the second traces the sad decline into 'pop' rather than rock & roll music." Wolff objects to this view on three grounds. First, such a simple dichotomy overlooks the very real accomplishments of Presley's post-1960 work. Second, it essentializes rock 'n' roll as one thing. Third, it demonizes Colonel Parker, Presley's manager, as the major if not sole cause of the downfall.

All three points relate also to Orbison's career. Of Guralnick's distinction between Presley's pre- and post-1960s recordings, Wolff observes:

> That definition only makes sense if you're willing to exclude from the rock pantheon Roy Orbison, Sam Cooke, the Platters, Roy Hamilton, the Everly Brothers, Jackie Wilson, and a number of other artists who produced melodic, sophisticated hits in the early Sixties, after the music "died." Their songs were not only good for slow dancing (as essential to the rock & roll phenomenon as the rip-'em-up sound), but they had a bravura emotional quality that could, indeed, be traced back to Jolson by way of Bing Crosby, Sinatra, Billy Eckstein, and—one of Presley's favorites—Dean Martin. For a purist, this doesn't count as rock history. What's it got to do after all, with leather jackets and shaking up the staid Eisenhower years? (Woolf 1999)

Wolff points out that such an essentialist notion of rock 'n' roll is inadequate to understanding the complexities of Presley's career. He quite rightly calls "Are You Lonesome Tonight?" a "great record," even though it is not a rip-'em-up rocker full of threatening rebellion.

Colonel Parker, Presley's infamous manager, is implicated in this scenario. Writing of "Are You Lonesome Tonight?" Wolff observes: "It's a ridiculously old-fashioned and inappropriate ballad, which had first been a hit for Al Jolson (!?) more than thirty years earlier. Supposedly, Presley agreed to record it only because it was one of Colonel Parker's favorites. If you buy the thesis put forward in *Careless Love*, here's a beginning to the downward side slide; Elvis as the Colonel's puppet, the wild boy tamed" (Wolff 1999).

The parallels between this view of Presley and common perceptions of Orbison's career are uncanny. The main difference is the time shift. The standard critical view of Orbison is that he was never a good rocker and that his only real claim to fame are the 1960–64 Fred Foster-Monument–produced ballads, with "Oh, Pretty Woman" the notable exception. Then, the story goes, the move to MGM marks Orbison's pathetic decline into pop mediocrity. Furthermore, Wesley Rose, Orbison's manager, is the villain who ruined Orbison in order to get a million-dollar, multi-film contract with MGM. Rose even took over producing Orbison's records. That Orbison did an album of Hank Williams songs and one of Don Gibson songs at MGM is offered as further proof of Rose's selfishness, since both songwriters were published by Acuff-Rose, a company in which Wesley Rose, son of Fred Rose, had a major interest.

Rick Kennedy and Randy McNutt, for example, call the move from Monument to MGM "disastrous" and attribute it to the fact that although Foster was willing to match the MGM dollar figure, he had no resources to match the movie deal:

> Orbison ultimately signed his first million-dollar contract with MGM. He owed Monument four more sides, but Rose attempted to dictate to Foster what songs would be released when. "So I said, 'Then *you* do it [produce the records],'" said Foster. "So we went from selling seven million copies of 'Oh, Pretty Woman' to less than 200,000 on the follow-up. It broke my heart. The next one didn't even break 100,000. That should have been the writing on the wall. I mean, a million dollars is nice, but if you can stay where you are and keep rolling, a million dollars is nothing. You can make more than that anyway. But that's the way it came down." (Kennedy and McNutt 1999, 147)

If Foster's recollection is accurate, it contradicts the credits on the *Orbisongs* album (1966) and all later albums, which list Fred Foster as the producer on both "Goodnight" and "(Say) You're My Girl. Here, however, Foster himself contributes to the myth. The problem is that "Goodnight" (the follow-up to "Oh, Pretty Woman) is a great song. In fact, it is a much better song than "Oh, Pretty Woman" and one of Orbison's crowning achievements at Monument. The production is superb. What happened between "Oh, Pretty Woman" and "Goodnight" was the solidification of the British invasion, something that would intensify even more between "Goodnight" and "(Say) You're My Girl," Orbison's next Monument release. Foster's claim that Orbison could have stayed where he was, turning out million-dollar hits, is unsupported by anything but sheer sentiment. Had Orbison stayed at Monument with Fred Foster producing, it is highly unlikely that the hits would have kept on coming; and it is this, rather than the loss of any "magic," that explains why, when the two re-teamed at Monument in 1978, their *Regeneration* album was a total failure.

Kennedy and McNutt, perpetuating Foster's account, conclude:

> Some critics contend Orbison never found another producer with Foster's touch. Foster believes that they had a special collaborative spirit together that could not be recaptured. Perhaps Foster's dual roles of producer and label president enabled the team to excel. Because he controlled session budgets, for example, he allowed Orbison an incredible 36 takes on "It's Over." By the time Rose produced Orbison's final Monument singles, "Goodnight" and "(Say) You're My Girl," the spark was gone. (Kennedy and McNutt 1999, 148–49)

In fact, a careful listen to the music reveals that the spark was not gone. What were gone were the audience and the reception context for such songs; they were neglected, forgotten, by an upheaval in popular culture so swift and dramatic that within a year the world had become a different place. In every way—the lyrics, the complex melodic shifts, the orchestration, the vocals—"Goodnight" sounded like a beautiful continuation of the Orbison-Foster collaboration, and in fact, until I learned that Rose actually produced the song, I always presumed that Foster had. "(Say) You're My Girl," while something of a departure for Orbison, is also a very good, well-produced record. It is energetic and fresh, perhaps a needed departure from the more typical orchestrated dramatic ballads.

In this book I will resist such narratives as Wolff's and Kennedy and McNutt's, with their pre- and post-army Presley dichotomy and Monument/MGM Orbison dichotomy, appealing as they may be. Artists like Presley and Orbison are too complex to be dealt with in simple terms of unblemished success and irreversible decline. Several of Orbison's MGM songs, for example, share profound connections with those of the Monument period.

This is not to say that these writers are entirely wrong. Their argument about the importance of producers and record companies is valid, and there was indeed a special bond between Orbison and Foster. Moreover, the daringly innovative music they created together at Monument was possible because Monument was a small, independent label, and Foster had total control. A major label probably would not have provided the creative freedom necessary for such an accomplishment. And the fact that MGM was a corporate giant, and that Rose and other MGM producers were not Foster's equals, surely accounted in part for the decline in quality and the move toward a more mainstream ballad sound. But one can grant these things without resorting to oversimplifications about dramatic career ruptures. That Fred Rose produced "Goodnight" (if he did in fact produce it) does not signal a dramatic shift in Orbison's fortunes.

During the MGM years, two tragedies struck Orbison's life. In 1966 his wife, Claudette, whom he had recently remarried, died in a motorcycle accident, and in 1968 two of his sons died in a fire at his home while he was touring in England. While these personal tragedies, combined with sinking fortunes, characterize the MGM period, it is not fair to say that they caused Orbison's decline. While the almost unimaginable horror of two such tragedies in quick succession would clearly have a devastating effect on anyone, their impact on Orbison's career is far from clear. Indeed, one of the MGM songs, a cover of Don Gibson's "Too Soon to Know," was a huge hit in England, and the song's emphasis on the uncertainty of forgetting a lost love was widely interpreted as referring to Claudette's death. That this song was a hit in England demonstrates that simplistic hypotheses cannot explain complex phenomena. If "Too Soon to Know" failed to become a hit in the United States because it represented a decline in quality (whether because of Fred Rose, MGM, or personal tragedy), then why was it a hit in England? The success of this song in England and of "Penny Arcade" in Australia show that the story is more complicated, that complex historical and cultural forces are at work here. Ironically, in the wake of the Beatles, the Rolling Stones, the Who, and the entire shift to band-based rock 'n' roll, the British remained more receptive to the American tradition of single male performers than did Americans themselves! Orbison enjoyed huge success in England and Australia at this time, even while he experienced near total eclipse in the United States.[4] So the simple narrative of rise and fall simply will not wash. Paradoxically, it was during the MGM period that what has come to be thought of as Orbison's image was solidified. It was not until 1963, for example, after nearly all of his Monument hits, that Orbison's ever-present sunglasses appeared. And although Orbison's persona is widely perceived as one fixed thing, it has in fact undergone numerous changes. In the late sixties he changed his hairstyle from a fifties pompadour to a post-Beatles "mod" style. With such MGM songs as "Southbound Jericho Parkway" and "Communication Breakdown," he also attempted, though in vain, to create hits that had a "contemporary" sound. Orbison's first MGM album was titled *There Is Only One Roy Orbison*, but in one sense there have been many Roy Orbisons.

After MGM Orbison recorded three albums, each for a different label: *I'm Still in Love with You* (Mercury, 1975), *Regeneration* (Monument, 1977) and *Laminar Flow* (Asylum, 1979). All were commercial and critical failures and involved production conflicts, and it would be ten more years before Orbison would do another solo studio album of original material. Although he did not have a recording contract, important new directions emerged in his work in the eighties. In 1980 he had a country hit with "That Lovin' You Feeling Again," a duet with Emmylou Harris. From that time until his death, Orbison was involved with duets and group projects with well-known singers, including the 1986 album *The Class of '55*, with Johnny Cash, Jerry Lee Lewis, and Carl Perkins, as well as the 1988 hit *The Traveling Wilburys, Vol. 1*, with Bob Dylan, George Harrison, Tom Petty, and Jeff Lynne. This period also saw the Cinemax special *Roy Orbison and Friends: A Black and White Night*, a live concert with backup by Bruce Springsteen, Elvis Costello, Tom Waits, and k. d. lang, to name just a few. Other duets of the period included "Indian Summer" with Larry Gatlin, "Leah" with Bertie Higgins, and "Crying" with k. d. lang. After a virtual absence of more than a decade, Orbison also toured the United States extensively through-out the 1980s.

It was not until the end of the decade, with the posthumous release of *Mystery Girl* (Virgin, 1989), that Orbison had another solo studio album of new material—a major album equaling the best of his Monument work and, significantly, showing a mature late-period style—that was a critical and commercial success. Songs like "In the Real World" make strong reference to the sixties hit "In Dreams." The album self-consciously develops, in a restrained and reflective mode, many motifs both in the music and lyrics that have run throughout his *oeuvre*. Orbison's work has moved through a full range of stylistic periods—the Sun, RCA, and very early Monument recordings are characterized by the search for a personal style; the Monument, MGM, and various seventies albums constitute a mature middle-period that elaborates and develops that style; and some of the mid-eighties work, such as "Comin' Home" (from *The Class of '55*), "Life Fades Away" (from the *Less Than Zero* soundtrack, 1987), and Mystery *Girl* are typically late-period songs preoccupied with death, self-conscious reference to the *oeuvre*, and stylistic restraint bordering at times on a deceptive simplicity. Never once on *Mystery Girl*, for example, does Orbison use the full power of his voice, pulling out all the stops and building to the crashing climaxes that characterized his middle-period.

In 1992 another posthumous album, *King of Hearts*, was released. It contained half a dozen songs that had been left as demos when Orbison died and finished by various producers and mixers, including Don Was, Jeff Lynne, Robbie Robertson, and k. d. lang. The album also includes a few of the various eighties songs released on other labels and the demo version of "Careless Heart," which appeared on *Mystery Girl*. At least one of the new songs, "Love in Time," is a major addition to the Orbison *oeuvre*, and the alternative version of "Careless Heart" includes a more unrestrained use of the powerful voice than the release version. The later version that Orbison chose for *Mystery Girl* highlights the late-period tendency to hold back on the fuller development of the middle period.

As this brief survey indicates, Orbison's *oeuvre* is extensive. Although I will concentrate on his major works and achievements, they will be placed within the entire career context, without which much would be missed and distorted. Orbison's work includes many contradictions and many aborted and forgotten attempts to move in new directions. During the MGM period alone, in addition to the songs of late sixties "relevance," he attempted a movie career (*The Fastest Guitar Alive*, 1967); recorded a "middle-of-the-road" album (*Roy Orbison's Many Moods*, 1969), and recorded two albums of country music (*Roy Orbison Sings Don Gibson*, 1967, and *Hank Williams the Roy Orbison Way*, 1970).

Over the course of his recording career and since his death, a bewildering number of cultural discourses have arisen about Orbison and his music. It is difficult to recall now that during his string of hits between 1960 and 1964, Orbison did not hire a publicist and was virtually unrepresented in U.S. fan magazines. Indeed, *Life* magazine called him an "anonymous celebrity." Even his most successful albums (*Greatest Hits, Vols. 1 and 2*) included no photos of him; and the photos that appeared on *Lonely and Blue*, *In Dreams*, and *Early Orbison* were not at all typical of what was to become and remain his dominant image—that of a mysterious man in black.

After all of Orbison's sixties hits had been written and recorded, a series of events occurred that was constructed into a discourse of tragedy that dominated Orbison's life story in the media and the public mind. As I have noted, this discourse was based primarily on the death in 1966 of his first wife, Claudette, in a motorcycle accident that occurred as she rode by Orbison's side, and the death of two of his three children in a 1968 fire that destroyed his Nashville home. Orbison's emergency heart surgery in 1978—a triple bypass—also became part of it. Orbison's obituaries confirmed just how widespread and pervasive this tragic image had become. *People* magazine ran a front-cover headline, "The Haunted Life of Rock Legend Roy Orbison," and the *Star* declared his death the final tragedy of a tragic life.

Orbison's ubiquitous black clothes and dark glasses, adopted in 1963, only reinforced his image as a dark, tragic figure. Indeed, careless commentators later attributed the pain and anguish of his sixties hits to his "tragic life," though the loss of his wife and sons occurred after all of his greatest hits had been produced. The title of Ellis Amburn's biography, *Dark Star*, underscored the dominant image of Orbison, and the discourse of tragedy has remained central to the reception of Orbison's music.

A clichéd view of rock history paints the early 1960s as a bland wasteland; Buddy Holly was dead and Elvis Presley was in uniform. This version of history has the Beatles stepping in, in 1964, to rescue rock 'n' roll from mediocrity. In the words of Daniel Wolff:

> For some, Presley's military induction did, indeed, mark the end of an era. "Elvis died the day he went into the army," John Lennon would declare. According to this mythic version of rock & roll, the music was born in a blinding flash in July 1954, when country-western, blues, and gospel music mutated in the body of a truck driver from Memphis. The resulting strain lasted four years. Then Elvis was drafted, Jerry Lee Lewis gutted his career by marrying his fourteen-year-old cousin, and Buddy Holly went down in a plane crash in early 1959: "the day the music died." This legend goes on to claim a resurrection, four years later, when the Beatles released "I Want to Hold Your Hand." (Wolff 1999)

Part of the reason why Orbison was underrated and overlooked is that his biggest hits occurred in the period between the alleged death and resurrection of rock 'n' roll. This was also the period of successful girl groups like the Shirelles, the Ronettes, and the Crystals, the latter two produced by Phil Spector. The manner in which this music has been marginalized suggests that the dominant death-and-resurrection narrative has a gender bias at its center. But these girl groups may share more in common with Orbison than being overlooked during the early sixties. Michael Jarrett has pointed out that there is a strong strain of masochism in the songs of the girl groups, and masochism is a central component of Orbison's aesthetic. Conventional wisdom has it, then, that there was no major figure during those years, even if implicitly that meant no major *male* figure. Yet there was a world of difference between Orbison and such "Bobbys" as Bobby Vinton, Bobby Vee, and Bobby Rydell.

Thanks to David Lynch and Bruce Springsteen, Orbison was later repositioned as a major figure in the history of rock 'n' roll, on a scale with Presley and the Beatles; and his music was seen as much darker and more sexually troubled than that of the teen idols who were his contemporaries. Orbison has gone from being a forgotten bad joke to perhaps the most revered "musician's musician" in the history of rock 'n' roll. An astonishing number of the greatest names in rock and country music played with him, contributed to his final albums, were planning future projects with him, and paid tribute to him at and after the time of his death.

A number of other discourses are closely related to that of the "musician's musician." Near the end of Orbison's life an *auteurist* discourse sprang up around this music that so many considered somehow "classical." In a 1987 article on Orbison's music, occasioned by the release of *In Dreams: Greatest Hits,* Dave Marsh hailed Orbison as one of the greatest singers of all time, a view he reiterated the following year, after Orbison's death, when he called him "more than just the owner of the greatest white pop voice in the last 30 years" (Marsh 1989b, 28). Marsh's comments in many ways paralleled those of the *auteurist* film critics. He claimed that Orbison created a complex personal and interconnected world in his songs: "These songs define a world unto themselves more completely than any other body of work in pop music" (Marsh 1987a, 7). After Orbison's final performance in New York, *New York Times* reviewer Peter Watrous contributed to this *auteurist* account of Orbison's music, calling him "a genuine American eccentric" and observing that "he has perfected an odd vision of popular music, one in which eccentricity and imagination beat back all the pressures toward conformity" (Watrous, 44).

There is indeed an unusually rich interconnection between the songs that prompted these remarks by Marsh and Watrous. In fact, the world of Orbison's music is so rich and self-contained that many of the well-known songs of which he recorded cover versions ("Danny Boy," "I Fought the Law," "Drift Away," "It's Too Soon to Know") take on unique personal dimensions within his *oeuvre.* Orbison's private world of loneliness and dreams contains an important, pervasive element of sexual masochism that has gone totally unnoticed. Watrous's assessment of Orbison as a "genuine American eccentric" who was able in the end to commit himself with integrity to his unorthodox music and personal style is accurate enough, but unfortunately Orbison was not always successful in "beating back the pressures of conformity." There were times in his career when Orbison in fact capitulated to those pressures, both musically and otherwise.

Musicians frequently compared Orbison's work to classical music and opera, and implied that his music was too good and too timeless to be categorized as pop. As we have seen, David Gates's obituary in *Newsweek* claimed that Orbison's music approached the "art song." During the filming of *A Black and White Night*, Jackson Browne called Orbison's music "symphonic." When he died Bob Dylan said simply, "Roy was an opera singer. He had the greatest voice." Tom Waits compared his songs to arias and described him as "a rockabilly Rigoletto, as important as Caruso in sunglasses and a leather jacket." Songwriter Will Jennings said, "The nearest thing to Roy—there's nothing like it in rock music—the nearest thing is Verdi and Puccini in grand opera" (Goldberg 1989, 32–33). Toward the end of his career Orbison uncharacteristically acknowledged that there might be some validity in the comparisons to classical musicians: "'I always felt each instrumental and vocal inflection had to be special. . . . I'd spend almost as much time on those as I'd spend on the song itself. Looking back on it now, I felt that I was blessed much like the masters, I guess—the guys who wrote the concertos'" (Amburn 1990, 129). Orbison's music and singing style do in fact depart from the popular rock norms of the times in a manner that helps account for this pervasive if at times baffling array of analogies to classical music. While Orbison's music is literally, of course, neither symphony nor opera nor art song, it does share elements with all of these forms.

The discourse of the classical musician whose music is artistic, complex, and timeless is related to the discourse of "The Voice," a common nickname first for Frank Sinatra and now, in the world of rock, for Orbison. "The Voice," of course, was a reference to Orbison's unusual vocal range, power, and nuance of phrasing, but one music magazine went to the logical extreme when it suggested that, in death, "The Voice" was all that was left, freed from the body. From this perspective, Orbison's voice was always on a trajectory of being severed from the body and soaring away on its own. If his body seemed troubled, unattractive, sickly, and frail, "The Voice" was strong and vital beyond compare in the world of rock.

These discourses of "The Voice," the classical musician, and the musician's musician suggest something of the hyperbole that has often marked statements about Orbison. Other highly regarded musicians spoke about Orbison in wildly exaggerated ways, frequently using the kind of language typical of that used by fans when talking about stars. Bono, the lead singer of U2, remarked of Orbison, "He was at the time of his death the finest white pop singer on the planet" (Zimmerman 1988, 2D). Emmylou Harris, who had years earlier claimed that she never wanted to sell her house after Orbison had sung in it, called him "one of the greatest singers that ever lived" (Zimmerman, 1D). When asked what it was like to open for Orbison, Chris Isaac remarked, "It's like doing card tricks before the Second Coming" (Holden 1991, C12). Emerging from the *Black and White Night* concert, Patrick Swayze said, "I saw God and the Boss [Bruce Springsteen] on the same night" (*People* 1987, 45).

Isaac's and Swayze's remarks also point to a religious discourse that has sprung up around Orbison, who is frequently characterized as god-like or not of this world. When he died, Billy Joel said, "He had the voice of an angel," and rock critic Dave Marsh wrote of the soon-to-be-released CD *Mystery Girl*, "Roy sings like a god across the whole record" (Marsh 1989a, 1). Dwight Yoakam described Orbison's voice as that of the cry of an angel falling backward through an open window. In a related vein, Springsteen, in his 1987 speech inducting Orbison into the Rock 'n' Roll Hall of Fame, said Orbison had the ability "to sound like he'd dropped in from another planet" (Springsteen 1987). Near the end of his life, Orbison himself contributed to this discourse by repeatedly telling interviewers that his writing and singing were a direct gift from God and that he could not personally take credit for his accomplishments; God spoke through him. He also remarked that he often felt that he was not long for this world; he was merely passing through. Though he did not bother to say where he came from or where he was going, such talk combined with Orbison's dark, mysterious persona, Springsteen's "visitor-from-another-planet" statement, and the religious imagery to give him a quality of other-worldliness—if he was not God, surely he was some kind of unique black angel.

Perhaps it is not altogether surprising that there was a strange and related discourse about Orbison's body. How could one be at once god-like, angelic, and not of this world, yet inhabit a normal corporeal body?

Orbison's body became a troubled site of attention. Once again Springsteen was particularly evocative when he observed that on first meeting Orbison, he felt that he could reach out and put his hand through Orbison's body. The body was somehow insubstantial, not entirely of this world. At the 1989 Roy Orbison tribute concert, Bernie Taupin referred to Orbison as "frail," an adjective not commonly applied to rock stars. James Dickerson, who was present throughout the recording sessions of *The Class of '55*, the 1985 collaboration with Johnny Cash, Jerry Lee Lewis, and Carl Perkins, echoes Taupin's remark when he observes: "For most of the Memphis sessions, Orbison looked shaky. His hands shook and his voice trembled. On the first takes of 'Coming Home' his voice was embarrassingly tenuous. He was a pitiful sight sitting in that darkened studio with a roomful of musicians" (Dickerson 1996, 14–15).

Indeed, Dickerson paints a portrait of a man who is shaky and frail mentally as well as physically. He claims that on the first day Orbison was "traumatized" (9) by the media and by the presence of the other legendary singers. The next day, when Orbison was scheduled for his first recording session, he didn't show up, and Chips Moman, the producer, explained that Orbison was ill with a virus; Dickerson, however, says he was merely emotionally distressed: "Eventually, Orbison showed up, several hours late, looking pale and nervous. He sang the first few bars of a song he had co-written, 'Coming Home,' then he left for the hotel, complaining of a sore throat. He had spent less than fifteen minutes at the studio" (9).

Although Dickerson attributes Orbison's lack of composure to the special circumstances surrounding the reunion with his former Sun stars, Orbison was typically nervous and shaky at the beginning of his concerts, a fact to which I can attest personally. I saw him perform many times during the seventies and eighties, and he always appeared to be suffering from a bad case of stage fright when he first appeared on stage. When he uncharacteristically appeared as a headliner at a Madison Square Garden oldies concert in the early seventies, he actually had to be helped onto the stage. He always began his concerts in those years with "Only the Lonely," and in addition to appearing shaky and nervous, his voice always sounded tenuous for the first part of the song. Yet without fail, by the midpoint of the song, the full strength of the voice returned and remained in force for the rest of the concert.

During the sixties and early seventies it was not unusual for Orbison to cancel a concert (including several for which I had tickets!). In the eighties he became a much more reliable performer, but he never got over his apparent terror of going out on stage and performing. Toward the end of his life, he seemed more relaxed and confident, and even appeared to enjoy himself after the inevitable attack of nerves. In short, it didn't require a reunion with music legends or the presence of the media to bring on the type of behavior Dickerson describes.

John Belushi's *Saturday Night Live* parody of Orbison in the late 1970s touched on what had by then become and would remain the three most notable aspects of the singer's body and performance style: its immobility, the totally black clothing that covered it, and the ever-present dark glasses. In the first part of the skit, Orbison's wife tries to get his attention by removing his glasses, only to find another pair beneath them. And another and another and another. The skit ends with a concert performance of "Oh, Pretty Woman." Rigid as a board, Belushi falls over while singing and playing guitar. He never misses a note as band members pick him up, and he finishes the song totally expressionless.

This perceptive caricature of Orbison raises the issue of his rejection of the traditional masculine posture in rock 'n' roll. Most rock singers of the period, most convincingly Elvis Presley, strutted around the stage, posturing in a sexually aggressive and overtly macho style. Critics have long pointed out that the display of the male body in rock 'n' roll is feminizing, in that the male body becomes the object of an erotic spectacle like that traditionally reserved in Western culture for women. This observation is fine as far as it goes, but it must equally be noted that the male body on the rock stage frequently goes to extremes to counter any connotation of femininity. Indeed, male rock performance sometimes reveals the same instabilities Richard Dyer has located in the male pinup. While these instabilities may still be present today, they were particularly present in Orbison's era, when Presley, Chuck Berry, and Jerry Lee Lewis, to name just a few, displayed an active and erotic male sexuality. Their bodies may have been spectacles, but they were spectacles that bespoke male (hetero)sexual power. Not so with Orbison.

This contrast between Orbison and other performers can be seen in *Hail! Hail! Rock 'n' Roll* (1988), a documentary about Chuck Berry, in which we can compare Orbison's scenes with those of Jerry Lee Lewis. Lewis, with trademark cigar and bourbon in hand, talks in typically braggadocio fashion about how Chuck Berry won Lewis's respect in a fight the two had. Predictably enough, Orbison appears in a black leather jacket, in fact totally enshrouded in black. Even with the jacket, however, he neither looks nor acts tough. If anything, the jacket looks like a shell that protects the soft-spoken Orbison, who talks about how Berry's being both a singer and a songwriter influenced him.

Orbison later contributed to this discourse by referring to the early sixties as a time when men weren't supposed to cry. Coming out of his 1988 recording session with k. d. lang, he joked that he had tried to be macho but failed. By 1988 the view of Orbison as feminine had emerged in the press, as in the earlier cited Watrous review in the *New York Times:* "Of all the rock-and-roll singers of his generation, Mr. Orbison is the least obsessed with masculinity; the music and his voice and words are unmenacing and complex" (Watrous 1988, 48). Here again Watrous is perceptive, but a more accurate assessment might be that Orbison's music and performance style were *most* obsessed with masculinity, but in reverse—that is, through its questioning of the machismo of the late 1950s and early 1960s. Watrous is also correct that Orbison's music lacks sexual menace, but it is important to distinguish this from Pat Boone's style of blandly watering down rock's sexuality to make it clean and safely middle class. Everything about Orbison's music, performance style, and persona is unusual with respect to gender stereotypes and defies generalizations about the rock music of his era. By not creating and circulating sexually desirable images of himself in fan magazines and on record albums, by minimizing the sexual display of his body in performance and hiding behind impenetrable dark glasses, by singing in an eerie high range, and most of all by writing songs explicitly about male anxiety and excessive emotion, Roy Orbison created a significant alternative to the sexual image of traditional male rock stars.

This difference extended also into the sphere of race. From the very beginning, Orbison's music bore an uneasy relationship to the black music that was such an influential model for white rock 'n' roll singers. Orbison's Monument recordings frequently showed little or none of the black influence so pervasive in the mainstream of rock at the time. Although no racial discourse sprang up around Orbison during his lifetime, a legal and racial discourse about him emerged in the highly publicized 1994 Supreme Court case involving 2 Live Crew's unauthorized version of "Oh, Pretty Woman."

Nearly all of the discourses I have identified reveal a sense of difference about Orbison. That the discourses of hyperbole and the musician's musician speak about him in such extreme language stems from a sense of difference or uniqueness. "There will never be another singer like Roy Orbison," Bonnie Raitt said at the tribute concert. And David Hinckley wrote: "All singers have someone who sounds like them—except Orbison. No one sounds even a little like Roy Orbison" (Hinckley 1988, D20). How could any single musician be hailed by such a diverse group of other musicians? They range from pop, country, and blues to nearly every form of rock 'n' roll, including punk, new wave, and new country, as well as current folk music. In an obituary, the jazz magazine *Down Beat* claimed that "Elvis Presley said Orbison had the grandest voice in pop music. A listen to 'Only the Lonely,' 'Blue Bayou,' 'Oh, Pretty Woman,' and 'Crying' proves it" (*Down Beat* 1989, 13). Robert Hilburn commented on this aspect of Orbison's music in his *Los Angeles Times* review of the tribute concert, when he noted that "the fact that artists as varied as Emmylou Harris, John Hiatt, Booker T. Jones, Joe Ely, Cindy Bullens, Michael McDonald and members of the Talking Heads can find common ground in the music of a single writer also underscores the richness and range of Orbison's grand musical legacy" (Hilburn 1989, F7).

Presumably Orbison's music means something much different to Ricky Skaggs than it does to David Lynch, and in that sense also there are many Roy Orbisons. In addition to the many Orbisons constructed over the years by the record companies and the artist himself, perhaps the common thread that dominates is one of mystery, be it the mystery of absence or the mysterious presence hidden behind dark glasses, seldom talking either in concerts or to the press. The press never got tired of shoving microphones in front of the Beatles or Bob Dylan and asking them questions of earth-shaking significance. But, to the day he died, very few Americans could have told anyone anything about what Orbison thought or believed about any subject of any importance. Was he a dove or a hawk during the Vietnam era? We don't know. Like Andy Warhol, whom in some ways he resembled, Orbison was a *tabula rasa* upon which different people projected different versions of the man. In a departure for our media-saturated society, there are so many Roy Orbisons precisely because the "real" one was so mysterious.

2

Mystery Man

The Evolution of a Dark, Mysterious Persona

ven if they knew nothing about the singer, anyone picking up Roy Orbison's posthumously released *Mystery Girl* CD (1989) might quickly conclude that the true mystery is not the girl of the title song but the dark, enigmatic figure on the cover. *Mystery Girl* shows two images of Orbison's face and arm, the second being an upside-down inversion of the first, with everything pitch black except the whiteness of the skin of his face and hand, the latter mysteriously cupped near his mouth. The lenses of his glasses are as black as the frames and the utterly black background against which he appears. The liner notes include two additional photographs of Orbison; he is dressed in black in both of them and the lenses of his glasses might as well be painted black. Even a small drawing of Orbison is totally black. In this chapter I will trace the origins, evolution, and meanings of Orbison's man-in-black persona.[1]

As the title of John Harvey's excellent book *Men in Black* suggests, Orbison is part of a longstanding tradition. Indeed, the question is not why Orbison, like so many others, assumed the persona, but why it was so successful that, in an era of countless men in black, his blackness somehow seemed unique. We need look no further than Johnny Cash,

Mystery Girl (1989, Virgin)

one of Orbison's fellow Sun recording artists and lifelong friend, to see
how common the man-in-black image was at that time. Indeed, it was
Cash, not Orbison, who was nicknamed "The Man in Black," from the
title of one of his best-known songs, in which Cash explains that he
wears black in mourning for the imprisoned, the beaten down, the hun-
gry, and the hopeless.

Harvey traces to the 1830s the popularity of men wearing black in
the Western world. Before that men wore many colors, even during the
Renaissance, when black was a fashion but not an altogether dominant
one. In the 1830s men's formal evening wear became black. "Men
wanted to dress in a smart kind of mourning," Harvey writes, and the
fashion became so pervasive that "the nineteenth century looked like

a funeral" (Harvey 1995, 24). Given the world of ever-changing fashion trends, it was remarkable, as Harvey notes, that "black fashions may come and go, but in 1820 or so black came and did not go" (29).

In the ensuing decades black acquired many meanings, both secular and religious. Indeed, so many different meanings have been attached to the color over the years that it is hard to say in what sense the color black means anything, since it seems to mean almost everything. Harvey offers a few meanings that seem particularly relevant to Orbison, however. "Black is rich and has many meanings, but still its most widespread and fundamental value lies in its association with darkness and night, and with the ancient natural imagery that connects night with death" (41). Images of darkness, night, and death form central motifs in Orbison's music in precisely such an interconnected manner.

Harvey continues:

> If black is the color of grieving love, it is also the colour of the grief of love, of the misery of a heartfelt unreturned love. . . . And if one wants someone one loves with the same intensity one wants back someone who has died, then the colour of mourning will be the colour of loving too. At the same time, the fact that the beloved will still be alive to see the lover grieving gives his black a more assertive and aggressive character, public as it is. There is an element of performance in it, there could easily be an element of pose. And the figure of the lover in black—the young man melancholy with yearning love—is a type that recurs in history. (51)

Harvey's observations apply very closely to Orbison's music, in which love is frequently unrequited and there is a pronounced public dimension to suffering. Needless to say, there is a huge element of performance and pose in Orbison's black persona. Although he opened up rock 'n' roll to the expression of a range of masculine emotions, those emotions (masculine doubt, vulnerability, fear, and so on) cannot be regarded as somehow more natural or authentic than the traditional macho self-confidence and strutting that characterized the music of the time. Orbison presented an alternative and an important, influential masculinity, but it too was a construction.

In the twentieth century, women begin wearing black as much as or even more than men did. In the nineteenth century, Harvey notes, black dress was a masculine phenomenon, and women continued to wear a variety of colors. Though Harvey does not mention it, this is still very much the case in the late-twentieth-century and early-twenty-first-century world of classical music, where during concerts and recitals the male soloists nearly always dress in black formal wear and the female soloists in colorful gowns. If the performance involves both men and women, the contrast is stark. But this, like so much about classical music, is an anachronism; part of its appeal lies precisely in how it harkens back to a nineteenth-century world that no longer exists. The black leather jackets worn by Joan Jett or Madonna show how black has, in fact, been taken up by women in our time.

During the second half of the twentieth century, black became strongly associated with power and authority, something Harvey traces through the World Wars (flyers' jackets and fascist regalia) and through the evolution of police uniforms. From there it migrated to bikers and "it has also become the standard youth uniform, a means of putting on toughness in readiness to hit the street" (245). Harvey concludes that "in putting on black leather you are putting on power: it may be the power that defies the law, it may be the power that enforces it" (245). To which I would add the power to hide from the law. Black may (and frequently does) bespeak power on both sides of the law, but this also suggests that black may be worn as a protective shell that hides weakness, fear, and sensitivity. Harvey writes of young people "putting on an extra skin" when they wear black (245) and the metaphor is apt. But of course one may don that extra layer of protection not because one is tough but precisely because one is not. In this case, wearing black becomes a masquerade and it is this meaning of black that I would argue is dominant in Orbison's image. The Orbison persona wears black to protect a masculinity that is anything but powerful, on either side of the law. Black in this sense is a barrier behind which a man hides—from the law, from lawbreakers, from tough guys, from women, from prying eyes, from public scrutiny, from whatever threatens from without.

The first glimpse of Roy Orbison offered to a large public is the photograph on the cover of his first Monument album, *Lonely and Blue* (1962). Orbison is sitting alone in a car at a drive-in restaurant. His head rests on his arm, which is propped on the food tray attached to the car door. He looks lonely but in no way unusual or mysterious. Indeed, he looks remarkably ordinary; none of the features of his trademark image are present—no emphasis on his black hair, no black clothes, no dark glasses.

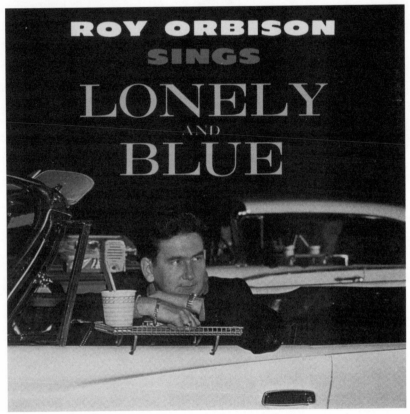

Lonely and Blue (1961, Monument [CD reissue])

As this image so clearly shows, there is no necessary connection between an image of loneliness and one of blackness or darkness. This was the dominant image of Orbison until 1963, when his album *In Dreams* was released, featuring another picture of the singer on the cover.

Between those two records, a collection of Sun recordings entitled *At the Rock House* (1961) was released, but it included no images of the singer on either the front or back cover. In 1962 Monument released two more albums: *Crying* and *Roy Orbison's Greatest Hits*. The cover of *Crying* featured a drawing of a theatrical mask with a tear running down its cheek. On the back side was a small black-and-white photograph of Orbison, now sporting a black pompadour and eyeglasses with black frames. The glasses, however, are clear, and he is smiling. His clothing is not primarily black or even dark; he wears a broad V-stripe-patterned sweater that reveals only the casually open collar of the black shirt beneath. What is striking about this picture is how ordinary Orbison looks. The *Greatest Hits* album cover contains no pictures at all—both sides simply list the song titles in bold, multicolored lettering, as if to proclaim that the songs speak for themselves.

In Dreams, released the following year, featured the most prominent picture of Orbison to date. A large color photo of Orbison fills the entire cover. It is similar to the small black-and-white picture on the back cover of *Crying* in terms of hairstyle, glasses, and clothing. Orbison wears a colored, broad-striped sweater, this time with a white shirt and tie underneath. He clutches a guitar across his body and looks directly out at the viewer, smiling broadly. He appears quite congenial.

In Dreams (1963, Monument)

In 1964 Orbison released two albums. The cover of *Early Orbison* is remarkable in terms of tracing the developing persona. It includes a baby picture of Orbison, over which is superimposed a drawing of eye-glass frames in black crayon. The empty frames, while foreshadowing the glasses that will become a crucial component of Orbison's persona, also gently and lovingly draw attention to Orbison's life-long vision problem. There is no hint of the ubiquitous dark lenses through which Orbison views the world. *More of Roy Orbison's Greatest Hits* continues the strategy of employing no image. Again, the front cover simply proclaims the titles of the songs, each title written on the label of a representation of a Monument 45 rpm. The copy on the back cover, by Tupper Saussy, reinforces the notion that the songs speak for themselves:

> Roy Orbison is possibly the most unusual phenomenon I have ever encountered in music. He has never been in a movie. He has only rarely been seen on network television. He has no press agent hawking his name and his songs in the pages of the fan magazines and the music business magazines. . . . It is not Roy's flashy clothes that sell his records; it's not the way he combs his hair, or the headlines he makes or the legends that promotion men weave about artists that sell his records; it is his music that sells his records. . . . Roy Orbison is living proof that the young American and European will go out—silently and deliberately and with little fanfare—and buy the music of an artist who, stripped of the usual gimmickry and glitter, has only his talent to sell.

This passage is an unusually direct acknowledgment of Monument's marketing strategy for Orbison, which paradoxically denies that there is a strategy. There are no pictures on this and other Monument albums, we are told, because appearance has nothing to do with Orbison's success; his music, not his looks, sells the records. Something of the peculiar nature of this strategy becomes clear with the assertion that Orbison has no publicity agent. Ironically, the liner notes publicize the fact he does not seek publicity! And of course Saussy's statement is ironic in that Orbison's hairstyle and dark glasses were about to become an important part of his persona.

Even so, there is something in what Saussy says. Orbison was unique among major rock stars of the time in both his absence from the fan magazines and the extreme de-emphasis on his looks as a major component of his image. He really had no press agent, something he would be proud of in later years and that would contribute to the discourse of "The Voice" that sprang up around Orbison, as if his great voice were almost disembodied. The liner notes to *Greatest Hits* also make clear that the Monument strategy was to keep Orbison off camera, as it were, rather than create an aura of mystery around his appearance. In 1964, Orbison's last full year under contract to Monument records, he was promoted as an exceptionally talented though seldom seen musician whose appeal had nothing to do with glamorous looks or gimmicks. This was a far cry from what his image would soon become and in some manner remain. Until the end of his career, Orbison's commercial and critical success would rest on these Monument recordings, all of which were made and marketed before his metamorphosis into a dark, mysterious, tragic figure. Although he signed with MGM in 1965 and his first MGM album appeared that year, Monument released an album of old and new material entitled *Orbisongs*, which included his biggest hit, "Oh, Pretty Woman" (1964). Once again, the album cover contained no images of Orbison. The front cover shows sheet music on which are written Orbison song titles. On top of the sheets is a pair of sunglasses with brown frames and green-lenses. The emphasis on the glasses begun with *Early Orbison* continues here, but with two important differences: the lenses are dark and the person does not appear—the dark glasses have become a metonymy for the artist himself. In 1966 Monument released *The Very Best of Roy Orbison*, another greatest-hits package with no pictures of the artist. Even after he left the label and developed his new dark image at MGM, Monument continued to minimize or avoid the display of the man. The image most people have of Roy Orbison was created after his most popular songs were recorded. Orbison's first album for MGM was, ironically, entitled *There Is Only One Roy Orbison* (1965), ironically because it was the first image on any album to present an aspect of the "new" Roy Orbison that would almost never change—the ubiquitous dark glasses. Every subsequent album photograph, performance, press event, and television appearance would maintain this image, with the sole exception of the 1967 film and soundtrack album, *The Fastest Guitar Alive*. The film was a disaster at the box office and had no perceptible effect on his persona.

The cover photograph on the 1965 album shows a large, low-angle image of the singer from the shoulders up. He wears an extremely dark blue jacket over a blue shirt with a prominent collar. The black frames of his prominent eyeglasses hold brown lenses. In a manner that would become fairly typical, the photo's composition and lighting make his eyes invisible. He stands against a predominantly blue sky, and a dark blue border frames the photograph. Awash in shades of blue, the album's front cover sets off Orbison's black pompadour hairstyle. The back cover shows a large image of Orbison riding a motorcycle. It has been removed from its original context and is simply placed over a white background. Here he is dressed entirely in black, and the lighting makes his glasses appear impenetrably black;

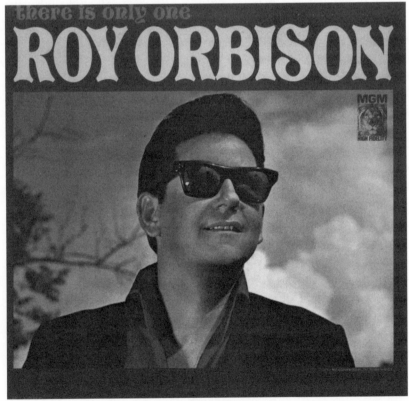

There Is Only One Roy Orbison (1965, MGM)

not only can we not look into them, it is hard to imagine that he can see through them.

By the time his second MGM album, *The Orbison Way* (1966), appeared, the blackness of the previous album's back cover has now moved front and center. A large image of Orbison leaning against a wall shows him dressed totally in black: boots, pants, belt, shirt, even his watchband. The lighting blackens the lenses of his black-framed eyeglasses. The black pompadour is still in place. Although the photo on *There Is Only One Roy Orbison* shows the hint of a smile on his slightly parted lips, here he is dead serious. The image is extremely stylized and highly posed in comparison to the seemingly more natural ones of the previous album. His arms are crossed and one leg is bent, the sole of his boot flat against the wall behind him. Here, for the first time in his album art, we have the full-blown mysterious black persona. This is not someone who just happens to be wearing black today—this is a person who defines himself through the color black and who appears to see the world through that color. (The manner in which Orbison's eyeglasses were frequently lit to appear impenetrable led many people to presume that he was blind, or at least to wonder.)

The next album, *The Classic Roy Orbison*, released later in 1966, absolutely cemented the evolving black persona. Orbison stands by a classic black convertible. His entirely black ensemble is now completed by black gloves. His open high collar reveals his neck; we see so little of his body that this photo eerily recalls Harvey's comparison of dressing in black with putting on another skin. The black pompadour and dark glasses are prominent. Again his expression betrays no trace of a smile. This mysterious dark figure is now marked as tragic by the dual personal tragedies that preceded the album's release. (I will discuss the images of motorcycles, cars, and even airplanes on Orbison's album covers in Chapter 4; for the moment I will simply note that the classy black car points to the manner in which Harvey links the color to power and ownership. Although I believe that Orbison's use of black is all on the side of loss in relation to sex and romance ["I Got Nothing," the title of a recently released 1969 MGM song, says it all], the recurring images of classic automobiles suggest the nearly opposite function of economic possession. If Orbison fails in one arena, he succeeds in the other; if he loses the girl, he wins the classic car.)

The Classic Roy Orbison (1966, MGM)

All of the remaining MGM albums include some of the now established Orbison iconography. In 1967 *Roy Orbison Sings Don Gibson* was
released in a manner recalling the Monument album *Orbisongs*. A drawing of the singer's white face emerges from a black background against
which his black hair is indistinguishable. The black glasses with brown
lenses are prominently drawn in, and identical images of Don Gibson
are reflected in each lens. The images of Gibson are marked by photo-
graphic detail, while the image of Orbison seems little more than
abstracted dark glasses against a pitch-black background. *Cry Softly
Lonely One* (1967) returned once again to the classic automobile motif,

this time showing Orbison, wearing a brown jacket, behind the wheel. The back cover, however, features a large black-and-white image of his face. The image is almost abstract in its stark contrast of black and white, with no realistic detail. The eyes are lost again behind the glasses and the black shirt covering his shoulders and part of his neck combine with the black hair to make the image one of the most extreme "unrealistic" depictions of black mystery to date. This no longer looks like a living man. *Roy Orbison's Many Moods* (1969) shows his image somewhat softened by the white shirt he wears under a black jacket and by the broad smile on his face. The eyes are once again invisible behind dark glasses. The back cover, however, includes an even darker black-and-white version of the cover from *The Orbison Way*. In this print, the left side of his face is blackened by a dark shadow. If the front covers of *Many Moods* and *Cry Softly* seem to vary or humanize the mysterious tragic figure, the back covers reassert it fully.

Nineteen-seventy saw the release of *The Great Songs of Roy Orbison* and *Hank Williams the Roy Orbison Way*. The former, mostly a collection of MGM singles, includes five photographs of Orbison on the cover. In four of them he is dressed primarily or entirely in black and in all four his eyes are invisible behind the dark lenses. In the fifth, he wears a light purple shirt with black pants. He is smiling, and his eyes are visible through the lenses. An important change in image occurs with the Hank Williams album. Once again he is dressed entirely in black, but the lighting is such that the colored lenses are minimized and his eyes can be seen clearly. The change involves his hairstyle: eight years after the initial impact of the Beatles, Orbison finally replaces his fifties pompadour with a "mod" sixties-style haircut. The hair was still black and would remain so, though for the remainder of his career its style would change gradually, in keeping with the times. When he died in 1988, he was sporting a then-fashionable ponytail.

The cover photo of the 1972 album *Roy Orbison Sings* is so dark as to appear black, but in fact Orbison is wearing a purple jumpsuit as he performs in front of a microphone. The same year his album *Memphis* was released, and the cover featured a drawing rather than a photograph, though the drawing included the familiar dark glasses. The last MGM album, *Milestones*, released the following year, included no image of

Orbison anywhere on the front or back covers. All of the remaining albums used variations on the Monument and MGM approaches. The Mercury album *I'm Still in Love with You* (1975) and the Monument album *Regeneration* (1977) both used drawings of Orbison featuring the trademark glasses. The Asylum album *Laminar Flow* used large photographs of Orbison on the front and back covers as well as the jacket sleeve, in all of which he was dressed totally in black, prominently including a black leather jacket.

The posthumous Virgin CDs *Mystery Girl* (1989) and *King of Hearts* (1992) make a conscious late-period reference to the mysterious black persona. Both are predominantly black covers that show Orbison clad entirely in black. *Mystery Girl*, as described earlier, presents a figure enshrouded in black, in an enigmatic pose that is doubled in a mirror image. *King of Hearts* shows a more "realistic" image of Orbison but it is nearly as black. In place of the totally abstract black background that seems to envelop Orbison on *Mystery Girl*, here we see a black-and-white photograph of him sitting on a stool holding his guitar, with a microphone in front of him. What appears to be a white spotlight whitens the area directly behind him and on the floor around him. He casts a prominent black shadow on the white floor, and the white area behind him is bordered by pitch black. As usual, the glasses appear black and opaque. Though anchored somewhat by what appears to be a performance space, the lack of any real-world detail contributes an otherworldly feeling to the space the black clad figure inhabits. This black space may resemble Hell, but Orbison looks more like a black angel than a devil. With the release of his last finished studio album, composed largely of new but unfinished material, the man-in-black persona reached its pinnacle. Orbison had by now become so associated with the color black that he seemed part of the surrounding blackness from which he emerged and into which he might momentarily dissolve again: he appeared to be at once surrounded by darkness and darkness itself.

The element of blackness in Orbison's persona is central to many of the other discourses about him and also to his lyrics. But why would the use of black stand out so starkly in an age when men and women alike dressed predominantly in black? Harvey observes that "what has seemed to me a curious point of interest for study is the way in which, through time, the use of this colour—the colour that is without colour, without light, the color of grief, of loss, of humility, of guilt, of shame—has been adopted in its use by men not as the colour of what they lack or have lost, but precisely as the signature of what they have: of standing, goods, mastery" (Harvey 1995, 10).

From this perspective Orbison is an anachronism, for his use of black is indeed a sign of what he lacks and what he has lost, both literally and symbolically. At the literal level, his music frequently centers on the lack of powerful, active, traditional masculinity, and on the loss of the woman he loves. Symbolically, and in psychoanalytic terms, he lacks the phallus and consequently has trouble occupying the position of the Father, while at the same time he has lost the mother and the unification with her that precedes the infant's experience of separation and ego formation.

Orbison's blackness is more noticeable, more defining, than the blackness of other rock singers for several reasons, most notably the dark glasses. On the face of it eyeglasses may not strike us as an essential element of any persona, but in Orbison's case they were the sine qua non. Starting in 1963, Orbison always wore dark glasses during live performances and in public, indoors and out, day and night. He was the first mainstream white pop or rock musician to do so, although so many have followed this practice that it can be easy to forget that dark glasses were not always the norm in pop and rock music. Even in the world of thirties and forties African American jazz, where sunglasses were a common accouterment, no musician was known for wearing them virtually all the time in public. In rock 'n' roll, Buddy Holly became associated with thick black frames similar to those that Orbison would wear, and pictures show Holly wearing sunglasses indoors, but they were not the same kind of defining element for Holly that they became for Orbison. Orbison's dark glasses somehow signified less that he was cool than that the man hidden behind them *always* looked at the world darkly. There was never, it seemed, a light moment in his life.

The evolution of the persona I have traced also heightened its impact. Had he started with a black persona, it might have been less shocking. But during the most successful phase of his career, his image was largely an absence. He was mysterious in the sense that the public had little idea of his presence as either a physical being or even someone with a private life. The few images of Orbison that did circulate before 1963 showed him with brown hair and no glasses, and then with black hair and black eyeglass frames with normal lenses. When, in the mid-sixties, his image crystallized as the man in black hidden behind dark glasses, he was transformed from one kind of mystery to another. Once the man was revealed, people thought he *looked* mysterious. Thus there is an uncanny (and I think unplanned) relationship between Orbison before he had a persona (beyond that of the talented musician of undistinguished looks) and the strange-looking figure enveloped in black. The initial lack of information about Orbison, visual or otherwise, helped set the stage for the mysterious persona who eventually appeared.

The startling contrast between what Orbison had once been and what he became underscored the blackness and revealed the construction of the persona. Central to this persona, as we have seen, were the overwhelming losses of his wife and two of his children that marked Orbison as a tragic figure, associating him with the color of mourning. Although he had transformed his appearance years before either tragedy occurred, his personal tragedies seemed to verify the real suffering and loss of the man in black. By a perverse logic, all that life could hold for such a darkened man was tragedy and loss. The real events of his life, in other words, seemed to confer on the carefully constructed persona the mark of absolute authenticity. The black persona, constructed between 1963 and 1966, dominated the years immediately preceding and following Orbison's death, gathering new inflections and merging with other discourses about Orbison. One of these was the discourse of tragedy that would never disappear.

In the 1980s a new generation of artists discovered Orbison as a major figure in the history of rock 'n' roll, one far removed from the pop singer of innocent teenage ballads that he was thought to be during the early sixties. Two events contributed to the creation of this new discourse: filmmaker David Lynch's emphasis on the dark, sexual side of "In Dreams," which he used in his cult hit, *Blue Velvet* (1986), and Bruce Springsteen's speech at Orbison's induction into the Rock 'n' Roll Hall of Fame in 1987. Springsteen described Orbison as a singer who "came out in dark glasses, a dark suit, and . . . played some dark music," music that Springsteen saw as the "underside of pop romance" and listened to "alone and in the dark" (Springsteen 1987). Both Springsteen and Lynch gave a new inflection to the Orbison persona. The dark sexuality that Lynch associates with "In Dreams" is closely connected to Springsteen's "underside" of romance; both link the dark persona to the music itself. At a Roy Orbison tribute concert in Los Angeles in 1989, Bernie Taupin confirmed this element of the persona when he described listening to Orbison's music as a boy, lying in bed in the dark. Orbison's music not only sprang from loneliness and darkness; it was received in the same lonely darkness.

This new critical discourse of darkness so drastically reinterpreted the music that it seemed to catch Orbison by surprise, and he distanced himself from it. He had been instrumental in developing his dark persona, and if he intended something like what Springsteen and Taupin described, he should have embraced the new discourse of the eighties. Why didn't he? I can only conjecture that he felt uncomfortable seeing what had been implicit in his work made so explicit. Before turning to the lyrics of the songs and their relationship to this discourse of darkness, in the next chapter I examine the music itself—the songwriting, the singing style, and the record production that created Orbison's sound and riveted attention on him. Not surprisingly, those aspects of his music were all as unusual as the lyrics and the persona of the man who wrote and sang them.

3

"Radical Left Turns"
The Voice and the Music

f Roy Orbison is a significant artist, what kind of artist is he? Obviously he is a singer, but he is also a prolific songwriter. To be more precise, he is not just a singer but a recording artist. He did not, however, produce most of his recordings, nor did he play instruments on many of them. He did perform live throughout his career, and so he was also an instrumentalist, always playing guitar and occasionally harmonica. Given all of these roles, the attempts of critics and musicians to draw parallels between Orbison's and classical music, comparing him to everyone from Schubert to Verde to Puccini to Caruso, have serious limitations—as do analogies between Orbison's songs and the art song, or *lieder,* and operatic traditions.

I have argued elsewhere that one of the most productive ways to approach authorship in the arts is via notational systems. That is, art forms with highly developed notational systems enable authorship to be clearly separated from performance (Lehman 1978, 1990). It might seem from this point of view that music is music, but it is not that simple. The Western tradition of classical music evolved hand in hand with what remains to this day the most sophisticated notational system in any of the arts. In Evan Eisenberg's words, "the work of the classical composer is usually complete on paper" (Eisenberg 1987, 128). The same cannot be said of, say, oil painting, for which there is of course no notational system. If you want to create an oil painting, you have to paint it yourself. You cannot leave instructions, as it were, for others. But if you want to write a symphony or an opera, you are not only not required to perform it yourself but in fact are unable to do so, as the performance of a symphony or opera requires many artists. In the Western tradition the conductor guides the performance, but Beethoven's Ninth Symphony would be no less Beethoven's had he never conducted it himself. Eisenberg notes, however, that since the advent of recording, some composers have taken a strong interest in the phonograph recording, and that, starting with Stravinsky, some of them have recorded all of their works. "When the composer is the performer, what the recording records is nothing less than the composer's intentions . . . if he is not composing in the recording studio, he may as well be. He is free to disregard his own markings but compelled to specify them—to indicate phrasing, dynamics, and the like by demonstration rather than description" (129). In such cases, classical music shares something with popular music.

The popular music tradition out of which rock 'n' roll grew involves a score, but not in the same way that the classical music tradition does. What Nelson Goodman calls the "constitutive features" of the aesthetic work have to be amenable to notation, and in rock 'n' roll they are not. The way that rock 'n' roll is sung, played, and produced is more important in constituting the identity of the work than how it is written. It is beside the point that popular music is amenable to notation in the sense that songs are "written," because the aesthetic complexity that constitutes a song's worth lies not in a complex notional system but in a complex performance/recording context. Like a screenplay, a popular song looks relatively simple on paper. To compare it in its written form to the score of a Schubert song is to condemn it to the aesthetic minor leagues in the same way that comparing the script of a Hollywood film to a Shakespeare play is to relegate it to insubstantiality, at best.

This being the case, a certain logic would dictate that the producer, not the singer, creates and controls the aesthetic production of rock music. In much the same way that a film director uses script, set design, and actors to create a complex whole, the record producer uses the song, the instruments, the singer's voice, and the electronic effects to create a unified aural experience. And there is an aesthetic history of rock 'n' roll that probably can and perhaps should be written within such a framework. Certainly isolated producers such as Phil Spector have attained precisely such an *auteur* status for just these reasons; many of the singers with whom Spector has worked are little more than components in his "wall-of-sound" creations, which, interestingly, have also been compared to works of classical music.

Indeed, Eisenberg has coined the term "phonographer" to describe the recording equivalent of an *auteur* film director. Eisenberg also draws upon analogies between film and music to make his argument, but he misses an important distinction between the two forms. Extending the analogy between record producers and film directors, the rock singer would be analogous to the film actor; but here is where the analogy falls apart. It is in the nature of filmmaking that film actors seldom have a comprehensive grasp of or control over their performance; it is pieced together from relatively brief shots over which they have little or no control and about which they frequently may not even know very much. Until they see the dailies, the rough cut, or in some cases the finished film, they have only a partial sense of their own "performance." (They are in a very different position in this sense from theater actors.) Even when rock 'n' roll is pieced together from many takes, the singer generally has full knowledge of the shape of the total vocal performance. While some rock 'n' roll is pieced together in such a manner, Orbison's, during his years at Monument, was not. Orbison was notorious for always insisting that songs be recorded in a single take and not spliced together from multiple takes. Furthermore, most if not all of the instruments were in the studio at the same time. Thus he not only heard his vocal performance but knew the primary elements of the arrangements as he sang. Even when following directions from his producer, Fred Foster, he understood, shaped, and controlled his vocal performance.

At MGM Orbison eventually lost control over the production process, including his preferred way of working with musicians in the studio. Newer recording techniques of building and layering tracks were used. Still, even under these circumstances, he did maintain control over the vocal track in the sense that he knew precisely how he was singing.

Snippets of never-released MGM tracks allow us to hear conversations between Orbison in the studio and the unidentified producer in the control booth. The producer frequently stops the recording to tell Orbison to modulate some aspect of his performance—for example, to increase the tempo, not to linger so long on the low notes, and so on. Orbison typically responds by trying it as directed. Even here, however, he can be said to have control over the shape and form of his vocal performance; my point is not that every phrasing idea originated with him any more than that every move of a stage actor originates with the actor. The crucial point is that Orbison had knowledge of and controlled his voice in that he produced and formed the sounds and grasped their overall shape, regardless of the extent to which that shape involved interaction between himself and others. Authorship is too frequently confused with romantic notions of complete originality and control, which is never the case, even with literary authors.

Recalling W. B. Yeats's observation that the dancer cannot be separated from the dance, it would seem that the rock singer cannot be separated from the recorded song any more than John Wayne can be separated from *The Searchers*. But in fact this is not true, either literally or metaphorically, and Eisenberg misses this point. It would in fact be easy to separate the vocal track from, say, "Running Scared." Until the era of digital image processing, it was not literally possible to extract John Wayne's performance from *The Searchers*. But even now, when it is possible, what can be extracted and "re-mixed" is not a unified, coherent performance over which Wayne had shaping knowledge and control; it is isolated moments of movement and posturing that can be recombined in a new manner. Indeed, such singers as Bob Dylan and the Beatles, whom Eisenberg identifies as moving "pop" toward "art," did not produce their own records.

Simon Frith observes that "voices, not songs, hold the key to our pop pleasures: musicologists may analyze the art of the Gershwins or Cole Porter, but we hear Bryan Ferry or Peggy Lee" (Frith 1996, 201). He is certainly right with reference to Orbison's vocal tradition, wherein the voice we hear is the central component of the pop aesthetic. Although both Eisenberg and Frith would agree that in pop music it is the recording and not the songwriting that we "hear," Eisenberg emphasizes the phonographer who records the song and Frith emphasizes the voice that sings the song. These views are not really opposed but exist on a continuum, and much good criticism can be written from both perspectives. The voice we hear in pop music is the recorded voice, inseparable from how it was recorded.

Not surprisingly, from the very beginning of his career, Orbison's interest in music extended well beyond his own writing, singing, and playing. In his history of Sun records, Colin Escott writes, "Orbison quickly developed a fascination for studio work—and it was the studio, rather than the stage, that became his true medium. He worked sessions for other artists and performed on commercials and radio spots that Sam Phillips continued to engineer" (Escott 1991, 149). Phillips himself remarks, "I'd kid him. I'd say, 'Roy, you're trying to get rid of the band and do it all yourself.' He just hated to lay his guitar down. He was either writing or developing a beat. He was totally preoccupied with making records" (quoted in Escott, 149). Similarly, Fred Foster confirmed years later that it was Orbison's idea, not his, to bring in strings on the Monument sessions, starting with "Uptown" and "Only the Lonely."

The first time I heard "Only the Lonely," upon its release in 1960, I heard something so new, so beautiful, so strange that nothing in the history of rock 'n' roll prepared me for it. First and foremost, the voice sounded like nothing I had ever heard or imagined, and this in spite of the fact that I had heard Roy Orbison's previous single, "Uptown," which had had little or no effect on me. How could a voice change so much between two songs? What had happened? Part of the answer, fittingly enough, lies in the production of the song, which Colin Escott has described in detail. "Fred Foster and Bill Porter placed him behind a coat rack laden with coats, which had the effect of isolating the voice from the other sounds in the studio. The RCA studio had a three-track recorder, which gave Porter the option of feeding Roy's vocal back upon itself in two loops to fatten it up, before committing it to one track of the three-track tape. . . . Porter also rethought the standard Nashville mix which built up from the platform of the rhythm section. He used Melson and the chorus as the platform, making them crowd the microphone for maximum intimacy, then built the mix around the vocal countermelody. The drums are almost inaudible" (Escott 2001, 35).

Clearly, the singer's voice cannot be separated from the recorded song, and what I refer to here as Orbison's voice is a complex aesthetic creation involving crucial input from Foster and Porter. It is remarkable that what I hear today in "Only the Lonely" is no different from what I heard forty years ago. When I listen to "Uptown"—and indeed everything that came before it (Sun, the Clovis sessions, the live Teen Kings, RCA)—I still don't understand it. Nothing in the earlier music hints at what that voice could do and would become, any more than the earlier songs foreshadow "Only the Lonely." It seemed to come from nowhere, or, as some would put it, from on high. Escott's research on the production and recording circumstances, however, reminds us that far from falling out of the heavens, the quality of Orbison's voice in "Only the Lonely" was the result of particular arrangements of coat racks, microphones, and tape loops.

Escott emphasizes the way circumstances in the studio created Orbison's unique sound, but Carl Perkins suggests that Orbison's live performances honed his voice. Reminiscing about the early Sun days, Perkins and David McGee write, "Of the cover versions Orbison performed live, one that 'absolutely warped' the audience . . . was 'Indian Love Call,' a song popularized in 1936 by Nelson Eddy and Jeanette MacDonald in the film *Rose Marie:* 'It was a killer . . . when he sang, "I'm callin' you-oo-oo-oo" you could hear a mosquito in that building, it got so quiet. People recognized something special. Roy was maybe one notch under raw greatness at that time'" (Perkins and McGee 1996, 200). Perkins's account of the audience's rapt attention sounds like an accurate description of what characterized his post-1960 concerts. That he was covering a Nelson Eddy and Jeanette MacDonald song is of equal interest, as it suggests that as early as the midfifties Orbison was interested in operettas that may have influenced his later work.

For those who had not heard Orbison in concert, "Only the Lonely" was the first opportunity to hear that "something special," that "greatness." The voice had a richness, a liquidity, a purity, a range, an eeriness not hinted at it in the earlier work. It was indescribably supple and intimate; it took your breath away, only to reveal even more breathtaking variations when it soared even higher, at the end of the song, in an unexpected melodic development. This attempt to put into words the effect of Orbison's voice—probably not much different from countless other attempts—is not particularly helpful in pinpointing what makes the singing on "Only the Lonely" unique. Although the special quality of the recordings is, finally, impossible to convey in words, in this chapter and in the Appendix I use some of Orbison's best-known compositions to try and come as close as possible to doing justice to Orbison's sound within the limitations of the written word. Orbison himself was quite aware of the accomplishment of "Only the Lonely," referring to it as one of the "flowerings" of his voice. He identified "Running Scared" as the other great "flowering" (*VH1: A Tribute to Roy Orbison*, 1988). Orbison was never very insightful (or perhaps forthcoming) or articulate in talking about his songs and persona, but he was quite perceptive when it came to his voice and vocal techniques. If "Only the Lonely" presented a richer voice than anything he had done before, "Running Scared" revealed a similarly startling power. Once he had achieved that rich range and the power, the main characteristics of his voice were established.

How the ending of "Running Scared" came to be recorded is a story that has been told often, but it is worth repeating briefly here, if only to reemphasize Foster's and Porter's roles in the creative process. Orbison had originally sung the ending in a soft falsetto voice. When both Foster and Porter complained that they couldn't hear it on the tape, Orbison redid the song, finishing with the now famous "operatic" ending. Since we now associate it with a dramatic, full-voice outburst, it is hard to imagine the song building toward a falsetto finale. Few alternate takes exist of the Monument recordings, because the technicians recorded over them in order to cut costs. Luckily, however, we have two versions of "(They Call You) Gigolette," a major song from this period that has received little attention. This song is treated more fully in the Appendix; here I want merely to point out that the two versions of it are parallel to the two versions of "Running Scared." In the release version on *In Dreams*, the song builds to an operatic conclusion very similar to, though more strained and less satisfying than, the conclusion of "Running Scared." On the alternate version, released posthumously in *The Legendary Roy Orbison* box set and later in *Orbison 1956–1965*, we hear a version that builds to a soft climax. In Orbison's *ouevre*, the notion of "building" to a climax and the "operatic" voice have become heavily intertwined, but these two versions of "Gigolette" show that Orbison actually developed his songwriting style, with its building climaxes, *separately* from the powerful voice we have come to associate with those songs. At the urging and with the coaching of Fred Foster, he learned how to develop and employ the powerful voice.

Many musicians paying tribute to Orbison quite rightly point out that the songs he wrote enabled him to use his powerful voice to the fullest, though it might be more accurate to say that the voice developed through interaction with the songs. We have an unfortunate tendency to think of the voice as something a singer is born with. Yet, even at the most superficial level, Orbison's career reveals that much of what we call the voice was in fact developed over time through hard work. Orbison's voice did indeed "flower" with "Only the Lonely" and "Running Scared," and it was not the same voice of "Ooby Dooby" or even "Uptown." But he did not just write songs that showcased the power of an already extant voice; the songs he wrote helped him develop that voice and discover its full possibilities.

"Only the Lonely" and "Running Scared" are revealing examples of how his songs enabled this development. The stories about how Orbison recorded "Only the Lonely" after Presley turned it down fail to acknowledge that the song Orbison wrote for Presley was not the same song he recorded himself. Because his career as a singer had not taken off, Orbison had come to think of himself, at the time, primarily as a songwriter. After Presley turned it down and he decided to record it himself, he continued to work on "Only the Lonely" for some time. He was working on another song at the time, and Fred Foster suggested that he combine the two.

Once more, the evolution of the recorded song reveals Fred Foster's role in Orbison's success. It was Foster who helped form the song we know as "Only the Lonely," and it was he who teased the power voice out of the soft, almost bashful voice Orbison had at the time. His RCA sessions with Chet Atkins sound fragile and tenuous next to the confident, powerful voice that would emerge under Foster's direction. The fruitful collaboration with Foster should remind us never to reduce authorship to the simplistic notion of individual genius. Orbison was certainly a genius of sorts, but his success involved significant contributions from others.

The evolution of "Only the Lonely" also points to Orbison's unorthodox writing style. The experience of combining what had been two separate songs into one (the now famous backup chorus that runs through the song and is inseparable from it was originally written for another song!) may have helped Orbison discover that he could write songs outside the usual constraints of pop formulae.

Several important singers and singer/songwriters have commented on Orbison's songwriting style. Bruce Springsteen has said, "Roy scrapped the idea that you needed verse-chorus-verse-chorus-bridge-verse-chorus to have a hit. His arrangements were complex and operatic; they had rhythm and movement" (Springsteen 1987). Similarly, k. d. lang has remarked, "I always am fascinated by 'Running Scared' because it's like verse, verse, verse, verse, verse and this kind of B section that is the end of the song. And it really boils down to one note. The story boils down to one word and to me that's great songwriting" (*Roy Orbison: The Anthology* 1999). But it is Bernie Taupin, a songwriter who is not a singer, who said it best:

> If somewhere within that song you can take a left turn from the obvious and put something in there that people aren't expecting or say something in a different way that is against the grain of the ways it's always been said before, that I think captures people's attention and their imagination and gives them something a little extra to think about. And . . . he was the quintessential artist in that respect. He always took those radical left turns. (*Roy Orbison: The Anthology* 1999).

Orbison himself remarked, "Songs like *Running Scared* were written because I wasn't aware of the limitations, I didn't know about verse, chorus and out, I just wrote how I felt. Wherever it went was fine and the voice went there as well" (Liner notes, *The Very Best of Roy Orbison*). Though Orbison may have made this statement in all sincerity, it is an inadequate account of his musical development. He may not have had formal training in the verse and chorus structure of pop song writing, but everyone, fans and musicians alike, absorbed this structure from listening to the radio and records. In any case, as a musician who played cover versions of others' hits as well as writing songs with the Teen Kings, Orbison did in fact have professional knowledge of the norm. Indeed, he wrote conventional songs later, at RCA. The Everly Brothers' recording of "Claudette," the greatest feather in Orbison's cap as a songwriter, made no departures from prevailing pop norms. Nor did the voice simply follow the writing. As I have argued, the relationship between song and voice was more dialectical, the song, with Foster's direction, sometimes leading to the development of a vocal technique. At other times, in the later works, the range and power of the voice shaped the songs.

The creative form of Orbison's music can be summarized schematically, using a different letter of the alphabet to indicate melodic development:

"In Dreams": Intro, A, B, C, D, E, F
"It's Over": Intro, A, C, B, C, A, C
"(They Call You) Gigolette": Intro, A, B, A, C, D, E
"Running Scared": A, A, A, A, B
"Crying": A, B, C, D, E, F, A, B slightly mod., C mod., D mod.,
    E mod., F mod.
"Goodnight": Intro, A, B, C, D, E
"Crawling Back": A, A, B, C, D, E, F, A, A
"(Say) You're My Girl": Intro, A, A, Ba, Bb, Bc, Bd, A mod. (instr.
    solo), Ba, Bb, Bc, Bd, Concluding Tag

Orbison departed from common verse-chorus forms of the time but, as the scheme above indicates, he did not simply repeat himself with a formula of his own. His compositions differ markedly from each other. His creativity extended to not only the dominant popular song form of the time but to his own previous work. The creative forms of the songs, the immense vocal range and power with which he sang them, and the complex orchestrations all contributed to the classical discourse that would arise around Orbison's music. His vocal range was extraordinary by any standard. "It's Over," for example, moves from D3 to B-flat 5 in full voice! This is an octave plus a fifth, or a thirteen-diatonic-note range in full voice. B-flat 5 is an octave above the full voice of a baritone, a fourth above the full voice of a tenor, and it is beyond the range of the full voice of an alto. Suffice it to say that few performers can do this. "Only the Lonely" has an even greater range. Here Orbison sings from B-flat 3 to C5, the C5 in falsetto. This represents two octaves plus a note, or a total of a seventeen-note range.

"Running Scared," however, plays a particularly important role in the classical discourse about Orbison for a very specific reason—its invocation of Ravel's *Bolero* (for a detailed discussion of this see the Appendix). According to Fred Foster, "I asked Roy if he ever heard Ravel's 'Bolero,' and he said he hadn't, so I gave him an album with 'Bolero' on it, and asked him to write something around that rhythm. He took that record home and loved it, but misread the time signature, which is 3/4. He heard it as 4/4, and wrote 'Running Scared' in 4/4" (Escott 2001, 40). Porter has also noted the similarity of the song's dynamic range to classical music, stressing how the range of twenty-five decibels approaches the forty-decibel range of classical music, "which was unheard of for a commercial release" (Porter quoted in Escott 2001, 40). Ravel's *Bolero* influenced not only "Running Scared" but Orbison's ballads in general. In comparison to lieder and arias, *Bolero* is often thought of in the United States as light classical music bordering on "pops" material. It has been popularized in a number of movies, most recently Blake Edwards's *10* (1979). Nevertheless, it foregrounds the classical discourse about Orbison in a very specific manner.

Jazz musician Don Byron has made a compelling case for collapsing these distinctions between "high" and "low," "art song" and "popular music," and even for erasing the artificial line we draw between classical, pop, and jazz.

> Has the art of writing arias and lieder been lost altogether? I think not. Rather even as various harmonic revolutions have propelled 20th-century classical music away from tonality as most people—listeners and musicians alike—understand it, and the hands-on nature of African-influenced popular music has placed the tools of romantic harmony in the hands of more composers, the art of arias and lieder—the sense of drama of great arias, and the matching of music and lyrics in lieder—may have grown stronger than ever, though completely outside of the classical music forum. I pose the question: Is there an aria greater than Roy Orbison's "It's Over"? (Byron 2000, Liner Notes)

Byron's CD *A Fine Line: Arias and Lieder* aims to erase the fine lines between various musical forms, and he covers "It's Over" on the CD along with the music of Leonard Bernstein, Giacomo Puccini, Frederic Chopin, Robert Schumann, Ornette Coleman, Henry Mancini, Stevie Wonder, and Stephen Sondheim. Unlike most of the other songs on the CD, which have a strong improvisational feel to them, "It's Over" follows the exact form and structure of Orbison's recording to within a second of the running time of the original! In this way Byron acknowledges the manner in which the essence of Orbison's music is tied to its unusual form.

It is significant that Byron articulates two criteria for the classical music analogies that are quite different from the assumptions of power and vocal range that seem to underlie the classical discourse I analyzed in Chapter 1. He notes the sense of drama associated with opera and the close fit between words and music in lieder. By using these criteria as definitive for the two musical forms, Byron places within them composers and singers who are ordinarily seen as belonging to other genres or traditions. Orbison is the only musician Byron singles out for mention in his notes, but instead of isolating him from musical traditions, he recognizes his unique accomplishments within them. Furthermore, Byron articulates a historical-aesthetic context—involving the direction of twentieth-century classical music combined with the influence of African-influenced popular music—in which to understand this development. (I will return to the African influence in the following chapters.) If, for Byron, Orbison's music possesses the drama of operatic arias, it is worth recalling that for David Gates (see Chapter 1) it embodies the special relationship between music and lyrics found in lieder.

Simon Frith and others have distinguished pop from classical music by emphasizing that pop requires no formal training. The pop music singer needs no formal training in established techniques such as projecting from the chest. Pop and rock musicians could learn on their own by using the recordings of other pop musicians as their only teachers. This is not to imply that anyone can be a pop singer, or that formal training is an impediment, only that many great pop vocalists and musicians learned their trade informally. This style is correctly linked to the invention of the microphone and electronic amplification. As Michael Jarrett

notes, "in the mid-1920s, advances in electronic amplification transformed singing in a manner analogous to the cinema's earlier transformation of acting. Just as the camera ... eliminated the need for the
broad gestures of stage performance, microphones and loudspeakers
eliminate the need to project the voice as in classical singing" (Jarrett
1998, 207). Jarrett, like others, identifies Bing Crosby as an important
figure in this transformation whereby singers (and actors) "were able to
broadcast (amplify and project) intimacy, to communicate emotional
directness through mass media" (207).

The first time one listens to any Orbison song, the intimacy and
emotional directness of a microphone-based, electronically amplified
singing style comes through. Orbison employs, in Jarrett's terms, a
"head" voice as opposed to a chest voice. This is true even when he
sings in full voice. As already noted, this marks Orbison as a pop and
rock singer, not an opera or lieder singer. But if pop music can be defined, in part, by its ability to be sung by an ordinary, untrained voice,
a problem arises when we come to Roy Orbison. Without significant
adjustments (which, incidentally, many published versions of the songs
indicate), very few, if any, of Orbison's professional contemporaries
could (or did) record cover versions of his hits. As for local bands playing at hops and dances, forget it. Indeed, as the analysis in the Appendix indicates, very few classically trained singers could perform Orbison's music with the full vocal range he employs. For this reason he is
frequently compared to Caruso, who had an equally broad vocal range.
So how can it be that Orbison is clearly part of the untrained popular
tradition and, at the same time, that his music is nearly inaccessible to
those within that tradition, whether professional or amateur? We seem
to confront a genuine paradox here, for he is a popular singer who is isolated from other popular singers, his music being beyond their grasp.
In other words, he is a popular singer who cannot be (and in fact was
not) popular in the usual sense of the word. This, combined with his
extraordinary vocal range and power, seems to align him with classically
trained singers (who also possess great range and power and perform difficult songs and arias that are outside the repertoire of untrained popular singers). When asked if he had learned anything from working with

Orbison, producer Jeff Lynne remarked that he had learned a great deal, all of it useless since no one but Orbison could sing the way he did. In short, although he is by several standards a popular singer, he is in a class by himself.

It is only within the context of this paradox that the phenomenon of "Oh, Pretty Woman" can be understood. At the time of its release this song was far and away Orbison's biggest hit, and it remains the song for which he is best known. It is the only Orbison song to place on a VH1 list of the all-time greatest hits and on similar *Rolling Stone* and MTV Top 100 lists. Yet the song least resembles Orbison's other Monument-period hits: it is a rocker rather than a ballad, and it lacks strings and elaborate orchestration in favor of a common drum- and guitar-based rock band sound. Most important, it could be and was played and sung by amateur teen bands as well as by professionals. Orbison's singing on "Oh, Pretty Woman" lacks both the vocal range and the power of his other self-penned Monument hits. And the song maintains a constant, driving, danceable drumbeat. "Oh, Pretty Woman" is a wonderfully produced and beautifully sung record, but it is atypical. Put most simply, it falls completely outside the classical discourse surrounding Orbison. They may not do it as well as Orbison, but everyone could (and did) play it and sing it and dance to it. No one could have confused this song with an operatic aria or Ravel's *Bolero*.

Drawing on Evan Eisenberg's analysis of Louis Armstrong and Enrico Caruso, among others, Jake Smith has located recorded music on a continuum within two poles, with what he calls the "rasp" at one extreme and the "bel canto" at the other. Such singers as Louis Armstrong, Tom Waits, Rod Stewart, and Bob Dylan typify the rasp, and singers like Paul McCartney and Roy Orbison typify the bel canto (literally, "beautiful singing"). There is a tendency to see the "rasp" sound as closer to quintessential rock 'n' roll and the bel canto voice as more closely related to the classical tradition (the term *bel canto*, after all, describes a style of operatic singing stressing purity and evenness of tone). But Roy Orbison is as true a rock singer as Bob Dylan or Tom Waits, and neither extreme is somehow a more authentic expression of the genre. Moreover, the rasp and the bel canto are two poles on a continuum, and many rock singers move between them with ease. The "pretty" voice of Paul McCartney, for example, is capable of producing a raspy, tortured scream ("Hey Jude"). And, needless to say, musicians from opposite ends of the spectrum collaborate with, complement, and influence each other all the time. Tom Petty, a member of the Traveling Wilburys who falls further toward the "rasp" end of the scale, was ecstatic when Orbison joined the group; the two singers alternate solo vocals on "Last Night." When Orbison died, Bob Dylan called him "an opera singer," and Tom Waits, who performed with Orbison on *Roy Orbison and Friends: A Black and White Night*, compared Orbison to Caruso. Tom Petty completed his *Full Moon Fever* CD, on which Orbison sings backup, just before Orbison's death, and Petty acknowledges Orbison's advice and support in the liner notes. The comparisons of Orbison to Caruso and Puccini basically reflect the awe in which musicians hold a popular singer so unusual that the language of classical tradition seems to be the best in which to describe his accomplishments. Orbison himself never mentioned a classical composer or musician when discussing the music he liked. On the contrary, he cited popular musicians such as Mantovani, Les Baxter, and Dean Martin, many of whom were despised as being particularly tasteless, middle-brow artists. And it was not Caruso whom Orbison admired but Mario Lanza, and this long before the recent reevaluation of Lanza as a serious musician. Remember that Orbison grew up in a small West Texas town, and that his only formal music training consisted of playing in his high school marching band and singing in the Glee Club and chorus. He achieved what he did not by copying classical music but by creating a unique form of popular music that drew upon a wide variety of music popular during his youth. Once, near the end of his life, when an interviewer compared his songs to classical music, Orbison did awkwardly acknowledge a similarity between himself and "the guys who wrote the concertos" (Amburn 1990, 129). But he was not talking about influence; he was talking about the care that goes into creating enduring music.

Don Byron has supplied an insightful way to understand the homage paid to Roy Orbison by fellow musicians. There really *is* a connection between Orbison and the opera and lieder traditions, so long as one understands that Orbison is a true microphone-based, head-voice rock 'n' roll singer—not a wannabe opera singer. In the next chapter I explore the key elements of pain and dreaming in Orbison's work, which Don Byron calls his dramatic "arias" and David Gates his "lieder." But of course these "arias," these "lieder," developed, in Byron's words, "entirely outside of the classical music forum."

The chapters that follow address Orbison's lyrics, as opposed to the qualities of his singing voice; and while it is much easier to talk about lyrics than about the voice, there is a connection between the unique songwriting, singing, and production styles of Orbison's recordings and more formal ideological analysis of the music. A sophisticated aesthetic is at work in Orbison's lyrics, and an equally profound challenge to dominant notions of masculinity and sexuality. His complex rejection of the traditional verse-chorus structure of pop and rock; his sophisticated singing style, employing nuanced delays and holds and rhythmical and temporal shifts; his powerful voice and eerie falsetto range; the carefully orchestrated nature of the productions, with their building intensities—all of these things combine with the lyrics, performance style, and persona to create an astonishing aesthetic, the meaning and value of which is the subject of much of the remainder of this book.

4

In (and Out of) Dreams

You hold me in and out of dreams.

—Orbison-Dees

ny discussion of the aesthetics of Roy Orbison's *oeuvre* must raise a number of theoretical as well as critical issues. In this chapter I will attempt to address those issues and to survey a few fundamental aspects of Orbison's aesthetics. In addition, I want to address the questions of authorship (in what sense does it even make sense to speak of Orbison's music as "his"?); style periods (early, middle, and late), and the melodramatic nature of much of Orbison's music. The argument that a major component of Orbison's music lies in a complex masochistic aesthetic is developed in Chapter 5, and since many of his characteristic motifs, his songwriting style, and his singing and performing styles relate to that aesthetic, I will not deal with them here.

Most of Orbison's major songs are sung in the first person. Songs written in the second and third person frequently invoke the fear, loneliness, darkness, and mystery associated with the Orbison persona. In a few songs, the narrative point of view shifts. Dave Marsh breaks Orbison's songs into two groups, those dealing with pain and loss and those dealing with dreaming; Marsh argues that "Orbison's music suggests a way to absorb pain this intense and stay alive: through dreams" (Marsh 1987a, 7). This perceptive argument is reminiscent of 1960s film *auteurism,* particularly of the way in which Robin Wood and Peter Wollen created complexity by combining Howard Hawks's comedies (e.g., *Bringing Up Baby*) with his male action films (e.g., *Rio Bravo*). In the action films, the world of masculine values is taken seriously, tested, and ultimately affirmed, while in the comedies masculine values are mocked, ridiculed, and ultimately vanquished by the feminine. Taken together Hawks's films make a full, complex picture that neither subgroup possesses by itself. Without discounting familiar arguments about the limitations of such *auteurism,* we can acknowledge that if we want to understand Orbison's music, we must recognize the consistent "persona," defined in part by extra-textual discourses, who sings the songs. Orbison was a constant presence in the Top 10 and on Top 40 radio between 1960 and 1964, and that presence coalesced into a persona of the type that Marsh describes (and that David Lynch invoked in his film *Blue Velvet,* as we shall see in Chapter 6). Unlike the work of classic Hollywood film directors who remained largely invisible to their public, Orbison's *oeuvre* was known to everyone who listened to Top 40 radio during those years. The man who cried at the touch of a woman's hand in "Crying," who was paralyzed with fear by the sight of a rival boyfriend in "Running Scared," who drifted into a dream world in "In Dreams," and who gave up to return home unfulfilled in "Oh, Pretty Woman" was the same man—the Orbison persona.

The Orbison persona, as I'm using the term, should not be confused with the conventional notion of the author in *auterist* film criticism. As we have seen, the Orbison persona was not the sole creative source of the music, nor did Orbison even always have creative control over it. Orbison wrote most of his hits, and so part of his persona was that he was an early archetype, along with Chuck Berry and Buddy Holly, of the singer-songwriter, a model that became prominent with the rise of the Beatles and thereafter. Most early rock singers—Elvis Presley, for example—did not write their own songs. Although Orbison helped form his persona through the songs he wrote, the songs that others wrote for him (e.g., "Dream Baby") or that he covered (e.g., "Beautiful Dreamer") are an important part of his persona and are, from this perspective, no less "his," even though he didn't write them. The same is true of the production of his recordings. Although Orbison produced his own records at MGM and later at Virgin, these self-produced recordings are no more "his" than those produced by Fred Foster.

The Orbison persona emerges through a complex interplay of musical practices and discourses, some of which he did not control. Obviously Orbison had no control over the accidental deaths of his first wife, Claudette, and his two children, and had at best limited control over how those deaths would become part of a media discourse of tragedy by the late 1960s. The various strategies employed in designing his album covers also figure prominently, though it is unlikely that he had a prominent role in formulating most of these marketing strategies. Minimizing his public image during the Monument years certainly contributed both to the initial sense of a mysterious absence and to the related sense that the music stood on its own, unaffected by the usual promotional tactics. Fans bought the music, in other words, because of the music, not because of how the singer looked. Later his peculiar appearance would become a central part of his still-mysterious persona.

Even his live performance style was not something over which he had total control. Orbison himself said frequently that he adopted his motionless performance style because the songs he wrote did not feature the characteristic instrumental breaks, which would allow him to leave the microphone and move around the stage. This is not the whole story, however; some of the songs he performed regularly (such as "Mean Woman Blues") did give him the opportunity, and he didn't take it. Nor was it the case that standing by the microphone forced him to avoid moving or talking to the audience. The oddity of his motionless style was heightened because the silent figure was frequently dressed in black and, after 1963, always wore dark glasses.

Indeed, Orbison rejected some of the elements that have become central to his persona. He never tired of telling people that he was shocked by and could not understand David Lynch's use of his song "In Dreams." How could such a "sweet song" (Amburn 1990, 192) be used in such a bizarre film? It was only after repeated viewings of the film that he changed his mind about *Blue Velvet* and about Lynch as an artist. As Lynch put it, "Roy, bless his heart, was the kind of guy, that just had a beautiful soul and open mind and he saw it again and he started changing his mind" (Lynch 2002). Clearly Orbison did not control—or even authorize—this use of his work. Similarly, he could not control whether or when he would be inducted into the Rock 'n' Roll Hall of Fame, much less what would be said about his achievements. Yet these events contributed to his mid- to late-1980s persona in the sense in which I am using the term.

The various producers with whom Orbison worked over the years also contributed strongly to the formation of the persona, sometimes against Orbison's wishes. Orbison's initial image as a rockabilly artist was, as we have seen, formed by Sam Phillips against Orbison's desire to write and sing a different kind of music. Similarly, Fred Foster played a role in developing Orbison's trademark Monument recording style and even his songwriting style. As noted earlier, Foster was instrumental in the revision of "Only the Lonely," his breakthrough hit, and in developing the powerful climax to "Running Scared."

Some of the most profoundly important aspects of the Orbison persona involve both contradictions and ideological dimensions over which Orbison as an artist had no conscious control, and of which he probably had no awareness. Some of his statements about music, his lifestyle, and his ideas conform to a conventional masculine ideology at odds with the radical break from such masculinity in much of his music. His traditionally masculine views about certain things might actually have provided a comfortable veneer behind which he was able to make the radical break that we hear in his music. In short, Orbison as author was not the sole source of all the meaning in his work; rather, his work has cultural and ideological dimensions and contradictions of which he was not fully aware. Unconscious elements are as important as (and at times more important than) conscious elements in the creative process. Nor are the two easily distinguishable, even for the artist. It is certainly possible that Orbison was sincere in his claim that he could not understand how David Lynch could use such a "sweet" song as "In Dreams" in such a disturbing manner in *Blue Velvet*. As David Lynch put it, "it *is* a beautiful song and it was written by Roy.... Those lyrics, that feel, meant something to him. And it just so happened that a song in a certain situation could mean something else. And the way that Frank Boothe [Dennis Hopper] used that song in two different places, it is just kind of unbelievable. But I can see why Roy was upset because for him it meant a third thing" (Lynch 2002).

Orbison's music may be partially understood in relation to Robin Wood's analysis of genre filmmaking. Wood has shown how the contemporary horror film has launched a strong critique of our culture's dominant notion of the nuclear family. The once warm, even sentimental and sometimes comic view of the family gives way in horror films to the monstrous family, a hotbed of perverse interactions and monstrous births. Wood recognized that genre entertainment can present a more radical social critique than can "serious" films, which tend to be basically committed to mainstream institutions and mores. Wood recognized that this was just as true for the creators of these films as for their audiences. While playing in the horror film playground of scaring their (mostly teen) audiences, they were able, in large part unconsciously, to explore the hidden horrors of family life. Orbison's exploration of the dark side of things may function similarly, the troubled nature of many of his lyrics couched in the presumably lighter form of rock 'n' roll produced for a teenage audience. Seen this way, Lynch unmasked an element of Orbison's music not only to the public but also, perhaps, to Orbison himself.

The Orbison persona, as outlined in Chapter 1, may have contributed to this confusion. Orbison's rockabilly persona, which persisted throughout his career, involved a very traditional masculinity. We can see this most clearly in his cover version of "Mean Woman Blues." It is worth noting that Orbison drastically altered the published lyrics of the song as attributed to Claude DeMetruis (*Roy Orbison: 24 Classic Hits* 1987, 42–43). Orbison's version begins "I ain't braggin', it's understood / But everything I do, well I sure do it good." What he does "good" in this song, it turns out, is the woman that he's "got." She's just as mean as he is, but this suits him fine. This overconfident braggadocio is the complete opposite of the frightened, anguished narrator of most other Orbison songs, who either lacks a woman or worries about losing the one he has. Orbison's very first song, which he performed regularly throughout the 1980s, is entitled "Go Go Go" (a.k.a. "Down the Line"), a rockabilly song about a confident man who is going to get a woman more "cool" than his old girlfriend. While this song conforms to a pattern discussed in the next chapter, in which the narrator sings about what he is *going* to do as opposed to what he is doing or what he has already done, its dominant tone is one of self-confident masculine action, a stark contrast to the fear and dreaming that are the subjects of so many of his other songs. Why did Orbison record "Mean Woman Blues" at the height of his success, side by side with the ballads that had established his dominant persona? And why did he continue to perform it and, later, "Ooby Dooby" and "Down the Line" in concert until the end of his life? There is no simple answer to these questions. Apart from "Oh, Pretty Woman," Orbison had no original up-tempo rockers to balance his ballads, as Fred Foster suggested he should (Morthland 1990). But why that song, why those lyrics? Either Orbison or Foster, or both, felt, quite perceptively, that Orbison needed something to counterbalance what had become his dominant ballad style. One reason was simply that variety breaks up monotony. Orbison's live concerts were always beautifully paced, lively rock songs spaced carefully among the ballads. But the choice was not purely musical, as the rockers have a different sexual ideology from the ballads. Most of them, including his covers of songs like "Let the Good Times Roll," are quite at odds with the "other" Roy Orbison, who could seldom be imagined singing the line "feel so good" in any context. I would suggest that Orbison needed this kind of variety—not only musically but emotionally—for two reasons. The dominant Orbison persona was too unrelentingly grim and dark to be sustained without letup; even an audience of older fans would be hard put to sit through a program entirely of ballads about pain, misery, loneliness, paranoia, and loss; something had to balance that side of the singer. In addition, and more importantly, he needed something not only to balance but perhaps also to mask the dark side of his persona—it was just too bizarre, too offbeat, too difficult, to be fully recognized and accepted for what it was. Some of the time he had to be seen as just another normal guy singing ordinary rock 'n' roll, swaggering in macho self-confidence about the woman he had, was going to get, or would dance with through the night. In this sense, the conventional rockabilly persona did not disappear between the Sun and Monument periods; elements of it survived and actually enabled the emergence of the radical Orbison persona who seemed such an odd figure in the world of rock 'n' roll. Robin Wood was right about entertainment, and this conventional persona was probably needed not only by the fans but by Orbison himself. Even he could not fully confront what he was doing in those ballads, which is why David Lynch's unmasking of "In Dreams" shocked Orbison as much as it did many of his fans.[1]

Furthermore, many of the extra-textual discourses surrounding Orbison were, like the rockabilly persona, traditionally masculine. As we have seen, beginning with the MGM period, his album covers regularly associated him with cars, motorcycles, and airplanes. That he was in fact a motorcyclist became widely known with the press coverage about the motorcycle accident that killed Claudette. He played football in high school, and he maintained a strong interest in building and flying model airplanes throughout his life (Ellis 1982). Orbison was not interviewed often, at least not in the United States, but when he did talk about gender issues, he did so in a conservative manner. For example, during the late 1960s, he criticized men's hair and clothing fashions. Emotionally as well as musically, Orbison developed a variety of conventional, conservative masculine views that not only counterbalanced but probably allowed the radical departures from conventional masculinity in his work.

One way in which Orbison embraced conventional ideals of masculinity was in trying to be "just one of the guys." This side of Orbison came to the fore in his collaborative projects of the 1980s, in his membership in the *Class of '55* group, in the Traveling Wilburys, and in the production of *Roy Orbison and Friends: A Black and White Night*. Hanging out with Johnny Cash, Carl Perkins, Jerry Lee Lewis, Bob Dylan, George Harrison, Tom Petty, and Bruce Springsteen, among others, went a long way toward making him seem—and perhaps feel—like just another one of the guys, part of the rock norm. Even within the context of *The Class of '55* and *The Traveling Wilburys, Vol. 1*, however, Orbison and his music stand somewhat awkwardly apart from the rest. Unlike the other members of those two groups, he contributed only one solo song to each CD: "Comin' Home" to the former and "Not Alone Any More" to the latter. In both cases, Orbison's songs bear virtually no resemblance to the other songs on the CDs in terms of how they are written, sung, orchestrated, or produced. They seem to come out of nowhere, and in fact Orbison himself seemed quickly to retreat back to nowhere, taking a backseat to his bandmates on the remaining songs.

At times these collaborations actually seemed to force Orbison into masculine positions far removed from those of his dominant solo persona. This is nowhere seen more clearly than in his collaboration with Tom Petty on "Last Night" on *The Traveling Wilburys, Vol. 1.* The song is about an encounter between a guitar player and a woman he meets in a bar. They go to her room, where she pulls out a knife and threatens to kill him if he doesn't give her his money. The song concludes with the man back in the bar, wryly observing that "she went a little too far." Tom Petty is the dominant soloist in this first-person narrative, though Orbison sings two solo passages: the first simply describes the street and, with sexual connotations, the "heat," while the second narrates the man's close call: "I asked her to marry me, she smiled and pulled out a knife / 'The party's just beginning,' she said, 'it's your money or your life.'"

It is highly uncharacteristic of the Orbison persona to pick up a woman in a bar and then describe what happens between them. Indeed, in "Twinkle Toes," discussed below, the Orbison persona desires a woman in a bar, but in this song, rather than narrate his actions and their consequences, in a fantasy state bordering on dreaming he describes how he is going to take the woman home. The song ends without revealing whether he has taken any action. By contrast, the masculine protagonist of "Last Night" is back in action at the song's conclusion. The song underlines how unusual the macho persona is for Orbison when he replaces Petty in the first-person narration. In a sense, he becomes Petty, a man of action, perhaps in fulfillment of some deep-seated fantasy. Although their voices are very different, both Petty and Orbison share the same first-person voice in this song, an unusual strategy under any circumstances; they are quite clearly two different men. Orbison's first two lines seem to be a third-person description of the scene, and it is somewhat jarring when he suddenly breaks in with the first-person pronoun. The song is clearly Petty's, not Orbison's, and the persona fits Petty well. Although Orbison sings beautifully and his voice supplies a strong contrast to Petty's, the events he narrates sound like nothing in the Orbison *oeuvre*.

Women in Orbison's songs do not pull knives; their danger, as we shall see in the next chapter, lies elsewhere. And Orbison's knives are metaphorical, not literal, as in "She's a Mystery to Me," in which Orbison sings about "A love so sharp, it cuts like a switchblade to my heart." The narrator in this song, enslaved by his love for a woman and under her "spell," is the victim not of some knife-yielding woman in a bar but of his own feverish dreams and passive paralysis. Like the supergroups to which he belonged, the widely publicized relationship between Orbison and Elvis Presley also functioned to "normalize" Orbison. He met Presley when the singer appeared as a guest on Orbison's Odessa television show, and soon thereafter Orbison joined Sun Records, where Presley recorded. When Orbison left Sun he signed with RCA, as Presley had, and when he left Monument for MGM, he hoped to have a film career like Presley's. Indeed, *The Fastest Guitar Alive* was originally planned for Presley under the title *The Fastest Gun in the West*. Roy Orbison's "Crying" was reported to be Presley's all-time favorite song and, near the end of his life, Presley introduced Orbison, who was in the audience at one of his concerts, as "the greatest singer in the world." This was a decade before other prominent rock stars gave Orbison similar accolades. Before he died, Presley left behind a rough demo of "Running Scared."

In fact, Orbison's relationship with Presley was not particularly close. The two seldom saw each other over the years, though each professed a musical kinship with the other. Although they both recorded covers of such songs as "Unchained Melody," "Mean Woman Blues," and "Pledging My Love," their music did not actually intersect much. In 1977, when Orbison returned to Monument Records and cut the LP *Regeneration* (Fred Foster once again producing), Dennis Linde, who had written "Burning Love" for Presley, wrote "Belinda" for Orbison. Early in his career Orbison covered "Blue Suede Shoes" with the Teen Kings (it appears on the box set *Orbison 1956–1965*), and in the eighties he performed a version of "Hound Dog" at the Super Bowl (although written by Carl Perkins and by Jerry Leiber and Mike Stoller, respectively, both songs were popularized by and associated with Presley). If Presley and Orbison were linked in the public mind, they were opposite sides of the same coin: Presley was the handsome, charismatic, sexual rock star, while Orbison was its gifted but awkward, somewhat bizarre underside. As is frequently the case with such opposites, apparently each was attracted to something the other possessed.

Just as Orbison's persona and style developed over time, so did his music. The musical development can be divided into early, middle, and late periods. Unlike most pop/rock singers from the fifties and early sixties, Orbison's recording career spanned four decades, although the span of his career cannot by itself account for this development. Unlike some long-lived male rock singers, who spend a lot of energy trying to deny the aging process, Orbison did not spend his mature years trying to recapture the glory of youth—perhaps because he had so little invested in proving his masculine prowess to begin with. Instead, Orbison's late period was a maturely reflective phase, in terms of both style and content.

Early, middle, and late periods can be characterized in a variety of ways. In *Music, the Arts, and Ideas: Patterns and Predictions in Twentieth-Century Culture,* Leonard B. Meyer applies the concept to both historical periods (e.g., Romantic music) and the works of individual composers (e.g., Beethoven). He notes that similar patterns frequently occur on both the macro level of historical period and the micro level of individual composers. The early work is comparatively simple and marked by the struggle to discover a style; the middle-period involves a complex development of the style; and the late period comprises either a baroque elaboration of the style or a deceptive paring down of the style. In this latter case, the work is characterized by a deceptive simplicity— deceptive because it is in fact the result of intertextual reference to the earlier works of the *oeuvre* or genre.

Meyer is concerned with classical music, but his observations are valid to all the arts, including painting and literature. Of course, style alone does not characterize early, middle, and late periods. In literature especially, late-period work tends toward introspection and a preoccupation with mortality. Furthermore, these periods are not neatly delineated chronologically. As the terms early, middle, and late suggest, the general process is one of chronological progression, but an individual artist may create what is stylistically a late-period work and follow it with one more characteristic of the middle period. There can be, in other words, some overlap, some jumping ahead, some looking back. Artists gradually move from period to period; they don't simply end one period and begin another.

Since my analysis of Orbison's masochist aesthetic, developed in the chapters that follow, ranges over his entire career, I want to situate his music within these stylistic periods. At the simplest level, the Sun and RCA recordings, along with the recently discovered and released 1956 live session *Are You Ready?* with the Teen Kings (all available on *Orbison 1956–1965*) constitute his early period; the Monument, MGM, Mercury, and Asylum recordings make up the middle period; and the Virgin recordings, along with his collaboration with *The Class of '55* and the Traveling Wilburys, the late period.

Orbison's middle period begins in 1960 with "Only the Lonely." Suddenly, with that one song, a number of his personal style elements fell into place: a new richness and fluidity to his voice; the strong, pure falsetto; his complex songwriting structure, which went beyond the pop formulae of the time; the use of strings; the building to a breathtaking climax; the intensity of emotional expression of feelings that conventional masculinity denied or contained; and the emphasis on extreme loneliness and crying. One year later "Running Scared" would solidify the middle-period style by adding the two major components missing from "Only the Lonely": the "operatic" vocal power of the climax, and the signature *Bolero*-style rhythm. "Only the Lonely" climaxed with an astonishingly high, pure falsetto, but it was not powerful. At the end of "Running Scared," by contrast, Orbison let loose for the first time in his career, giving the note all he had. Unlike the climax to "Only the Lonely," which seems to come from nowhere, the climax of "Running Scared" is the culmination of a slowly building rhythm to which the whole song leads inexorably. Here again Foster's influence was important, for it was only at his urging that Orbison gave it this powerful reading; originally he had sung it in a soft voice.

In other ways the song cemented the stylistics of "Only the Lonely": the complex writing, which here abandons the common verse-chorus-verse structure and includes a surprising rhythmic shift that nearly divides the song in two, beginning with the line "Then all at once . . ."; the unusual intensity of male emotion, including the expression of fear;

and the first-person narrator. While both songs are melodramatic in tone and style, "Running Scared" adds an element of narrative melodrama lacking in the other song. Such melodrama, as I will discuss below, is a central component of the Orbison aesthetic.

Both songs are pivotal in establishing Orbison's mature middle-period style. Nevertheless, they both appear on albums that also contain the kind of early songs typified by conventional structures and a sweet, even hesitant voice. "Only the Lonely" (1960) appeared on the album *Lonely and Blue* (1961). Early-period songs on that album include "Come Back to Me (My Love)" and "Raindrops." Several songs straddle the middle ground between the mature phase and the early phase, including "Twenty-two Days," "I'll Say It's My Fault," and "Blue Avenue." Several, such as "Blue Angel" and "I'm Hurtin'," along with "Only the Lonely," help develop the middle-period style.

The boundaries of the late period are even less clear-cut. Orbison's late-period songs are characterized by lyrics preoccupied with death, particularly his own mortality, and a stylistic tendency to make brief references to his middle-period work combined with a paring down of his full-blown, pull-out-all-the stops, operatic style with crashing climaxes. The late period begins in the mid-1980s with the Larry Gatlin duet "Indian Summer," on which, as soon as Orbison starts singing, a chorus briefly quotes the chorus from "Only the Lonely." The fact that no such chorus is heard in the first part of the song, sung by Gatlin, makes the reference highly stylized and almost jarring. It is a pure example of late-period style, as it is not developed centrally within the song; its sole purpose is as a self-conscious reference to Orbison's *oeuvre*. Orbison would use the same device in such later songs as "Not Alone Anymore," performed with the Traveling Wilburys, and, to profound effect, in "The Only One" from *Mystery Girl*, a song that comments on Orbison's immersion in self-pity during parts of his middle period. The title is an ironic reference to the singer's belief that he is the only one in the world to suffer as he has (Gates 1988). The distorted, deep, sloweddown invocation of the choruses from the Monument era is a characteristic late-period device.

Several songs on *Mystery Girl* derive an added complexity from their late-period references to middle-period work. The most extreme instance of this is heard in "In the Real World," a companion piece to "In Dreams." Whereas the earlier song celebrated escape into dreams, the latter emphasizes the real world to which we awaken when we are done dreaming, the world in which "endings come to us in ways we can't rearrange." "All I Can Do Is Dream You" recalls "Dream Baby" in the manner in which the Orbison persona celebrates a woman he possesses only in his dreams. Whereas the earlier song expresses the hope that "You can make my dreams come true," the later one cherishes no such illusion. "The Comedians," with its characteristic middle-period rhythms and building crescendos, recalls "Running Scared" and "It's Over," among others.

The first song in which Orbison was clearly preoccupied with his own mortality also occurs in the mid-eighties, with "Comin' Home" (1985). This song was Orbison's sole written contribution to *The Class of '55*, and its title alone suggests a musical homecoming. And this, of course, is how the project was presented: Johnny Cash, Jerry Lee Lewis, Carl Perkins, and Roy Orbison were coming home to Memphis, where it all began in the 1950s at Sun Records. But in spite of its title, Orbison's song is not really about music or a musical homecoming, as, for example, Cash's "I Will Rock 'n' Roll with You" and Perkins's "The Birth of Rock 'n' Roll" are. The song, characteristically sung in the first person, is about a man who is returning home after a wayward period in his life. What calls him back is his impending death: "I heard the angels cry / As you live so shall you die." The ultimate meaning of "Comin' Home" is not the singer's literal homecoming with the woman who is waiting for him, but his being called home by God and the angels.

"Life Fades Away," Orbison's contribution to the soundtrack of *Less Than Zero* (1987) is, as its title indicates, an even more direct invocation of death and mortality. Although in this case the death motif is motivated by the song's placement in the film's narrative (it is heard at the end of the film, when one of its central characters has died), it also resonates in terms of its placement within Orbison's *oeuvre*. Even while it seems to comment on a fictional, third-person character, Orbison, surprisingly, sings in the first person. As the song progresses, death is raised to the level of desire. The opening, like "Comin' Home," invokes the singer's imminent death, declaring, "All at once, it's too late, life fades away." Here death is presented as a fateful inevitability, though as we shall see in the next chapter, it involves the characteristic bad timing of the masochist: "It's too late." The Orbison persona repeatedly takes comfort in the knowledge that he will live on in the memory of the woman to whom he addresses his song as he lies dying alone in his bed. But the idea of time recurs, this time coupled with a surprising desire for death: "I'm tired of tomorrow, lost for today / I long to be at peace for ever." Here death is less a matter of fate and more like a form of suicide. Lest there be any misunderstanding about this, the singer asks the forgiveness of the woman he is leaving behind. It makes no sense to ask to be forgiven for dying if the death is involuntary, external, and cannot be helped. But the guilt implied in that line makes perfect sense in the context of, if not suicide, at least complicity in one's own death. The emotional climax of the song occurs when Orbison's voice soars over the repeated line, "I long to be at peace," this time replacing the word "ever" with "forevermore." The song's last line—"One last thing to say, life fades away"—is utterly grim in its insistence on summing up life as a process of fading toward death.

Although, like everyone else, I was stunned by the news of Orbison's death in 1988, I remembered thinking that in light of these songs it was not really all that surprising. It is perhaps also not surprising that death in the form of literal suicide occurs in "Windsurfer," a song from the posthumously released *Mystery Girl*. Despairing about his failed romance, the song's third-person protagonist leaves a suicide message in the sand and windsurfs to his death at sea.

The next chapter places this preoccupation with death within the masochist aesthetic, but for now I simply want to document its characteristic late-period presence and also briefly differentiate it from the references to death in such middle-period songs as "Tennessee Owns My Soul," "Southbound Jericho Parkway," "Best Friend," "There Won't Be Many Coming Home," "The Three Bells," and "Danny Boy." The mere presence of so many songs dealing with death indicates Orbison's longstanding preoccupation with it, and, indeed, in *Death Discs: An Account of Fatality in the Popular Song*, Alan Clayson discusses Orbison seven times, in a variety of different contexts, in relation to death. Orbison's early period includes "Come Back to Me (My Love)" (1961), a song, like "Teen Angel," that belongs to the romantic teen death-ballad genre. Other Monument songs involving death include "Indian Wedding" (1964), also a genre song (like "Running Bear") that ends in the death of the newlywed couple.

Of the later MGM songs, "Danny Boy" is certainly the easiest to explain in light of the death of two of Orbison's own children. Similarly, "There Won't Be Many Comin' Home" is about death in war and was recorded during the Vietnam War. "Southbound Jericho Parkway" is about a man who commits suicide, but the song is concerned with death primarily in terms of "relevant" social issues such as dysfunctional families and empty lives. Perhaps revealingly, neither "Southbound Jericho Parkway" nor "There Won't Be Many Comin' Home" are sung in Orbison's characteristic first-person style. "The Three Bells" chronicles a life from birth to death. And in the first-person "Danny Boy," the narrator is preoccupied less with his own death than with the possible death of his child. All four of these songs are about someone else's death, not the narrator's or even death in general. The Orbison persona is, in short, distanced from death caused by social ills such as war, or simply by old age, although in the case of "Danny Boy" there is obviously an autobiographical dimension.

"Best Friend" and "Tennessee Owns My Soul" are somewhat different. The former is a first-person narration in which the singer tells of an old man's death. Again, the Orbison persona is distanced from death and in fact only passes along the wisdom of the old man's dying words: "So laugh when it's time to laugh / Cry when it's time to cry / … You'll die when it's time to die." That it is an old man who dies mutes somewhat the song's preoccupation with death, but the repetition of the line "You'll die when it's time to die," sung with an almost grim relish, hints at a closer involvement for Orbison. In "Tennessee Owns My Soul," the Orbison persona does die, and in fact narrates his own death, but the song is a genre piece involving jailbreaks, shootings, and the like. Again, this works to distance the Orbison persona's death somewhat; he is not "real" so much as a character in an action narrative.

The late-period death songs are another story. It is the Orbison persona who directly confronts his own death or, in the case of "Windsurfer," as David Gates has perceptively observed, the death of a figure who is clearly autobiographical. The uncharacteristic third-person voice on "Windsurfer" enables the song to continue after the death and disappearance of the windsurfer. Death in the late-period songs is removed from social significance and even social contexts; here the Orbison persona or his stand-in contemplates his own death, on occasion even longing for and contributing to it.

The prevalence of death in Orbison's music points to the frequently melodramatic nature of his work, and this raises another preliminary aesthetic issue. Melodrama, as a genre in literature and film, is typically addressed to women, and as such it tends to be devalued by male critics. In film criticism, "women's weepies" was originally a derogatory term indicating both the intended audience and the devalued nature of the form. It is not, of course, surprising that in a patriarchal culture "women's weepies" should be taken less seriously than a "men's genre" such as the Western or the war film. Many of Orbison's songs might be dubbed "men's weepies," since his music is neither addressed primarily to women nor is primarily about women, as, for example, Douglas Sirk's film melodramas were. Orbison's music raises the issue of male melodrama but brings with it the longstanding devaluation of the form. There are many reasons why Orbison was never fully recognized or taken seriously as a major musician during most of his lifetime, but the frankly melodramatic nature of many of his best-known hits is undoubtedly one of them.

Theorists and critics have defined melodrama in so many ways that the term no longer has one precise meaning, if it ever did. For our purposes, however, the term can be defined simply as excessive in relation to prevailing dramatic norms. Serious drama sets a standard of realism and plausibility against which melodrama appears as overblown excess. Too much may happen in the allotted time, the nature of what happens (e.g., illness and death) or the nature in which it happens (e.g., reliance on coincidence) may be "unbelievable" by dramatic standards, and so on. Of course melodrama is always a relative term: what is considered believable or "realistic" in one era may be perceived as melodramatic in another. Our response to the excesses of melodrama likewise shifts between tears and laughter, depending upon whether we take it "seriously." Both laughing and crying are different physiological responses, of course, to the perceived excess of melodrama. Roy Orbison's hits between 1960 and 1964, as well as many of his later recordings, constitute a multifaceted excess when listened to against the pop/rock norms of the time. They are melodramatic in terms of the amount of narrative that transpires in their two-minute-thirty-second format, in terms of what happens, and in the manner in which they are written, sung, and even produced. Indeed, the classical discourse identified in Chapter 1 is relevant here; the term most often used to describe Orbison's music is "operatic." One of the main reasons for this, I would suggest, is that opera is a form of melodramatic excess in several ways. The exaggerated singing style (and the exaggerated gestures that accompany it), the stock themes (star-crossed love, unrequited love, death), the lavish sets—all of these are larger than life, excessive in emotion and setting. Opera is, to many minds, the perfect meeting ground of high art and melodrama.

David Gates's comparison of Orbison's music to the European art song, discussed in Chapter 1, in many ways makes more sense than the more common comparison to opera. Orbison wrote and sang pop songs, not arias, and these songs were not part of large narrative works with plots that lasted several hours on the stage. In addition, during concert performances he sang one after another in a motionless manner characteristic of the art song; he did not change costumes between songs or enact them within a narrative framework. Yet many observers persisted in calling his music operatic and in calling him an opera singer. Why?

What can best be termed Orbison's operatic outbursts—at the end of such songs as "Running Scared," "Crying," "The Crowd," and "It's Over," among many others—combine his extraordinary vocal power with an extraordinary outpouring of emotional intensity, whether it be intense emotions of fear, as in "Running Scared"; of loss of emotional self-control, as in "Crying"; of feverish wish fulfillment, as in "The Crowd"; or of hopeless pessimism about a love affair, as in "It's Over." Orbison reserved maximum volume—and frequently maximum vocal range—for those moments of melodramatic emotional excess. Someone once remarked that in "It's Over," the end of a love affair sounded like the end of the world. It is precisely this inflated notion of romance that constitutes one of the markers of melodramatic excess in Orbison's music. At other times, as in "Running Scared," the melodrama stems from an exaggerated buildup of suspense. The suddenness with which the rival boyfriend appears ("Then all at once he was standing there") and the paralyzed fear of the Orbison persona ("Which one would it be?") are the musical equivalent of melodramatic techniques used in film to keep audiences on the edge of their seats. Sometimes the sheer number of things that happen to the Orbison persona in the course of approximately two and a half minutes make the melodrama: in "Oh, Pretty Woman," he goes from seeing a woman, to desiring her, to dreaming about her, to giving up and turning away, to unexpectedly having her come to him.

"The Crowd" is particularly interesting in this respect. Of all Orbison's singles—indeed, perhaps of all his songs—it is the one with the most excessive operatic outburst at the end in terms of sheer power and vocal pyrotechnics. If one were going to compare his songs with actual opera (which I do not think is the best way to understand or appreciate them), "The Crowd" is the one in which he sounds the most "operatic." Yet the song was not as successful as most of his other singles, and Orbison spoke of it as a mistake and as too "fussy." When he rerecorded his greatest hits on Virgin as *In Dreams: Greatest Hits*, "The Crowd" was the only song not included. But in fact it stands with his very best work; it builds a complex shifting melody in conjunction with shifting rhythms. Perhaps the song's relative commercial failure and Orbison's resulting displeasure with it show that, even by the standards of his operatic melodramatic excess, this one went too far. Perhaps not coincidentally, Orbison's choice of the word "fussy" has feminine and homosexual connotations. For once, the melodramatic excess may have been too much for all involved, even considering Orbison's unusual masculine image.

Excess also characterizes Fred Foster's production style on the Monument recordings.[2] It is often claimed that "Uptown" and "Only the Lonely" were the first Nashville songs to use strings as opposed to fiddles, and Foster himself has acknowledged that it was Orbison's idea to use the strings (*Roy Orbison: In Dreams*). As with all claims about "firsts," we should be suspicious of this one. For one thing, such claims are often wrong; earlier examples are often uncovered. Moreover, such claims are usually irrelevant. The real issue is not so much who did something first (Buddy Holly's last recordings, for example, though not made in Nashville, experimented with a string orchestral sound) but who first did it in a meaningful way. Strings, and specifically strings that invoke the classical music tradition, became a central component of Foster's Orbison productions. That they were violins instead of fiddles is not of major significance—what matters is that these strings were featured prominently and produced using a technique in excess of the norms of the time. The manner in which Foster produced Orbison's voice, and the general production ambiance of operatic string excess, combined with the lyrics and the structure of the songs to produce an aesthetic of male melodramatic excess. Men trembling with fear and crying uncontrollably were simply not part of the formulaic pop/rock songs of the time—nor were the operatic production techniques that accompanied them. Anyone unwilling to take melodrama seriously cannot begin to understand Orbison's aesthetic.

The complex, multifaceted nature of melodramatic excess in the Monument recordings helps explain what happened to Orbison when he moved to MGM. Although, as we shall see, Orbison made some important recordings at MGM, in general the operatic nature of Foster's production techniques were replaced by a much more conventional string orchestra sound. Orbison's producers at MGM seemed at times to confuse the quantity of string sound with quality—they believed that the more orchestration, the better. Indeed, Orbison is quoted on the liner notes of his second MGM album, *The Orbison Way*, as saying, "On several of these tunes we have a big orchestral sound as background—about 25 musicians and voices backing me up. The sound is wonderful" (O'Donnell 1996). But in fact Foster's greatest results showed restraint in that area; he did not overwhelm the voice with a huge orchestra but produced a sound mix that emphasized a few string instruments (sometimes as few as four). Many of the string arrangements in Orbison's MGM recordings are highly conventional, and the use of so many strings simply emphasizes this banality. Far from the world of operatic excess, the MGM productions frequently sound like a middle-of-the-road pop orchestra.

The distinction between Orbison's Monument and MGM periods supplies yet another parallel between Orbison and Presley. If Peter Guralnick (quoted in Wolff 1999) sees Presley's post-1960 RCA recordings as "The Unmaking of Elvis Presley," most critics similarly see Orbsion's MGM recordings as his unmaking. The standard cliché about Orbison, as I indicated in Chapter 1, is that the move from Monument and Foster to MGM ruined his career. Colin Escott documents that the Monument recordings took much more care and time than did those at MGM. Orbison's decline in popularity, however, needs to be understood within a much more complex historical context. Given the rise of the Beatles and the British invasion, along with the profound social and cultural turmoil of the late 1960s, it is unlikely that Orbison would have remained as successful and popular had he stayed at Monument, even if the quality of his recordings had been undiminished. Not one singer from the pre-Beatles era managed to sustain his level of success during the invasion. It is worth repeating that while Orbison's MGM work generally does not match the quality of his Monument work, he did cut some very good songs, and even a few great ones, at MGM, while some of the Monument songs were mediocre. Orbison's MGM period needs to be assessed carefully, not simply dismissed as a steady decline. Daniel Wolff points out that Guralnick's lavish praise of Presley's early work at Sun and RCA set up the dismissal of the post-1960 work. "To Guralnick, this kind of singing is 'Italianate' and defines 'pop' rather than rock & roll music." But, as Wolfe points out, "Are You Lonesome Tonight" is a great Presley song, and the tradition to which it belongs (to which Roy Orbison also belongs) is central to rock 'n' roll. The case for Orbison at MGM and Monument is similar. In short, there are many ways in which Roy Orbison's songs can be productively grouped: rockabilly vs. ballads; Sun vs. Monument vs. MGM; dream songs vs. songs of lonely reality; middle period as opposed to late period; operatic ballads vs. songs of more normative restraint (e.g., "Dream Baby" and "Candy Man").[3] Indeed, it is productive to explore and layer all of these groupings, creating not just a richer picture of the *oeuvre* but, perhaps, an understanding of how one aspect interacts with another. I want to turn now to some of the central motifs that emerge from the lyrics of Orbison's songs. Dave Marsh's division of Orbison's work into dream songs

and songs of lonely reality, with which this chapter began, is a good starting point for this discussion. Although Marsh does not develop his
insight in detail, his groupings point to the centrality of dreams in Orbison's work, and it will be useful to explore this idea more thoroughly.
A dream, needless to say, is often more than just a dream. While songs
such as "In Dreams," "Leah," "Dream Baby," "All I Have to Do Is
Dream," and "Dream" all deal quite explicitly with literal dreaming,
many of Orbison's songs that seem to deal with waking reality are in
fact permeated by a feverish dreamlike quality. If he isn't literally
dreaming in his sleep, the Orbison persona is frequently daydreaming.
Of Orbison's hits, "Blue Bayou" best illustrates this type of dreaming.
In this song he sings of how he's going to save all his money to return
to a place where he has no troubles: "Working 'til the sun don't shine /
Looking forward to happier times on Blue Bayou / I'm going back some
day / gonna stay on Blue Bayou." The blue bayou is an unobtainable
utopia, accessible only in dreams. In "Uptown," a bellhop sings about
how the woman he loves will one day be his: "One of these days I'm
gonna have money / She'll wanna be my everlovin' honey / It won't be
long just wait and see / I'll have a big car, fine clothes and then I'll be
uptown." There is nothing in these lyrics to indicate that this wishful
scenario is anything but a dream. "Working for the Man" is more of the
same. Orbison sings about working all day at hard labor while antici-
pating a romantic rendezvous with the boss's daughter. The song ends
euphorically: "So I slave all day without much pay / But I'm just a-bidin'
my time. / 'Cause the company and the daughter you see / They both
gonna be all mine." The worker with shovel and ax in hand will meta-
morphose into the successful lover who owns the company only in his
dreams. In "Ride Away," the first single Orbison released for MGM, he
sings with total confidence about how he will leave his cheating girlfriend. He repeatedly promises, "I'll just ride away," yet the final line,
"Tonight I'll ride away," puts a telling emphasis on the word "tonight,"
suggesting that the singer has told himself many times before that
"tonight" will be the night.

The relationship between the dream songs and the songs of real
loneliness is further complicated by songs that stress the connection
between the two states, what Orbison characteristically calls "drifting."

In "In Dreams," he sings, "I close my eyes, then I drift away / Into the magic night." In "You Got It" he sings, "One look from you / I drift away." He also recorded a song about a disintegrating relationship entitled "Drifting" and a cover version of the Dobie Gray hit "Drift Away." In addition to drifting and, in particular, the state of drifting between waking and sleep, Orbison's songs sometimes reveal a confusion about which is which. "Darkness," an early Monument song written for Orbison by Gene Piney but unreleased until the posthumous 1989 CD *Rare Orbison II,* is the earliest example of this confusion: "Voices, I hear voices, sounds in the still night everywhere / But you're not there, no you're not there / Imagination brings you so near, I reach for your lips but they're not here." The song is extreme in its hallucinatory imagery, in which Orbison not only hears voices but sees shadows: "How can I hold shadows in my arms?" Orbison wrote with Bill Dees and recorded two versions of a song entitled "Heartache," first for MGM and later for Mercury. Between the two versions he changed the lyrics substantially. The first version begins with the singer describing how at midnight, when he is "halfway weeping halfway sleeping," the woman he desires appears: "You reached out and touched me and then you faded away / It's unreal the way I feel." Here the Orbison persona does not even distinguish between an apparition and the real thing; he sings as if she had been there and touched him rather than as if he had imagined it. "Halfway sleeping" perfectly describes this zone of delirious confusion that the Orbison persona so frequently inhabits. The close juxtaposition of the assertion that she both touched him and faded away (fading is a little like drifting) makes clear how confused he is; touching is an act of physical presence and fading away is an acknowledgment of the woman's nature as an apparition.

This gray zone between waking and dreams, which Orbison here calls "unreal," is neither dream nor daydream. At times, instead of drifting from one state into another, Orbison gets stuck in a feverish no-man's-land between the two ("Tossing turning trembling burning"). In "I'm In a Blue, Blue Mood," a song Orbison recorded for MGM, he sings, "I reach out to touch you, but you're not there." In "Penny Arcade," also from the MGM period, a dreamlike arcade suddenly appears in the distance of the night and the singer cannot believe his eyes.

A number of Orbison songs that at first glance have nothing to do with dreams (e.g., "Blue Angel," "Cry Softly Lonely One," "[Say] You're My Girl," and "Twinkle Toes") have an important place within the dream works, for if they are not literally about any form of dreaming they betray a deep, almost frightening dreamlike quality. Unlike his classic hits, these songs are not about the Orbison persona as much as they are about the women to whom they are addressed. In "Blue Angel," "Cry Softly Lonely One," and "Twinkle Toes," for example, it is *their* loneliness, not his, that lies at the center of the song. Indeed, instead of singing of his loneliness, he offers to cure theirs.

So what do these somewhat uncharacteristic songs have to do with dreaming? "Blue Angel," which belongs to the same period as "Only the Lonely" and "I'm Hurtin'," is a good place to start. "Only the Lonely" begins with the line, "Only the lonely know the way I feel tonight," and the first-person pronoun makes clear that the narrator's loneliness is the Orbison persona's loneliness. The title of "I'm Hurtin'" similarly says it all. "Blue Angel," by contrast, begins with the line, "Oh blue angel don't *you* cry" (emphasis added); here the lonely one is the person at the song's center. Orbison offers solace to the woman, assuring her that she shouldn't cry or despair because he loves her and always will. The dream element begins precisely here, as there is no evidence that the woman wants the Orbison persona to be her lover, something that becomes clear when he sings to her about the "divine" and "magic" moments they will have: "If you'll just say you're mine, / I'll love you 'til the end of time." The song clearly implies that this is merely a feverish wish-fulfillment dream on the part of the Orbison persona.

Similarly, as the title indicates, in "Cry Softly Lonely One" the Orbison persona offers to console a lonely woman by letting her cry to him: "You can cry to me tonight and forever, lonely one." Here again the singer is expressing his desire, not the reality of the case, which in no way suggests that his feelings are reciprocated. All of these songs are marked by the revelation, which comes at or near their conclusion, that the Orbison persona is only *imagining* an eternal relationship with these women. In "Cry Softly Lonely One" he tells her that she can come, run, and cry to him "tonight and forever." "Blue Angel" builds toward its conclusion with such lines as "I'll love you 'til the end of time." This nearly apocalyptic notion of love lasting until the end of time is characteristic of the most intensely romantic wish-fulfillment dreaming, and it bears little or no relation to the actual case.

Orbison's attraction to Simon and Garfunkel's "Bridge over Troubled Water" is interesting within this context. Nothing in their performance of that song seems to be about anything other than a real, tangible relationship; nothing suggests the offer of love and support is an unfulfilled fantasy. But it is not surprising that the song resonated richly for Orbison; and its content is similar to that of his songs, in which he, in effect, repeatedly offers to lay himself down as a bridge over troubled water for women whom he addresses in a near-hallucinatory state. Orbison recorded "Bridge over Troubled Water" at MGM in the 1970s (as yet unreleased) and performed it live in his concerts at the time (several bootleg versions exist). More recently, Raul Malo has taken the Orbison vocal track from the MGM recording and used it to record a new duet (also unreleased as yet).

"Twinkle Toes" supplies a complex variation on these songs and makes clear how, in addition to dreaming about his role in saving the woman, the Orbison persona *identifies* with the woman. The song is about a go-go dancer and the singer sings to her while she dances. Again it is the woman who is lonely and crying, or at least the singer thinks she is. He describes her as someone whose carefree exterior masks an inner sadness: "Yeah, behind the smile, I know you're crying." Again he offers emotional support, telling her to be tough and hang on. The song concludes with his fantasy of saving her; he tells her to get ready, "'cause I bet I take you home tonight / . . . now when the dance is through / You won't be lonely, you won't be blue tonight, / I'll be with you."

This song makes explicit what is implicit in the others—namely, that there is no evidence that the woman to whom Orbison is singing even knows that he exists. Literally speaking, the dancing woman in this bar cannot be hearing the Orbison persona, who is just another man among a crowd of men, something the dubbed-in voices of a male crowd further emphasize. And, as always, the song is about an imagined future, not a real present. The singer dreams of this woman in a smoke-filled bar, just another man among a crowd of men—but with, of course, one crucial difference. In stark contrast to the crudity of the other men we hear shouting, the Orbison persona sensitively identifies with the woman whom he wants to save. He desires her just as strongly as they do, but unlike them, he sees her loneliness. I will return to this pattern of identification in the next chapter.

"(Say) You're My Girl" supplies yet another variation on this type of dream song. Here again the title says it all: although the song seems to be about a man addressing "his" girl, in fact the man is merely imploring the woman to be his. This time, however, the Orbison persona knows the woman; she has been his best friend's girlfriend but the two have just broken up. He tells her that he has been waiting for this and has always been in love with her. Again, there is no indication that his feelings are reciprocated, and the fascinating repetition of the title line makes clear that, once again, the Orbison persona is hopelessly confused between his dreams and the reality. The line "Be my girl, you're my girl" is a remarkable condensation of the split between the wish and the reality. The entire song leads up to an intensely emotional outburst structured around precisely this contradiction: "Be my girl, be my girl, you're my girl, you're mine, you're my girl." The delusion here is that if he says it enough times with enough conviction, she *will* be his girl. He slides from asking her to be his girl, to describing her as if she were his girl, to declaring that she *is* his girl. But this is just his fantasy.

On the album *In Dreams* Orbison acknowledges that dreams have long been a staple of American popular music and rock 'n' roll. In addition to the title song, which he wrote, the album contains cover versions of Stephen Foster's "Beautiful Dreamer," Johnny Mercer's "Dream," and the Everly Brothers' hit "All I Have to Do Is Dream," written by Boudleaux Bryant. I mention this here because many of the motifs Orbison develops in his music are far from original. His use of images of crying, loneliness, and the color blue are, like dreaming, all common in rock 'n' roll and country music. But Orbison takes the most common tropes of rock and country and transforms them into a poetic and complex tapestry.

Not surprisingly, Orbison's music shows a fascination with night and the dark. One of the earliest recorded examples of this is "Darkness," a song that describes night in detail. Other songs associate darkness not only with night but also with gloom and a virtually surreal world of wakeful dreaming. For Orbison the "magic night" could be jubilant, as in "Nightlife," where he revels in the sunset and the onset of nighttime activities; or optimistic, as in "We'll Take the Night," a song celebrating night as an opportunity for lovers; or, as in "Penny Arcade," the time of dreamlike pleasures, when the lights of an arcade suddenly appear through the darkness; or ominous, as in "Wait," where illicit love must be postponed, as the singer once again promises, in an almost dreamlike state, "I promise you I'll be with you tomorrow night / We have to wait until the time is right."

As with so many of the motifs in Orbison's music, darkness receives late-period development in "She's a Mystery to Me" from the *Mystery Girl* album. The song opens with the words "Darkness falls" and is full of references to twilight, nighttime, and darkness. The song invokes Orbison's persona through the first-person narration and tells of a night of love so dark and mysterious as to border on the perverse. The unnamed woman takes him to a "twilight land" where "night falls" and he cannot see without her. He is captivated by the "darkness in her eyes." Their "night of love" is described in ambiguous terms, though the pain it causes is graphically clear. "She's a Mystery to Me" makes clear the frequent relationship between darkness, nighttime, mystery, and perverse sexuality in Orbison's music, as we shall see in more detail in the next chapter.

The song also reveals a surprising displacement of the dark, mysterious figure in Orbison's music, for in this case it is the "girl" who is the dark mystery. Of course, the real mystery, throughout his career, was Orbison himself. "She's a Mystery to Me" gave the CD its title, but the cover art emphasizes a very dark and mysterious Roy Orbison. Let us turn now to the dark sexual undercurrents that form the basis of the masochist aesthetic that so much defined the work of this mysterious man.

5

"Crawling Back"
The Masochist Aesthetic

"You are dreaming," she cried. "Wake up!" She grasped my arm with her marble hand. "Wake up!" she repeated, this time in a low, gruff voice. I strained to open my eyes. I could see the hand that was shaking me, but suddenly it turned a tawny brown, and the voice became the husky alcoholic voice of my Cossack, who stood towering above me.

—Leopold von Sacher-Masoch, *Venus in Furs* (147)

This scene opens the best-known novel of Leopold von Sacher-Masoch, from whose name the term masochism derives. We are following a conversation between a man and a beautiful woman, when suddenly we discover that it is all a dream. Later in the novel the protagonist awakens from another dream: "I wake after a feverish night troubled by night-mares. . . . Which of my confused memories are real? What have I experienced, what have I merely dreamed?" (187). When he examines his body and realizes that the beating of which he has dreamed has actually occurred, he declares, "My dream has come true."

The dreaming protagonist of this quintessential masochist novel clearly resembles the dreaming Orbison persona, who also at times does not know the difference between dream and reality. Dreaming is both a motif in Orbison's music and relates to the centrality of masochism in his aesthetics. In Orbison's dream songs, the protagonist frequently awakens to a painful reality; that the pain is psychological rather than physiological should not obscure the masochist aesthetic of songs like "Crying," "Crawling Back," "I'm Hurtin'," and "Love Hurts."

As I have demonstrated, during his first period of major success, from 1960 to 1964, everything about Roy Orbison was unusual by the standards of rock at the time: the songs he wrote, his vocal style, his performance style, and his persona. Masculinity supplies the common point at which all these unique attributes intersect: Orbison did not occupy any of rock's conventional masculine positions. He constructed a complex masochist aesthetic based on a dark, passive, frightened, overly emotional figure, who either reveled in loss and pain or lost himself in a world of dreams. The origins of this unusual masculinity surface explicitly in "Chicken Hearted," a Sun song released in 1956, in which Orbison revels in his cowardice ("I'd like to be a hero but I ain't got the nerve, I'm chicken hearted") and his failure as a lover ("I'd like to be a lover but I ain't got no girls, I'm chicken-hearted"). An alternate version of this song, on the same theme of masculinity but with quite different lyrics, is included in the box set *Orbison 1956–1965*.

Orbison called "Chicken Hearted" "one of the worst recordings in the history of the world," and Colin Escott heartily agrees, asserting, "The record was the flop it deserved to be" (Escott 2001, 21). Whether one agrees with this assessment or not (I do not), such glib judgments and dismissals obscure important issues. Bill Justis, who wrote the song, seems to have been the first person to see in Orbison the potential for a masculinity far removed from the norm. Orbison's own lyrics tend not to be so explicit about masculinity, preferring a more muted, subtextual approach.

The two versions of "Chicken Hearted," taken together, represent a particularly creative moment in the Sun sessions. The alternate take has an almost punk attitude that sounds twenty years ahead of its time. But even if the record were one of the worst ever made, it is instructive for our purposes and should not be dismissed. Its daring assertion of an alternative masculinity is significant as the first major exploration of Orbison's masculine persona. Similarly, "The Clown," another minor, overlooked Sun recording, introduces the first of several clown and "fool" images wherein the Orbison persona is laughed at and humiliated.

Remember When, a recently issued bootleg of newly discovered, early but undated Orbison demos reveals more of the early signs of this evolving masochist aesthetic. In his composition "Defeated," the Orbison persona wallows in the loss suggested by the title, repeating the word "defeated" twelve times in a song less than two minutes long. His loss of the woman he loves to another man only intensifies his love for her: "Defeated, defeated, now I know the score / Defeated, defeated, yet I love you even more." In "Yesterday and You," another Orbison composition, time and desire flow backward: "Time goes by much too slow, my blues have turned to gray / I love you less than tomorrow, more than yesterday." The laughable clown persona, the defeated lover who loves even more in loss, and the perverse distortion in which time intensifies loss instead of healing it, are all components of a formal masochist aesthetic.

Not surprisingly, Orbison was eulogized as the singer who, more than any other, made hurting so bad feel so good. Although primarily pop rock, this aspect of Orbison's music speaks to its strong country influence. All of his major hits between 1960 ("Only the Lonely") and 1964 ("Oh, Pretty Woman") were recorded in Nashville. Placing country music within the context of literature (Mark Twain) and art (Edward Hopper), Cecilia Tichi writes of experiencing the loneliness of the figures in Hopper's *Nighthawks* at the Chicago Art Institute while on a road trip:

> Back on the interstate you complete the theme by playing some more country tapes: Roy Orbison singing the uptempo "Only the Lonely" or Patsy Cline, Tammy Wynette, or Emmylou Harris singing the haunting slow ballad "Lonely Street." Together these texts become a sensory surround of a prominent American trait, loneliness—a part of a national experience so deeply embedded in the culture that it continues over centuries to insist on its own message in our literature, social commentary, and art, prominent among these the art of country music. (Tichi 1994, 5–6)

Somewhat similarly, writing of music used in Clint Eastwood's films, Dennis Bingham notes, "Eastwood's fondness for the rueful suffering of country ballads, which reverberates in the loneliness of many of his protagonists, seems to be an overlooked symptom of male masochism in his films" (Bingham 1994, 231). These perceptive observations offer a temptation to simply throw Orbison in with all the other country singers whose songs deal with suffering and loneliness, but doing so would conceal what is distinct about Orbison's masculine persona.

The general notion of male masochism (reveling, for example, in loneliness) is different from a male masochist aesthetic. Certainly this aesthetic includes such emotions as suffering and loneliness, but it extends well beyond them. And country ballads, written and sung by men, of suffering and loneliness may very well involve masochism, but they do not usually embody a formal masochist aesthetic. Hank Williams's "I'm So Lonesome I could Cry," for example, is quite distinct from Orbison's "Crying." The loneliness of which Orbison sings in "Only the Lonely," his first big hit, derives from the male desire to relinquish power and control for passivity and loss. Roy Orbison's songs, frequently sung in an eerie falsetto, are not sung, in the terms of Lacanian psychoanalysis, from the symbolic, powerful Place of the Father or in the Voice of the Father. While the Law of the Father sometimes makes an appearance in Orbison's songs, it is usually as a socially oppressive and frequently deadly law, as in the case of the police who kill the protagonist in "Tennessee Owns My Soul" (1969) or the military, which leads to the death of most of the combatants in "There Won't Be Many Coming Home" (1967). Orbison's cover version of Sonny Curtis's classic "I Fought the Law" (1972), in which the protagonist declares, "I fought the law and the law won," continues this theme. Perhaps the presumed suicide of Bobby Fuller, who popularized the song, played some part in Orbison's decision. Orbison later recorded a cover version of "Pledging My Love," by Johnny Ace, who died in a game of Russian roulette shortly after recording it.[1] Crying and dying constitute a continuum of loss in Orbison's music, his embrace of death and his identification with artists who committed suicide being the most extreme point of masochism.

Orbison's composition "Mama" (1962) stands in strong contrast to these songs about the deadly Law of the Father. Dealing with the literal mother rather than the symbolic father, the song overtly holds up the mother as the man's object of desire. It is undeniably a love song from a grown man to his mother, in which the singer displaces his lost love onto the figure of the mother. The mother is in fact the woman he has lost and to whom he wishes to return. Indeed, the song summarizes the dilemma of the male masochist: "Oh mama, I'd like to run to you," and follows it shortly and regretfully with society's dictum: "Gotta stay, be a man, if I can." Near the end of the song he consoles his mother through a series of regressions: "Yes, I'll take care of myself, no I'll be alright / I'll go to bed early tonight." Like a little boy, he asks after his "puppy Cocoa." The song concludes with desire for infantile reunification with the mother, "Yes, I'll always be your baby through all the years." Orbison's voice on this song is full of wistful, melancholic desire.

In a bizarre instance of life imitating art, Orbison died on a visit to his mother's home. Nick Kent, who interviewed Orbison days before his death, wrote, "he died from a heart attack 'cradled in the arms of his mother' at his home in Nashville. That image would end up providing the media with a final tragic closing-shot for their emotive vision of Roy Orbison's life as one long, remorseless tale of woe" (Kent 1994, 285). Although the extensive U.S. media coverage of Orbison's death regularly mentioned that he was in Nashville visiting his mother while his wife was in Germany, I have come across no article that referred to him dying "cradled in the arms of his mother." Whether or not that is an accurate quotation from the British press, Kent's use of the phrase has an uncanny echo within the context of the male masochist's desire for renunification with the mother—a reunification that ends in death.

How, then, should we understand the nature of Orbison's masochist aesthetic? Gaylyn Studlar has argued that male masochism derives from the boy child's pre-Oedipal desire to reunite with the nurturing mother, before this goal is threatened and thwarted by the castrating figure of the father. Kaja Silverman, by contrast, has argued for a form of male masochism based precisely upon the genital stage of psychoanalytic development, with the specter of the castrating father in full force. According to Silverman, rather than desiring union with the mother, the male masochist refuses to take the symbolic place of the father. By Silverman's account, Orbison's killed, defeated, and suicidal characters seem to have more in common with the protagonist of Fassbinder's *Berlin Alexanderplatz* than with the Sternbergian protagonists who suffer at the hands of a coldly powerful Marlene Dietrich. The as yet unreleased Orbison song from the MGM period entitled "The Defector" relates significantly to this strain of his masochism. The song is about a military defector during the Vietnam War, a clear instance of someone refusing to take up his rightful position within the symbolic law of the Father. Indeed, the entire song traces a trajectory of loss in the name of the Father. The song opens in the third person: "And the boys can't stand the pace of the war." The narrator loses the clear sense of purpose with which he went off to war: "And anymore I'm not sure what to think." The entire Vietnam War is reduced to a backdrop for the quintessential Orbison declaration, "For now I walk alone." The song ends with the lonely defector wondering if they will send his body back home after he has died.

In my view, the Studlar/Silverman dichotomy represents a false opposition. Male masochism can have multiple determinations that stem from different stages in psychoanalytic development and take quite different forms. Orbison's music fluctuates between both types of masochism—at times being punished by the Father and his law and at other times yearning for a return to the powerful pre-Oedipal mother. Clearly, however, it is the latter form that predominates in his ballads of romantic anguish.

Orbison also recorded a song entitled "Mother," written for him by one of his band members, R. C. Price, in 1978, though it was not released until after his death on the compilation CD *Rare Orbison II*. An unusually enigmatic song, it is about mother/son relationships, the repeated chorus asking: "Mother, what have we done to you? / Mother, can we make it up to you? / Mother, what can we do to start anew?" The song has a strong emphasis on reestablishing the mother/son bond that has been ominously broken in an unspecified manner by the sons. Indeed, the crime of the sons (the use of the word "we" indicates either literally more than one son or symbolically a generalized notion of all sons, or perhaps both things) seems to be nothing other than the Oedipal trajectory of growing up. At one point, the Orbison persona asks, "And why can't it be like it's been . . . ?" If "Mama" and "Mother" are literally about reunification with the mother, "Sweet Mama Blue" (Roy Orbison-Joe Melson) is about a symbolic unification with the mother figure of the title, "an old sweet black woman [who] sings and plays piano like a dream." The center of the song deals with a night the

Orbison persona spends with an old, black woman musician, an experience that is clearly, if metaphorically, sexual: "One night I stayed past closing time / Sweet Mama blew my troubled mind / She sang the night away for me." Even the play on words, where instead of the expected name •Sweet Mama Blue" we hear "Sweet Mama blew," has sexual connotations. The song is literally about the insight into life that the Orbison persona gains from this mother figure. In this case, however, she is the one who dies, and he vows to remember her.

The narrative of the song is in some ways a variation on the young boy/older woman narrative so common in our culture. In such coming-of-age narratives, an adolescent boy loses his virginity and innocence. By the story's end, he has become a man. In this odd love song, however, the woman is not merely older but "old," and the singer not an adolescent but a grown man. Yet he also in some way grows up from the experience, declaring that he has learned to see the truth from her. Like the boy who becomes a man via the loss of sexual innocence, and who remembers forever after the older woman who initiates him, the Orbison persona here gains insight into life through his intimate bond with the old mother figure, who then passes from his life but not his memory.

"Indian Summer," a 1985 duet with Larry Gatlin, conforms to the conventional scenario in a revealing manner. Like the film *The Summer of '42*, "Indian Summer" is a tale of a young boy initiated into the pleasures of love by an older woman. In the first part of the song, Gatlin sings about the manner in which this experienced woman fulfills him; all is bliss and plenitude. Revealingly, Orbison sings the second part of the song, about the breakup of the relationship; it is all pain and loss. In Gatlin's verse the boy is empty until the woman fills him, whereas in Orbison's, the boy cries out "I'm still empty, come fill me." It is precisely this sense of wallowing in the pain of loss and emptiness that characterizes Orbison's masochist aesthetic.

The masochism of these songs goes beyond an emphasis on loneliness and suffering; it is more precisely defined in relation to temporality. As the titles of such songs as "Wait," "Time Changed Everything," "All I Need Is Time," "Love in Time," "Twenty-Two Days," and "Wild Hearts (Run Out of Time)" indicate, time plays a key role in some of the songs, and this relates to structure and composition as well as lyrics.

Many of the songs place the Orbison persona in a context in which time is critical, drawn out, or suspended. At the end of "Running Scared," Orbison's voice thrills at the unbearable suspense of wondering whether his girlfriend will chose him or his phallic rival: "Then all at once he was standing there / So sure of himself, his head in the air / My heart was breaking, which one would it be? / You turned around and walked away with me." I will return later to the importance of the Orbison persona's passivity and paralysis, but notice here the suddenness with which the rival appears ("all at once") and the drawn-out moment during which the outcome is unknown ("my heart was breaking, which one would it be?"). Only the last word of the song relieves the suspense. The song's happy ending is almost irrelevant given the virtual panic that pervades the song. Orbison himself has somewhat innocently remarked of the song: "Every relationship I'd ever been in, the girl already had one going when we first met. Even as far back as kindergarten" (Kent 1994, 291). Although Orbison seems unaware of it, such a pattern itself bespeaks masochistic desire, since being attracted to a woman who already has a boyfriend raises not only the risk of failure but also, in the event of success, the specter of the rival's return. That he traces this pattern all the way back to early childhood is remarkable, though, within the context of his masochist aesthetic, not entirely surprising.

"Running Scared" is about passive suffering, and the way the melody, the arrangement, and Orbison's voice all build to the suspense of the rival's appearance make the outcome secondary to the mounting terror. Indeed, the outcome is almost lost in the instrumentation; it is difficult to tell whether Orbison sings "You turned around and walked away with *me*" or "You turned around and walked away with *him*." When I first heard the song in 1961, this was a crisis for me: I was dying to know what happened and could not hear the answer!

Several years later, Orbison made this structure clear in "Time Changed Everything" (1966), a song about a man's return to the town where he left his girlfriend a year earlier. The entire song deals with his mounting anxiety, as, as the title indicates, time has changed everything in the town. The song builds to his first glimpse of her where he discovers that time has changed everything *but* her. But once again, the discovery is delayed—this time by Orbison repeating the line "Time changed everything" three times before adding "but her." The happy ending is, once again, anticlimactic; the thrill is all about wondering what the delayed outcome will be.

In short, it hardly seems to matter whether the Orbison persona gets the girl, an insight that Nick Cave and the Bad Seeds developed explicitly in their 1985 cover version of "Running Scared," in which they end the song with the woman walking away. The history of "Oh, Pretty Woman" also makes this very clear. In the original version, the Orbison persona does not get the girl, going home alone and consoling himself with the thought that there are "other fish in the sea." His producer Fed Foster thought this was too depressing an ending and asked that Orbison change it. In the revised version, this song too works on the principle of delayed gratification, emphasizing the question ("But wait, what do I see?") more than the answer. "Oh, Pretty Woman," more than any of the others, makes formally explicit the need to draw out the suspense. After the question is phrased, the opening drum beat returns with the opening guitar riff, which once again involves a frustrating, almost stuttering repetition of part of the melody before the whole theme is finally stated. The instrumental delay, that is, also works on the principle of suspension. Moreover, the question is initially answered with another question: "Is she walking back to me?" While the affirmative answer gives the song the upbeat ending Foster wanted, the form makes clear that the long moment of suspense is what really counts. When Orbison sings "But wait," he means it.

If time momentarily freezes in these songs at an unbearably suspenseful moment, in the song entitled "Wait" (1966) it works to keep Orbison suspended in a virtually permanent state of crisis. In this song, which he also cowrote, he tells his illicit lover that she must wait for him until they can be together. Though Orbison sings, "We walk in shadows dark and cold," their transgression is never specified. Time, however, is the focus of the song, as Orbison implores, "I promise you I'll be with you tomorrow night / We have to wait until the time is right." In this and a number of similar songs, the time is never "right." The chorus of this song has Orbison repeatedly crying "wait," until it becomes a virtual incantation, one on which the song fades out, suggesting a seemingly endless delay. We do not really believe that he will act "tomorrow night";

it seems more likely that he has repeatedly appealed to his lover to wait for him, without ever reaching the point of consummation.

Tomorrow night will never come—or if it does, it will not be what the lovers anticipate. Indeed, temporal concepts in Orbison's music are frequently part of a dream world in which the singer envisions action he will never take or imagines that magical changes will take place. Orbison even cowrote and recorded a song entitled "Where Is Tomorrow" (also 1966) in which he repeatedly expresses his desire for that elusive concept: "I long for tomorrow, I'll be strong tomorrow." Time appears to be the enemy of the masochist, but in fact it is the agent by which he prolongs his pain. Masochistic time does not move in the same way as ordinary time. If the pain is in the past, the passage of time doesn't deliver the usual relief, because time is experienced as standing still or as passing with no effect. In "I Can't Stop Loving You," Orbison sings, "They say that time heals a broken heart / But time has stood still since we've been apart." In "I'm Hurtin'," "Time goes by, right on by / And I, I'm still hurtin', yeah hurtin'."

In "Harlem Woman" (1972), the masochistic Orbison persona tells the woman of his dreams, "Someday I'll take you away." But "someday" joins the temporal category of "tomorrow" and "tonight," and the song ends with him pleading to her to "hang on." The masochist ethic is the reverse of the maxim "Don't put off till tomorrow what you can do today." But we know that the Orbison persona will not really be "strong tomorrow"; he never is.

In several of his songs, Orbison writes in what appears to be a traditional male voice, from the point of view of the strong, self-confident man of action. But even these songs live in the future tense, and what are supposed to be plans or actions are in fact daydreams. The most interesting of these from the Monument years is "Working for the Man" (1962), a song that, like "In Dreams" (1963), he uncharacteristically wrote by himself. Both songs are intense expressions of Orbison's interest in both unconscious night dreams and conscious daydreams, as we saw with respect to "Working for the Man" in Chapter 4. "Leah," one of Orbison's most important nighttime dream songs, is particularly interesting within this context. Dreaming would seem to bypass the thicket of temporality and verb tense, for in dreams we fulfill our desires only to discover upon waking that "it was just a dream." Remarkably, however, in "Leah" the Orbison persona dreams about action he will take in the future. He sings about how he's going to go diving for pearls for a necklace for Leah. Most of the song is predicated on future action that culminates in the anticipation of how she will respond: "I'll bet my Leah will be surprised tonight." Even in dreams, the emphasis is on "tonight." Only in the end, when the action turns into a nightmare as the diver's leg is caught and he begins to drown, do we find out the song is a dream about a lost love. In a more conventional narrative, the protagonist would dream about putting the necklace around the lover's neck and then awaken with just the necklace; that is, the dreamer performs the desired action, then awakes to disappointment. The Orbison persona, however, dreams about daydreaming about the desired action. He never acts, even in the dream! "Leah" is a night dream about a daydream.

During the MGM period, the song that most clearly postpones action to the future is "Ride Away" (1965), his first single for the label. In contrast to his total passivity in songs like "Running Scared," here, as the title implies, the Orbison persona is a man of action. Referring to images of a powerful, phallic motorcycle and a desiring woman, he describes the manner in which he will leave his cheating girlfriend by riding his motorcycle away from her. The last lines of the song, however, are "Ride away, ride away / from tears and sorrow / like there's no tomorrow. / Tonight I ride away." Orbison gives a wistful emphasis to the word "Tonight," which has additional resonance from directly following the word "tomorrow." Orbison's masochistic persona always dwells on and defers action to "tonight" or "tomorrow," preferring daydreams to action. The songs with "happy endings" depend on the action of the woman. The late-period "I Drove All Night" bears an interesting relation to "Ride Away"; as the title indicates, it is another song about mobility. Written specifically for Orbison but not used on the *Mystery Girl* CD, the song was released on the posthumous CD *King of Hearts*. Rather than a planned drive (or, rather, dreamed drive), this song is about actually driving. If the Orbison persona uncharacteristically takes action in this song, that action takes a strange form and is undermined by the even stranger position he takes in regard to the action. Another dark, nighttime song, the song strongly implies sexual transgression. This time, instead of dreaming about taking action, he dreams *while* taking action: "I was dreaming while I drove." This is one of those moments, described in Chapter 4, in which Orbison confuses or blurs the line between waking and sleeping. He drives in the midst of a feverish hallucination of sexual pleasure; for a change, this is something he *is* experiencing rather than something he will experience when he arrives at his destination. The line "Maybe I should have called you first" characterizes the action as an inappropriate one. This dark, improper, feverish sexual desire leads to a surprisingly graphic image of sexual deviance: "I drove all night, crept in your room / woke you from your sleep / To make love to you / Is that all right?" The image of the feverish lover creeping into a sleeping woman's bedroom at night to fulfill his sexual desires without first asking her permission borders on explicit perversion. Asking the question "Is that all right?" afterward simply highlights the obvious answer: no, it is not all right. Remarkably, the question is asked six times in this three-minute-forty-five-second song. The Orbison persona seems to hope that by repeatedly asking if it is all right he will be forgiven; clearly he knows that he has done wrong. The song ends with no response from the lover; instead, the repeated question juxtaposed with the title line of the song underscores the sexual urgency that "drives" the man to the dark act. Clearly this action could (indeed, should) cost him the very relationship he seeks to preserve.

His feelings for the woman are particularly dark and obsessive. Exclaiming that he thinks about their two hearts as one and that he thinks of her in the dark, cold night makes him sound delusional and creepy. Everything about the man is characterized as out of control. Nothing anywhere in the song suggests that she feels the same way about him. Indeed, this song may be seen as a bizarre variation on the dream songs. Rather than dreaming about a deferred action, the Orbison persona in this song acts, but the action may be based upon nothing but a feverishly perverse dream. Perhaps the reason he is not together with this woman is that she has rejected him. Perhaps she does not even know him; the single heartbeat may be nothing but his own fantasy— the man's desperation strongly hints that it is. In this way, the song is similar to "Blue Angel," "Cry Softly Lonely One," "Twinkle Toes" and "(Say) You're My Girl," discussed in Chapter 4, where the Orbison persona comforts a lonely woman. In none of these songs, however, is there any indication that the woman wants his comfort and attention.

In one way, "I Drove All Night" is the obverse of the masochist's usual deferral of action. Here, having undertaken an action, the Orbison persona wonders whether he should have. All indications are that he should not have and that this action will thus cost him the woman he desires. For in addition to not acting, the masochist can act improperly in a manner likely to lead to his ruin. Regardless of how one reads the song, whether or not their relationship actually exists, or, if it does, whether it corresponds to his desires, the Orbison persona is ready to assume guilt and remorse.

For the masochist, the crisis of action is linked to countless forms of bad timing: there is too much time or not enough; he acts too quickly or waits too long; he stands paralyzed in an eternity of time or rushes madly off on the spur of the moment. Perhaps Orbison's most intense song of exquisite masochistic pain is the late-period "Love in Time" (1987). The song was left unfinished and was not included on *Mystery Girl*. It was finished and beautifully produced by Robbie Robertson for *King of Hearts*. The unbearable pain of the present in this song is seemingly mitigated by reference to a future time when everything will be all right. But once again, the future is nothing but a desperate dream of a time that will never actually arrive. The images of loneliness in this song are the starkest in the entire Orbison *oeuvre;* he seems to have taken the pain of the world into himself. Indeed, the external world becomes internalized in a series of impossibly sad and lonely images. The river, the winds, and the rain are all inside him, along with the calls of lost souls. It is not just his pain that he carries but that of everyone and everything. What starts out as a firm belief that his time will come turns from certainty to mere hope, with such repeated lines as "I hope I find love in time," and "I hope it's there for me." The juxtaposition of internalized suffering with intense hope of relief, as expressed by the sweetly melancholic voice in which Orbison sings this song, raises it to an intensity unusual even for him. In keeping with the late-period characteristic of scaling back the middle-period melodramatic outbursts, the song is comparatively restrained. Interestingly, the moment at which Orbison sings in his most powerful voice comes when he emphasizes the phrase "in time," immediately before the instrumental break featuring Robertson's guitar solo.

The word "time" receives many forms of emphasis in this song. The title itself is ambiguous, referring both to love occurring *in* time and also to the suggestion that in time love will come, if one waits long enough. In "So Young: The Love Theme from *Zabriskie Point*," Orbison describes love as "space in line, a place in time." For Orbison, love occurs in time not only in the sense of the time for love, when it comes, but also as *within* or *inside* time. That love is a temporal thing is good news for the masochist, for these varieties of time open up a seemingly endless set of possibilities for loss and pain. Time is always and only an enemy of love. In "So Young," "time runs out on love too good to last"; at the end of the song the Orbison persona declares, "too late I find, when tomorrow's come and love is lost." Sometimes, as in "Wild Hearts (Run Out of Time)," there is not enough time. In that song, Orbison implores the lover who has left him, "Please don't let your heart run out of time," but, as the title tells us, wild hearts do run out of time. At the end of "All I Need Is Time," Orbison cries desperately, "I need time." The masochist either has abundant time to suffer endlessly, or not enough time in which to act and resolve his suffering.

In an alternate, unreleased version of "Twinkle Toes," the Orbison persona's behavior is so extreme as to be incoherent. For no stated reason, he leaves the woman of the title, "Tell Twinkle Toes that I love her, / but I've got a train that just won't wait, / Tell Twinkle Toes I'm dreaming of her, / I tried to get by but its too late, too late." There is absolutely nothing in the song to explain this train that won't wait or why it's too late—and for what? The singer inexplicably jumps a train that takes him away from his lover and then bemoans his loss, placing the action within an irreversible temporal sequence. To further heighten his unhappiness, he addresses this song to his friends, telling them to have a good time and asking that they remember him. Were it not for his unexplained leave-taking, he would be having a good time with his friends and his lover. Instead he worries that he'll "die in misery." The released version of "Twinkle Toes" is coherent, although its dreamlike reverie does not tell us if the Orbison persona's relationship to the girl is anything but feverish hallucination. In contrast, the incoherent masochism in the alternate version risks tearing the surface and laying bare the manner in which the singer brings this terrible suffering on himself.

The masochist is, of course, happiest when there is an audience for his suffering, and Orbison frequently describes that audience in his songs. In "Crawling Back" (1965), probably his most explicitly masochistic song, he sings, "People stop, they talk and they stare." He then concocts a fiction for himself about how the staring people don't understand his lover's cruel behavior or that she really "needs" him. The song concludes with the affirmation that "Where ever you may lead me, [once again the woman is active] / I will come crawling back." "I'll Say It's My Fault" is, as the title suggests, constructed entirely around the attention a broken love affairs draws, with the Orbison persona offering to "take all the blame" and accept the fault: "I'll give a good show." This song makes crystal clear the masochist's desire to take on pain (no reason is given why he should take the blame) and suffer it in front of others. The lyrics "Everyone will be wondering / all our friends will inquire" emphasize how pervasive this public scrutiny is.

In "Pantomime" (1966), another MGM-period Orbison composition, he opens the song by singing, "Well thank you, thanks a lot / Now I am the talk of the town." In the late-period "The Comedians," written by Elvis Costello for the *Mystery Girl* CD (1989), the Orbison persona is the victim of a very public "practical joke": he is left "dangling" at the top of a stopped Ferris wheel as his girlfriend walks way with another man: "It's always something cruel that laughter drowns."

Not coincidentally, "Crawling Back," "Pantomime," and "The Comedians" present the image of the clown and the butt of the joke. In "Crawling Back" Orbison sings, "I'll be your faithful clown because I love you"; in "Pantomime," he sings "Of all the fools they drink to / I am the king of the clowns"; in "The Comedians" he is the pathetic butt of the joke, characterizing his girlfriend and her lover as the comedians of the title. And in "The Actress" (1962), an early Monument B side that Orbison cowrote, he sings, "You keep me around to be your faithful clown / 'till someone you can love comes along." Here the imagery uncannily recalls Professor Rath as the publicly humiliated clown in the film *The Blue Angel*—a man humiliated not coincidentally by his wife's choosing a "strong man."

Both "The Actress" and "Pantomime" point to a related feature of the masochist aesthetic: acting and masquerades. As is made clear in Sacher-Masoch's novel *Venus in Furs* and in Sternberg's Dietrich films, masochism commonly involves role playing, charades, masquerades, costume parties, and theatrics. In "The Actress," Orbison tells his cruel lover that she should be an actress since she is so good at role playing. Using theatrical metaphors, the song builds to one of his typically emotional climaxes: "But I'll go all the way to the end of the play / I'll be a part of your masquerade, / Although I know it may be the saddest show / In the life of a fool on parade." Theatrics also surface in the cover art of Orbison's 1962 album *Crying*, which features a large drawing of the conventional theatrical mask representing tragedy. Although none of the songs included on that album explicitly raises the issue of or refers to the theater (inexplicably, "The Actress" is not included), the cover art enigmatically points to the way in which all of Orbison's music is part of the intensified world of masochistic emotional theatrics and role playing.

Orbison's masochism fluctuates between two opposing poles: at one extreme his persona recognizes that he is to blame for his misery and pain, while at the other he seems victimized by circumstances beyond his control, frequently blaming social and cultural circumstances that "justify" his situation. I place in the first category the love songs in which he punishes himself. "Careless Heart," the last song on *Mystery Girl* (1989), is a nonstop lamentation about the singer's loss of perfect love through his own fault. It is a form of emotional self-flagellation full of such laments as "I let you slip away," "I had my chances," "I took it all too far," "I let it fall apart," and "I didn't care enough." In "A Love So Beautiful," from the same CD, a variation appears in the line referring to the perfect love of the title: "We let it slip away." Even in this modified form, the Orbison persona takes his share of the responsibility. These songs come close to acknowledging that Orbison prefers to revel in the pain of lost love for which he bears some or all of the responsibility to acting in a manner that guarantees his continued happiness. Even this, however, sometimes drifts into a form of fatalism closely resembling displacement. In "A Love so Beautiful" he cynically declares, "We were too young to understand, to ever know that lovers drift apart, and that's the way love goes." The bleakness here is not even qualified by acknowledging that *sometimes* lovers fall apart; this insight is presented as an inexorable fact of life.

The bizarre composition "Harlem Woman" relies on displacement strategy. In love with a (presumably black) prostitute, a single mother fallen on hard times, Orbison urges the woman to "Go on and do what you must do," even as he declares his love for her. Although framed with reference to social problems, this song does not amount to the serious social commentary of such songs as "Communication Breakdown" and "Southbound Jericho Parkway" (see Chapter 1); it is pure Orbison romantic melodrama. Even though "Harlem Woman" is ostensibly about the prostitute's life, the Orbison persona is its center; he breaks down in the middle of it, singing of his pain and tears in the first person. "Sometimes I cry, but I'll get by." This song is riddled with so many contradictions that it simply doesn't add up—Orbison revels in the pain caused by her need to have a never-ending series of other men. He never explains why he doesn't offer her financial assistance or marry her. As before, the masochist's action is deferred (she doesn't even know how much he loves her), so that he may suffer in the present. The "benevolent" racism of the song (he understands the need of this Harlem woman to be a prostitute) further obscures the Orbison persona's involvement with her in the first place. How and why did he fall in love with a black, single-mother prostitute? The answer is that he was a client: "Yes you walk at night / I have held you tight." At any rate, the excesses of this song are a match for any Von Sternberg film. The Orbison persona and his actions are clearly to blame for the pain he bears, but he in turn blames the flawed society that fails to help her. Thus, like so many Sternberg heroes, he can watch his beloved in the arms of other men.

If "The Actress" recalls *The Blue Angel,* "Harlem Woman" recalls *Blonde Venus.* In the latter film, a husband and father sells his body for medical experimentation in order to support his family. The wife and mother, played by Marlene Dietrich, decides that she must leave the home and become a showgirl to support herself. Eventually, destitute and hiding from the law with her child, she falls into a life of prostitution. As in "Harlem Woman," dire economic necessity seems the cause of these unfortunate events, in both cases involving prostitution for the "fallen woman." But Sternberg is not primarily interested in poverty in *Blonde Venus;* it serves merely as a catalyst for the action. The film is more a maternal melodrama than a social-problem film. Similarly, Orbison is not primarily interested in the economics and racism of the ghetto, though they provide the catalyst for his emotional melodrama.

A somewhat less melodramatic version of the same impulse found in "Harlem Woman" can be found in "The Loner," where the Orbison persona declares to his girlfriend that, as a loner, he cannot run with her crowd. Once again, however, he is "understanding" and declares that he will see her at night, urging her, "So go on laugh and walk and talk with other guys / I'll never let them see the love that's in my eyes." Even when he has a lover, the masochist flirts with disaster by throwing her into the arms of other men.

Indeed, Orbison's songs have a dual masochistic structure of identification. In one group, he dwells on his imagining other men in the arms of a woman he has loved and lost. In "Come Back to Me (My Love)", for example, he sings, "Now today is her birthday my baby's sweet sixteen / But someone is in my place to hold my every dream." There is frequently someone in his place and he obsesses about that person in a manner that can only intensify his pain. In "How Are Things in Paradise," he characterizes a lover who left him for another man as presumably being in paradise with her new lover. At one point he asks, "Does he try to hold you like I used to do? . . . Oh, does he take your hand and whisper I love you? / Oh, don't you know that I love you too."

On the other side of the coin, Orbison dreams of being in another man's place. "Blue Angel" is an extremely important song in this respect. It departs from the usual first-person narratives in which he suffers the pain; in this variation, he comforts the woman who has suffered at the hands of another man. At the beginning of the song, he disapprovingly describes the other man as someone who "thought love was a game," assuring the woman that he, by contrast, will "never say goodbye." Yet as the song progresses we discover that the love he sings about is displaced into the future, and (again) there is no indication that the woman has any interest in him, though he offers himself up to her unconditionally, describing the wonderful love they will have: "If you'll just say you're mine / I'll love you 'til the end of time." Rather than having had heavenly moments with the woman, he imagines himself in the place of the other man, who actually experienced such moments. Although the Orbison persona wants (dreams) her to "say you're mine," there is no indication that she will. Indeed, the song has a bizarre, remote feeling, implying that there has been no relationship between the singer and the woman and that there will never be. As in "(Say) You're My Girl," all that exists is his feverish desire to replace the other man and, unlike him, stay true forever. The obsessive intensity with which the Orbison persona imagines himself in another man's place is the obverse of imagining the man who has replaced him with the woman whom he once had. In short, just as the time is never right, the "place" is never right, either.

"She's a Mystery to Me," from the *Mystery Girl* CD, gives an unusual inflection to Orbison's masochist aesthetic. As we saw at the end of the previous chapter, the song is generally dark and mysterious. But it is clear, to say the least, that this is not a blissful night of normal love. The ambiguity of the song's setting and actions stands in stark contrast to its detailed description of the sharp pain of love. The images of a switch-blade cutting the heart, the bleeding heart and the body being pulled apart, are intense images of masochistic pain, but they are atypical of Orbison's *oeuvre* in that they are images of physical pain. Indeed, taken out of context, these images conjure up someone being drawn and quartered. Although masochism is linked in the popular imagination to physical pain, psychological pain is what many masochists chiefly crave. There is no necessary physical dimension to masochistic pain: masochists do not need to be tied up and whipped, though that is how they are most often depicted in popular culture. "She's a Mystery to Me" gives a symbolic physical referent to the masochistic pain that is typically more psychological in Orbison's music.

The song does, however, emphasize several themes typical of Orbison's masochism. Once again, the Orbison persona is paralyzed, though he makes clear his desire to run. The song concludes with an intense image of both physical pain and frozen time: "Am I left to burn / And burn eternally." These images of Hell invoke the most extreme, indeed an eternal, form of that masochistic time that seeks to slow down and stop at the moment of greatest suffering. The image of the paralyzed figure who wants to run but cannot and instead "melts away" points to the total dissolution of the self that lies at the heart of the masochist aesthetic. The desire for reunification with the powerful oral mother means death for the male masochist. The development of the ego involves a series of splits from the original, blissful unity with the powerful mother of the oral phase. In order to develop a sense of its own identity, the infant has to break the original unity with the mother and become aware of itself as a separate being. Once that original bond is broken, the individual will be prey to desire until the final dissolution of death.

If melting away poetically but indirectly means the dissolution of the self, "Windsurfer" expresses clearly the masochist's desire for death. "Windsurfer" was included on the *Mystery Girl* CD only at Orbison's insistence. Executives at Virgin Records did not like the song and urged him to use another. Orbison, however, felt a particular commitment to the song and decided that it should stay on the CD. In his final interviews, he was particularly pleased with advance critical reception for the song among European critics. That this song meant so much to Orbison makes perfect sense within the context of his masochist aesthetic.

Like "Windsurfer," discussed in Chapter 4, "Southbound Jericho Parkway" is also sung in the third person, although, unlike Windsurfer, the song is more about the causes and effects of a suicide than about the desire for death. Here, a character named Mr. Henry Johnson commits suicide by driving his speeding car directly into a wall. Johnson is the perfect image of the failed symbolic father. The first part of the song details his personal failures, which include divorce and estrangement from his children. The unnamed man in "Windsurfer" is also a failure, but of a different sort. Remarkably, this song suggests that the masochist really wants to be a "regular guy" so that he can impress a woman. Although not sung in the first person, the man in this song bears a close relationship to the Orbison persona, and the song implies that the Orbison persona's unconventional position arises out of a failed desire to be a traditional male. Recalling the double movement in "Mama," where the masochist wants both to stay and be a man and to run to his mother, the windsurfer wants both to fit in with the guys and at the same time to be a loner. This doubleness expresses the pressure to conform to the conventional masculinity that the masochist rejects—whether of his own free will or because he cannot measure up to the standard. The windsurfer "practiced in his dreams" and "sailed alone."

The woman's rejection of this man's desire achieves a heightened poetic expression: "He said, 'Let's sail away together.' / She told him, 'No, no, never, no.'" The rejection is so powerful not only because of the repetition of the word "no" but because of the startling presence of the word "never." Being told no three times is final enough, but being told never is more than the protagonist can take.

The pain being too much to bear, the protagonist literally dissolves, "melts," and disappears, leaving only a message in the sand asking why we always want something "out of reach." In an early draft of the song by Bill Dees, the body is washed up on the beach. Orbison insisted that it simply disappear, a change that gives poignant expression to the masochist's desire to be rid of the ego, to "melt away." For the masochist there is, in fact, a perfectly logical reason for wanting the unattainable: it guarantees the pain of loss. In this song, the loss is literal and final.

It is important that we try to identify the masochist aesthetic in terms of its various tropes (e.g., the seeming victim of social and personal injustice who must suffer from the pain inflicted on him from "without"), as well as in its various forms (e.g., temporal delay, postponement, bad timing, and so on). In "(They Call You) Gigolette," an Orbison composition from the Monument period, he warns of a dangerous woman ("the devil's pet") who has ruined many men. She is the masochist's dream of the cold, cruel woman: "They say that you laugh when lovers cry." Although the first part of the song is a detailed warning of her dangerous charms, in true masochist form the Orbison persona nonetheless becomes the victim of bad timing: "It's too late for me, too late now to forget." Describing himself as under her spell, he laments that the time for escaping her is past, as he finds himself in her arms. For Orbison it is always either too late or too soon, and he can never act, either by running away from the woman (as in "She's a Mystery to Me") or by running to her (as in "Running Scared"). When trapped, through his own fault, by the devil's pet, he does what any good masochist would do; he flings open his arms and in an operatic outburst embraces her: "So come on and hold me, hold me close to you," he sings with a thrill in his voice as he anticipates his night of doom. "She's a Mystery to Me" can be read as a sort of sequel to "Gigolette": it is the night of doom, switchblade, bleeding heart, and all.

I want to conclude this discussion of Orbison's masochist aesthetic with a final posthumous song, "You May Feel Me Crying," released nearly ten years after the posthumous "She's a Mystery to Me." The lyrics articulate an important sexual theme that runs through much of Orbison's music as a subtext. The Orbison persona sings to his former lover. The lyrics describe her having sexual intercourse ("so when you take him deep inside") and present the perverse notion of the Orbison persona making physical contact with her new lover ("Remember I'm there with you and you may feel me crying"). The lyrics are so explicit that Orbison may very well have felt uncomfortable with finishing this song for public release. Indeed, the emotional high point of the singing coincides with an almost shockingly clear, poetic account of Orbison's removal from conventional masculinity and sexuality. "There are stronger men than me," he cries out, declaring, "And you will desire what they want." The stronger men take the woman to a mountain where she will see the new things that only they can give her. The mountain and the surrounding language suggest a metaphor for the astonishing sexual acts these men perform. The passage also acknowledges that this form of masculine performance is not really about female pleasure—men who perform these acts do so to prove their masculinity to themselves and others. Women have to be complicit in learning to desire what these men want.

The Orbison persona is incapable of performing this kind of sex. Outside this masculine norm, he inhabits a no-man's-land that may be the most extreme form of masochism imaginable: he is simultaneously inside the woman, feeling the penetration of her new lover, and "out there all alone," with nothing but memories of what he has lost. Both positions are represented as ones of extreme pain and suffering. The combination of these two positions, impossible if taken literally, creates something reminiscent of the inner circles of Hell in Dante's *Inferno*. And in fact, in "She's a Mystery to Me," the Orbison persona's description of his passion sounds like Hell: "I will burn and burn eternally." Far from making women desire what he wants on a mountaintop, the Orbison persona masochistically revels in the depths of his self-made hell.

6

In David Lynch's Dreams

Roy Orbison at the Movies

oy Orbison has become a movie star, but not a conventional one, nor the one he initially envisioned becoming. Following Elvis Presley's successful entry into films, it became almost expected that rock 'n' roll stars would attempt the same transition. A successful career as a pop singer led naturally to film acting. The Beatles continued this tradition with *A Hard Day's Night* (1964) and *Help* (1965), coming shortly after they attained superstar status, much as Presley's *Love Me Tender* (1956) came shortly after he signed with RCA and attained that status. Since Presley's and Orbison's careers had intersected several times before, it was no surprise that Orbison would model his career on that of his phenomenally successful friend and fellow Sun recording artist. Orbison's career also intersected with the Beatles, with whom he toured England in 1963, and their successful films would have supplied further incentive for him to follow suit.

Roy Orbison made only one movie, *The Fastest Guitar Alive* (1968), by all accounts a failure. The low-budget film is poorly made and has mediocre music. MGM did little to promote it, the critical reception was minimal, and the box office was poor. It did nothing for Orbison's career, though for my purposes it provides a revealing, if momentary, aberration. Originally planned as a serious Western after the success of

Cat Ballou (1965), *The Fastest Guitar Alive* was quickly converted into a comedy. The three best songs on the soundtrack album never even appeared in the film. These songs (*Best Friend, Heading South,* and *There Won't Be Many Coming Home*) are quite different from the others in tone and were reportedly written for the film by Orbison and Bill Dees, before it was transformed into a comedy.

Perhaps the film's main legacy is its documentation of a radical re-invention of Orbison's image. The film's total failure ensured that the reinvented image would be discarded and indirectly contributed to the myth of the Orbison persona, with the ever-present dark glasses. The publicity photos surrounding the film, like the film itself, are the only public images made after 1963 in which Orbison's dark glasses are not essential. The publicity photos present a heavily made-up Orbison as a would-be matinee idol, a persona almost unimaginable now. Had the film succeeded, Orbison's career and self-presentation might have taken him in a very different direction. This attempt at transformation underscores Orbison's willingness by the late 1960s to make conces-sions that might promote commercial success. Along with the film and glamorized image, I regard his writing and recording of the Simon and Garfunkel–influenced "Communication Breakdown" as an exper-iment in his career development.

This is not to fault Orbison's integrity. In the main, his career choices point to a highly committed musician who pursued his music with lit-tle regard for the commercial environment of rock at the time. The coherence of vision in his *oeuvre*, however, results in part from the fail-ure of such projects as *The Fastest Guitar Alive.* Orbison's willingness to try different things suggests that he would have pursued commercially successful ones further. His MGM contract, for instance, called for a number of movies that were never made. If "Southbound Jericho Park-way" and "Communication Breakdown" had succeeded, he could have become a late sixties singer of socially serious songs; had *The Fastest Guitar Alive* succeeded, he could have become an Elvis Presley–type MGM musical star. In a significant sense, then, these failures drove him back to what we now consider quintessential Orbison.

Orbison switched from Monument to MGM in part to develop a film career; when his only film failed dismally and the studio dropped all future film plans, he was enlisted to compose and sing songs for three other MGM films. None of the songs—"So Young" from *Zabriskie Point* (1970), "It Takes All Kinds of People" from *The Moonshine War* (1970), and "Zig Zag" from *Zig Zag* (1970)—became hits or were central to the films. None of the films brought significant attention to Orbison's music. "So Young" was added to *Zabriskie Point* after the film's release, when MGM decided that something was needed over the film's closing credits. The release prints were called back and the song was added, but the soundtrack had already been completed without its inclusion. Whereas *Zabriskie Point* was well received on the art film circuit, *The Moonshine War* and *Zig Zag* were critical and box office failures. Many Orbison fans at the time, myself included, were not even aware of these movies or the use of Orbison songs in them.

If his plans for movie stardom failed, how then did Orbison become one? By accident, according to David Lynch, whose use of "In Dreams" in *Blue Velvet* (1986) marked the first of several highly successful, prominent uses of Orbison's music in movies. Lynch says, "I listened to Shostakovich while I was writing *Blue Velvet* and that's one of the things I talked to Angelo [Badalamenti] about when I asked him to score the picture." Lynch sometimes makes notes about music in his scripts, but he does not recall indicating anything about Roy Orbison in the script for *Blue Velvet*. He heard "Crying" on a cab radio while riding through Central Park with Kyle McLachlan during pre-production on *Blue Velvet*. "And on the cab's radio came 'Crying' by Roy Orbsion," Lynch recalled. "And I started listening to that and thought that that might be a great song for *Blue Velvet*." He then got an album of Orbison's greatest hits and realized that "In Dreams," not "Crying," was the song for his picture (Lynch 2002).

Lynch later used "Crying" to stunning effect in *Mulholland Drive* (2001), but not because he retained a deep interest in or love for the song. "That was a total accident, just as that song being on the cab radio was an accident," says Lynch. An agent who sometimes introduced musicians to Lynch arranged a meeting for him with Rebekkah Del Rio, a singer, thinking that Lynch would be interested in her music. "So he brought a girl over for coffee and she said she would like to just stand and sing something in front of me, and four minutes off the street she was in the booth and sings what was exactly in the movie. It ["Crying," translated as "Llorando"] was a song that she had translated into Spanish and it was a very special song to her and she just got through singing it at Carnegie Hall." Lynch had never even heard of Del Rio. "I started getting ideas based on that and that led to her being in the film" (Lynch 2002).

In the sense that neither was planned in the original conception of the film, the use of both "In Dreams" in *Blue Velvet* and "Crying" in *Mulholland Drive* are accidents. Had Lynch not heard "Crying" on the cab radio and had an agent not brought Rebekkah Del Rio over to his house, Orbison's music would have been in neither of these films. Accidents often play an important part in the creation of a film or other artwork. As Lynch says, "things happen every day." But only certain artists manage to weave them into their work. Lynch actually wrote both "In Dreams" and "Crying" into the films, beyond just using the songs. In *Blue Velvet*, Frank Boothe cites lines from the song before we hear it, and in *Mulholland Drive*, Lynch introduces a visual motif of crying during the scene in which the song is heard, and he returns to it later. In both movies, the action comes to a literal halt when the songs are "performed" by characters within the films, rather than merely heard on the soundtrack. In both films the "performances" are lip-synched—in *Blue Velvet* into a trouble light, and in *Mulholland Drive* into a microphone that appears to be "real" until the singer collapses on stage and the song keeps playing. Whether Lynch had planned to use the songs or accidentally stumbled upon them makes no difference within this context. Lynch told me that he had been an Orbison fan since first hearing Orbison's music in the 1950s, growing up in Boise, Idaho. Otherwise, it is likely that his hearing it on the cab radio would have had no particular effect upon him. Similarly, had he not briefly thought of using "Crying" in *Blue Velvet* years earlier, and had the extraordinary success he had with "In Dreams" not occurred, he might have responded entirely differently to the "accident" of hearing Del Rio sing it.

Lynch's use of "In Dreams" in *Blue Velvet* was the first time an Orbison song had "starred" in a movie, but it was not the first time his music had been used in a film. His duet of "That Loving You Feeling Again" with Emmylou Harris from *Roadie* (1980) earned him his first Grammy

Award and ignited his remarkable eighties comeback. Some films have made incidental use of his music or used it as period-setting material. More frequently, filmmakers with a special reverence for Orbison's music have given his songs a central place in their films, and some have even named their films after the songs. Much of this has occurred since his death.

In an obscure footnote to the use of Orbison's music in films, *The Living Legend* was released in 1980. Earl Owensby produced the film, about an Elvis Presley–type rock star for the southern drive-in circuit. Orbison, who had no recording contract at the time, composed and recorded original songs for the film and even participated in a live concert, singing from behind the stage while Owensby, the star, lip-synched for an actual audience. The film received no critical or box office attention and has never even been released on video. Nor was a soundtrack album released. The recordings are of poor quality, though Orbison later rerecorded several of the songs for his *Laminar Flow* album, which appeared in 1979, prior to the release of the film.

Initially, independent and art film directors made use of Orbison's music, as in Nicholas Roeg's *The Man Who Fell to Earth* (1976) and *Insignificance* (1985); Wim Wenders's *The Goalie's Anxiety at the Penalty Kick* (1971), David Lynch's *Blue Velvet* (1986), Jim Jarmusch's *Mystery Train* (1989), and Alan Rudolph's *Roadie* (1980). Later examples of this trend include Wenders's *The End of Violence* (1996), Harmony Korine's *Gummo* (1997) and Neil Jordan's *In Dreams* (1999).

The movement to mainstream Hollywood came with *Pretty Woman* (1990), *Only the Lonely* (1991), *Indecent Proposal* (1993), *Star Trek: First Contact* (1996), *You've Got Mail* (1998), and *For Love of the Game* (1999). Indeed, Orbison's music was becoming so popular that when Mike Clark reviewed *Only the Lonely* for *USA Today* he quipped, "Like everyone else, I adore the Orbison oeuvre, but let's draw the line before we get *Ooby Dooby* (The Movie)—all right?" (Clark, 1991). We haven't, so far, but it's been close. Orbison's rendition of "Ooby Dooby" plays a pivotal role in *Star Trek: First Contact*. The song marks two dramatic high points in the film. The first introduces the character who will pilot the ship from earth that first makes contact with extraterrestrials, and the second marks the extraterrestrials' first visit to earth. "Ooby Dooby" thus becomes the music associated with one of the most profoundly important events in the history of the planet earth.

This use of "Ooby Dooby" was, in the first place, a pop music response to the use of "serious" classical music (Richard Strauss's *Also Sprach Zarathustra*) in Stanley Kubrick's *2001: A Space Odyssey*. Strauss's weighty composition, based on Nietzsche's philosophical work, may strike many viewers as a more appropriate way to mark a profound moment in human development. The pop sensibility of *Star Trek*, however, revels in the notion that a seemingly ephemeral "novelty" song from the 1950s could survive into the future and be part of the most extraordinary of moments. Yet the song is clearly used with affection—this is not a send-up of *Ooby Dooby* that contrasts the profound with the trivial to devalue the song. On the contrary, it is an homage to the widespread critical reevaluation that Orbison's music was undergoing at the time. It also serves to contrast the association of Patrick Stewart's character in the *Star Trek* television series with classical music; this pilot is cut from a much different cloth.

Pretty Woman and *Only the Lonely* are, of course, both films that draw their titles from the Orbison songs they use, and "A Love So Beautiful" is heard over the closing credits of *Indecent Proposal*. In *Pretty Woman*, Orbison's song is used over the transformation scene, when the character played by Julia Roberts (a poor call girl) tries on stylish clothes in an upscale boutique, thus becoming the pretty woman of the title. The song is played again over the closing credits. *Pretty Woman* was not the working title of the film; that it became the title after the song was used on the soundtrack indicates how popular the Orbison song had become; to this day it remains his most popular hit. Yet, aside from its popularity and obvious reference to a beautiful woman, the song has no special connection to the film. As I will show in the next chapter, the song is not really about the pretty woman of the title but rather the intense sexual longing of its feverishly daydreaming male protagonist. The film thus reverses the emphasis of the song's lyrics; the music becomes associated with the spectacle of an attractive Hollywood star being transformed before our eyes into an even more attractive woman.

In *Only the Lonely*, the title song is played over the opening, in a reference to the romance between a lonely undertaker (John Candy) and the woman who beautifies the corpses for public viewing. Here the connection between the song and the action is more logical than that in *Pretty Woman*. Both the song and the movie's plot deal with the sexual desires of a lonely man. Furthermore, John Candy's obesity places him well outside the realm of conventional male leads, creating a parallel between the actor/character and the Orbison persona. Like Orbison himself, Candy and his character are odd and offbeat. Even the funeral home setting fits the emphasis on death in Orbison's work.

In *For Love of the Game*, "The Only One" is played at the dramatic moment when the Kelly Preston character discovers that her lover (Kevin Costner) is having an affair. As with *Pretty Woman*, the only connection is a simple reference to a title that has nothing to do with the song, which in this case is about a man mocking his tendency to wallow in excessive self-pity. *You've Got Mail* is unique in that it uses a little-known Orbison cover version of Johnny Mercer's "Dream" rather than one of his well-known hits. While the song fits the general tone of the romantic comedy, its inclusion does little more than document the surprising appeal Orbison's music has for so many Hollywood filmmakers.

The extent of Orbison's appeal to independent art cinema directors is apparent from the fact that both Roeg and Wenders used his music in more than one film, and that Lynch even collaborated with Orbison on a musical project. Roeg has the title character (David Bowie) in *The Man Who Fell to Earth* play "Blue Bayou" to evoke the profound beauty he longs for on earth. Roeg returned to Orbison years later for *Insignificance*, shot at a time when Orbison had no recording contract. Roeg in effect handed Orbison two opportunities—to record, and to collaborate (on "Wild Hearts") for the first time with Will Jennings, the man who would become his most important collaborator during his late period.

Wenders's return to Orbison's music also reveals an abiding commitment to Orbison. He initially used "Dream Baby" as a song played on a jukebox in *The Goalie's Anxiety at the Penalty Kick*, but by the time he made *The End of Violence* Orbison had been dead for nearly a decade. Rather than simply use an old Orbison hit (as most filmmakers do), Wenders used a new song that had been left uncompleted at the time of Orbison's death. "You May Feel Me Crying" was completed by Brian Eno and is a major addition to the Orbison *oeuvre* (see Chapter 5). Wenders not only made the song part of a film but also part of an excellent soundtrack CD that attracted critical attention, signaling his enduring love and respect for Orbison.

The attraction of Orbison's music for independent and mainstream Hollywood filmmakers alike points to the ambiguity surrounding the music itself and to Orbison's mysterious persona. Deliberately or not, Orbison invited people to hear his music and interpret his persona in quite different ways, and this may explain why, not just in movies but even in the music world, his music appealed to a bewildering variety of artists who seemed to have nothing in common with one another. The musicians who have paid homage to Orbison are as varied as the filmmakers.

After completing *Blue Velvet*, David Lynch learned of Orbison's project of rerecording his greatest hits, which were unavailable in their original Monument versions at the time. He was invited to join T-Bone Burnett, the producer, during the recording session. Although Lynch shares a coproducer credit with Burnett and Orbison, he downplays his involvement: "Roy said, 'You know, David, in the old days there was a guy just like you that would talk to me before I sang, just like an actor and a director kind of thing. He'd remind me of why I wrote it and get me back in that space, help me get there, just remind me and make sure I was there.' And that was my small role in that" (Lynch 2002). Orbison later claimed that he was deeply indebted to Lynch for opening up a rich new approach that helped him revitalize his old material dramatically. He served as a visual consultant on the music video for the new version of the song and appeared in a videotaped interview with Orbison on VH1 when the song and video were released. The two men became friends, and Lynch accompanied Barbara Orbison onstage at the end of the February 24, 1990, Los Angeles Tribute Concert, a concert that culminated with Dean Stockwell's re-creation of his film role, in which he lip-synched "In Dreams" into a trouble light used as a microphone. Jim Jarmusch also returned to Orbison. His most extensive use of Orbison's songs occurs in *Mystery Train*, a film about foreigners visiting Memphis, the home of Sun Records. The Sun studios appear as a setting in the film and the soundtrack includes a couple of Orbison's songs among its many Sun songs. In *Down by Law* (1986), the character played by Tom Waits sings a few bars of "Crying" (Waits was later featured in the band at the *Roy Orbison and Friends: A Black and White Night* concert).

At least three Orbison covers were used in unusually prominent ways in other films. As far as I can determine, the first use of an Orbison song in a film occurs in Radley Metzger's soft-core porn film *Carmen, Baby* (1966). Using "Candy Man," a song about a man's promises to a woman whom he tries to lure to him, the film retells the well-known Carmen story of Bizet's opera. Undoubtedly Metzger uses a cover rather than Orbison's original for financial and legal reasons. His films from this period are quite interesting but very low budget. Indeed, the credits for *Carmen, Baby* list no song titles, composers, or even musicians. We first hear the song in the quite ordinary context of a bar scene. It returns, however, quite unexpectedly, at the film's climax, the well-known scene of Carmen's death. Again, it is heard first in a bar; but then Metzger cuts to the dramatic action outside, the song playing in an extremely muted fashion as a jealous lover approaches Carmen in a dark, deserted town square, where he stabs her to death. As the murderer begins his approach, we hear the lyrics, "C'mon woman, gonna hold you tight." After the murder we hear the voiceover of the murderer tell us that after burying the body he turned himself in to the police. But the last line is particularly ominous for my purposes—he adds that he never revealed to the authorities where the body was buried. Metzger may not only be the first filmmaker to use Orbison's music; he may also be the first to associate it with dark, perverse deeds.

In *Little Voice* (1998), the central male character (Michael Caine), a concert promoter, takes the stage when his scheduled performer fails to appear. During a particularly emotional scene, he sings a snarling, gut-wrenching version of "It's Over," a song about the cataclysmic effects of the end of a love affair. A London commentator on the Internet Movie Database remarks, "He [Caine] cannot sing a note but his raging punk rendition of Roy Orbison's 'It's Over' reduced the nightclub audience in the movie, and cinema audience at the Odeon West End, to jaw-dropping silence" (www.us.imdb.com). Like so many other uses of Orbison's music in movies, the use of "It's Over" in this film has an unexpected dark impact, and as the reviewer suggests, the scene is riveting. (Caine later sang an ensemble version of "Blue Bayou" with his male comrades in Fred Schepisi's *Last Orders* [2001].)

The third major use of an Orbison cover is David Lynch's use of "Crying" in *Mulholland Drive*. The two central female characters are mysteriously drawn, one night, to a bizarre, nearly empty theater (the few filmgoers are an odd-looking bunch) and an enigmatic master of ceremonies who introduces Rebekkah Del Rio. The singer approaches the microphone and begins singing "Llorando," then collapses. The song continues to play. Del Rio's beautiful rendition of the song brings tears to the eyes of the two women. "Crying" is associated here with a surreal, dreamlike world and a profound sense of loss, as it will be again later, when one of the women finds the man she desires in the arms of her "friend." It is also during the theatrical performance of "Crying" that the women find a key piece of information in their quest to solve the film's central mystery. It is also the only song in the film that we hear in its entirety, and both the characters and the audience give it their full attention. The song is woven tightly into the narrative, and it is yet another instance of a dark, emotionally powerful use of Orbison's music in movies.

Lynch's use of "In Dreams" in *Blue Velvet* has special importance for my purposes, for it was Lynch's shocking use of the song in the context of true perversity that sparked the critical discourse of darkness that has come to occupy such a central place in interpreting Orbison's music. It is no exaggeration to say that Lynch's use of "In Dreams" changed forever the way in which Orbison's music would be received. The use of the song also marks one of the most memorable incorporations of a pop song into a film. Deeply embedded in the narrative, the song functions formally as a complex component not only of the scenes in which it is used but of the entire film. "In Dreams" is the key to understanding *Blue Velvet* and, at this point in the song's history, *Blue Velvet* has assumed central importance in the critical commentary on the song. For these reasons, I have chosen to devote much of this chapter to the use of that one song in the film and the critical commentary on it.

In an article on the greatest rock films of all time, Robert Hilburn notes that pop music "serves as an emotional shorthand" and that young

rock artists use music both to define feelings for themselves and to recognize that others share those feelings. Pop fans share a similar bond
through records, and this accounts for the effect of pop music in movies.
To illustrate his point Hilburn cites *Blue Velvet*'s use of "In Dreams."
"One of the most memorable things about David Lynch's *Blue Velvet*,"
he writes, "was the way he used a tension-filled Roy Orbison song, *In
Dreams*, to convey a character's whacked-out sensibilities" (Hilburn
2000, 6).

Hilburn, a professional pop music critic, is more perceptive in this
observation than many academic film scholars have been. Surprisingly,
since both film and pop music are generally considered popular culture
rather than "high art," many film scholars overlook or minimize popular music in their analyses of films. Some films, however, *Blue Velvet*
among them, have entered the arena of art cinema and thus seem far
removed from pop and rock music, in effect replaying the outmoded
high art/low art dichotomy between film and the arts, with film now
becoming the high art form and popular music the low form. In his
monograph on *Blue Velvet*, Michael Atkinson describes the second scene
in which "In Dreams" is used as

> all set to the overripe, ridiculous pop song (which even more than the titular
> song, can never be listened to calmly again). This scene manifests most
> clearly the role that pop songs play in Lynch's, and Frank's, cosmology: as
> sweet innocuous tissues of lies. Like Lynch, whose adoration of pop music
> belies a cynical fascination with its daydreamy innocence, Frank is drawn to
> them even as they enrage him with their betrayals, their false sense of hope.
> (Atkinson 1997, 61)

In dismissing the song's emotional fervor as "overripe" and "ridiculous," Atkinson is similar to the critics who once condescendingly dismissed "women's weepies." As I have argued throughout this book,
Orbison's melodramatic style is part of a complex and original rock aesthetic that challenges conventional, normative masculinity. Atkinson's
generalization about Lynch's attraction to and use of pop songs sheds
little light on the film or the song.

Lynch, by contrast, has said that "'In Dreams' explained to me so
much of what the film was all about" (Rodley 1997, 128). Orbison's
music has explanatory value for Lynch because it presents a complex

vision of dreams and their relationship to a dark, alternative sexuality and masculinity. Lynch acknowledges what his critics do not: that his film not only influenced how we now hear the Orbison song—the song also influenced Lynch's film. The respectful manner in which Lynch talks about Orbison suggests two unique artists interacting with, influencing, and eventually working with each other; it is clearly not a case of a serious artist appropriating and transforming a pop song it into something of greater significance than it had on its own. Lynch even jokingly says, when asked about all the crying in the television series *Twin Peaks*, "Like Andy. He's a man and he's crying. It's a rare thing, you know, to see a policeman crying. It comes from Roy Orbison, I guess!" (Rodley 1997, 167). And indeed there is a profound connection between such male crying in Orbison's music and in Lynch's work.

Lynch is also much more perceptive than Atkinson about pop music in general. Chris Rodley characterizes the lyrics of much fifties pop and rock music as "deceptively simple and naïve." Lynch agrees: "All of it was simple, but it's not what you're saying, it's the way you say it, and how it works as a texture against a bottleneck guitar. . . . It's unbelievable when it works, and to do that you've got to know so deep in yourself where you are and what it is. It's like High Art. And those guys *know* it. And then you get a guy like Pat Boone. He's doing everything, and it's a million miles away from working . . . between him and Little Richard there's nothing to talk about!" (Rodley 1997, 127). Pop and rock, in other words, are not one simple thing to which, as Atkinson crudely implies, Lynch is attracted, as if with some fascination for a simple surface that he can see beneath. Lynch himself uses the word "deep" in characterizing good pop and rock, recognizing that even when the lyrics in such music are simple, the complex manner in which *some* pop and rock musicians play the music justifies its designation as art.

The use of "In Dreams" in *Blue Velvet* is so prominent and unusual that nearly all critics remark on it, however briefly. Although Michel Chion, in his critical study of Lynch, quotes Lynch on the fetishistic qualities of velvet, oddly neither he nor any of the other authors of books on Lynch note the most obvious thing about the song and cinema. Kenneth Anger used "Blue Velvet" years earlier in *Scorpio Rising* (1964) in a manner that associated it perversely with fetishism—in this case, the blue denim of cyclists within a homoerotic context. Indeed, the use of "Blue Velvet" in that film—in a scene where we see a cyclist dress in tight jeans—has precisely the startling, unsettling effect that many critics attribute to it in Lynch's film.

Chion does, however, note that the songs in the film are "used for their lyrics" (Chion 1995, 89). After observing that "the film is a dream, but a structured one," he returns to "In Dreams": "If, at the end, Jeffrey takes his place in Sandy's dream, that is to say, in a sugary-sweet world recalling the idyllic paradise she described to him, one may think that he is there to stay ('In dreams you are mine' says the song Frank plays for Jeffrey) but that he will always find a way (via the ear?) of escaping it, from the inside" (91).

Kenneth C. Kaleta gives more prominence to the Orbison song in his analysis of the sequence, claiming, "Lynch succeeds in molding the music into an anthem in the film for secrets within each of us," adding, "Typical of Lynch's auditory style, the song has different uses in quick succession" (Kaleta 1995, 124). Kaleta argues that Ben first sings to Frank with homosexual overtones. Frank then similarly sings to Jeffrey: "The suggestion of the lyrics is still that singer and listener are two of a kind in their dreams" (125). Kaleta concludes his discussion of the role of the song by posing the question, "Is there in the lyrics' message of violent sexual attraction between singer and listener another level of painful understanding now hideously awakened in Frank and Jeffrey?" (125).

Martha P. Nochimson discusses the song within the context of the film's gender framework. For her, the ideal Lynchian hero has to learn the limitations of the phallocentric masculinity of both the "good" and the "bad" fathers, and become receptive to the feminine. The feminine is associated with the true dream world and is far removed from the masculine realms of control, violence, and sexual perversion: "Ben is the keeper of the dream only in Frank's terms, a base form of fantasy that is constructed, sterile, and toxic—one totally opposite the Lynchian dream. It is a phallocentric fantasy, a poor excuse for the dream, as we see when Frank compulsively puts a tape of Roy Orbison's 'In Dreams'— which Frank tellingly refers to as 'candy-colored clown'—in the tape recorder at Ben's" (Nochimson 1997, 114). For her, Ben's mouthing of the lyrics is "a pathetic reduction of dreams. . . . The rapture to which it moves Frank represents Frank's profound alienation from the real and from the dream, a pairing that is the core of the Lynchian narrative; for Lynch realists are by definition dreamers" (114). For her, Jeffrey's dreams, imbued with light, are visionary, whereas Ben's resort to an artificial light signals his impoverishment.

All four of the book-length critical studies of David Lynch's work emphasize the role of dreaming in *Blue Velvet* and thus implicitly recognize the special place of "In Dreams" in the film. Nochimson puts the heaviest emphasis on this aspect of the film, and indeed she is the only one to address the manner in which songs are used *differently* in the film. Writing of the credit sequence, she notes, "It is augmented by the soundtrack's use of the song 'Blue Velvet,' which sets the images into the context of performance even though what we see is very ordinary. (Later in the film, as we shall see, the performing of popular music will take on a more profound and complex meaning as it evokes not only surfaces but depths as well)" (105).

Nochimson's emphasis on the central role of dreaming in the Lynch *ouevre* directly links her analysis of the use of Orbison's song in the film to my analysis of his music and aesthetic. Dreams are as central to Orbison's world as they are to Lynch's. In an odd moment, during the VH1 interview, Orbison off-handedly remarked that he did not know whether Lynch was a "dreamer," whereupon Lynch enthusiastically affirmed that he was. In fact, dreams are part of a complex aesthetic in the work of both men. When Nochimson notes that for Lynch realists are dreamers, she might as well be writing of Orbison. Unfortunately, she stops short of saying why Frank's invocation of the candy-colored clown is "telling."

My reading of both the use of the Orbison song and Frank's line stand in sharp contrast to that of Nochimson, who neatly severs Frank and Ben from Jeffrey and Lynch. One of the most extraordinary things about the film is the way in which it links many of the characters—and the cinema audience—to Frank.

The opening lyrics to Orbison's "In Dreams" supply an ironic counterpoint to much of the film: "A candy colored clown they call the sandman / Tiptoes to my room every night, / Just to sprinkle stardust and to whisper, / 'Go to sleep, everything is alright.'"[1] The film begins with a series of images of small-town America that suggest a veneer of security and safety: the proverbial white picket fence of the opening shot, the image of a fire truck motoring slowly down the street as a fireman grins and waves, a school crossing guard stopping traffic to allow children to cross the street safely. Father is even out watering the lawn. Indeed, everything seems all right in this version of the American dream. Not surprisingly, then, at the time of its release critics seized on *Blue Velvet* as a film that tears away this clichéd view of small-town America to reveal the drugs and sexual perversion lying beneath the placid surface.

Predictably, much of the initial reaction to the film centered on whether it was a critique of the disturbing sexual acts it portrays or merely an exploitation of them. One critic changed his mind about the film after he saw it a second time, whereupon he discovered that the film was "also fiercely moral, and that explains its stunning force" (Campbell 1986). Several of my students initially found the film disturbingly ambiguous; it was not clear to them why Lynch showed bizarre sadomasochistic scenes in such detail. They could not, in other words, detect any critique of such behavior, and they felt reluctant to praise a film that implicated them in such activities. But looking for a moral critique in *Blue Velvet* seems to me simultaneously symptomatic of the film's disturbing complexity and an inadequate way to interpret it.

Blue Velvet blurs the lines between its apparently "normal" characters and its clearly "perverse" ones. This is most obvious when Frank (Dennis Hopper), a drug-crazed, sadistic fetishist tells Jeffrey (Kyle MacLachlan), a naïve college student, "You're just like me."[2] As Jeffrey begins to show strong interest in the mystery he stumbles upon, Sandy (Laura Dern), his high school accomplice, says to him, "I don't know if you're a detective or a pervert," to which he replies with sadistic delight, "That's for me to know and you to find out." After getting involved sexually with Dorothy (Isabella Rossellini), he hits her during lovemaking, though his initial response to her request is one of horror ("I want to save you, not hurt you.") The two, of course, are not really opposites, since, as Laura Mulvey has argued, the male desire to save women gives men power over the women they save.

Even Jeffrey's position of voyeur in the closet links him to Frank, though it seems to do the opposite. Is he not, after all, trapped in the closet, forced to watch Frank's perverse behavior? Yes, but only on the surface. Lynch emphasizes the connection between Jeffrey's excitement over the growing mystery and his sexual perversion. Although this is most clear when Sandy despairs over knowing whether he is a detective or a pervert, Jeffrey too articulates the connection between his desire to solve the mystery in Dorothy Valens's apartment and his sexuality, when he tells Sandy, "I'm in the middle of a mystery.... You're a mystery, and I like you very much." The answer to Sandy's question is, of course, that he is both a detective and a pervert.

But Frank and Jeffery are not the only characters implicated in the perversity. Indeed, the film becomes a strange echoing of characters resembling other characters. Dorothy seems to be the terrified victim of Frank's sadistic behavior, but she later reveals to Jeffrey that she masochistically loves it. This appalls him, but soon he becomes a willing sadistic partner to her masochistic desires. Dorothy even talks like Frank. When she finds Jeffery hiding in her closet, she forces him at knifepoint to undress, while ordering, "Don't you look at me." Moments later, when Jeffrey is again hiding in the closet watching Frank and Dorothy, Frank repeatedly yells, "Don't fuckin' look at me!"

Toward the end of the film, Jeffrey and Sandy are driving when a car races up behind them and attempts to run them off the road. "It's Frank!" Jeffrey yells, Frank being the only person Jeffrey knows who is capable of such behavior. But moments later Sandy screams, "It's Mike!" her boyfriend. Even Jeffrey's mother gets implicated in all of this, as she is constantly seen sitting at home watching crime and mystery movies on television.

It comes as no surprise within this context that the police department itself is part of the crime. Frank's partner turns out to be Detective Williams's partner: the same man is the partner of both the man who should be solving the crime and the man who commits the crime. Indeed, near the beginning of the film, Jeffrey goes to Detective Williams after finding a human ear in a deserted field. They go to the coroner, who examines the ear and remarks that it was cut off with scissors. The film cuts to a shot of a pair of scissors cutting a yellow police ribbon.

Are they the same scissors? This complex mixing of the seemingly normal with the seemingly perverse achieves its ultimate expression in Frank's "well-dressed-man disguise." If everyone else in the film seems a bit like Frank, Frank can also seem a bit like them.

So much for the characters in the film being like Frank. What about us, the spectators, those of us who want to find some kind of moral critique that can justify what we are doing sitting in the dark watching all these weird goings-on? When Jeffrey first hides in Dorothy's closet, we see shots of him looking and point-of-view shots of her undressing. When she is in her underwear, the camera is out in the room with her as she crawls on the floor. Then, when she goes into the bathroom, the camera stays in a long-shot view from the living room. We see both the closet door at the left and Dorothy as she takes off her bra and underpants and stands nude, her back to the camera. Jeffrey is still hiding in the closet and his point of view is exactly ninety degrees different from the camera angle. He can't even see the hallway at his left, let alone the bathroom at the end of that hallway. So who is seeing Dorothy undress, and why? Is it the film audience, we who are in our "well-dressed-man disguise"?

David Lynch remarked of *Blue Velvet* at the time of its release that it was a sort of "Hardy Boys go to Hell" story, and that he was originally driven to make the movie because of his attraction to certain scenes and images that then required a narrative justification. Watching the film, we can feel the validity of both points. The Hardy Boys–go-to-Hell aspect of the film is clearly the contrived narrative that gets us into the intense scenes and images that lurk at its center. (In this sense, the film has its own well-dressed-man disguise.) And, like the filmmaker, we are driven by our desire to see those things, however repugnant we may find them on one level. There is, after all, a disturbing kind of fascination that simultaneously involves the need to look away from something and the desire to take it in. Lynch has supplied Jeffrey, our Hardy Boy, as our excuse for looking at these sordid things. But, like Jeffrey, whose amateur detecting is linked to an erotic desire to see the hidden and forbidden, our position in the movie theater is not entirely innocent. And, like Jeffrey, although we may be horrified by Frank's conduct, we are not entirely different from Frank—at least not unless the desire to watch erotically charged scenes with Isabella Rossellini has nothing to do with fetishism.

What, then, is the nature of these dark sexual scenes that lie at the center of *Blue Velvet*? They are a cinematic illustration of key moments in psychoanalytic accounts of sexual development. First and foremost, of course, is fetishism. Frank may be the ultimate fetishist in the history of movies. He kidnaps a father and son in order to force the mother to participate in his fantasies, which involve listening to her sing "Blue Velvet" in a nightclub and having sex with her while she wears a blue velvet robe. As if this were not extreme enough, he cuts off a piece of her robe, thus literally possessing the fetishized object.

Jeffrey witnesses this bizarre spectacle from his hiding place in the closet, a virtual re-creation of the Freudian primal scene. The child discovers a fearful image of violent intercourse, a point later underscored by a primal animalistic roar on the soundtrack. Just prior to this primal scene, he has similarly witnessed a re-creation of the Freudian scenario of the origins of fetishism. He watches Dorothy undress; she discovers him hiding in the closet and, waving a knife at him, orders him to undress. The image of the woman with a knife standing over the naked man is the exact visual embodiment of castration anxiety.

But things don't quite make sense. It is Frank, after all, not Jeffrey, who is the fetishist. Furthermore, Frank's fetishistic behavior cannot be adequately explained by the standard Freudian account. Frank's sexual behavior is inextricably tied to the little boy's desire to possess his mother sexually. Before Frank appears in the film, Jeffrey overhears Dorothy talking to him on the phone. "Mommy loves you," she tells him. Later, while having sex with her, he repeats "Mommy, Mommy" several times and even says, "Baby wants to fuck."

Although the Freudian account of fetishism is the most well known, it has been strongly contested by a school of thought that places the origins of fetishism in the oral, pre-Oedipal phase of childhood development. According to this view, the mother nursing the baby is a powerful figure. The child develops the fetish to ease the crisis of separation from the desired image of the powerful mother, a direct contradiction of the Freudian emphasis on the fetish displacing the undesired, feared image of the castrating/castrated woman. Frank's desire to be the baby who returns to and has sex with the mother, and then cuts off a piece of the robe she is wearing, could certainly be interpreted as fitting the pre-genital model. If this is the case, Dorothy is in one scene the Freudian woman who raises the threat of castration for the infant hiding in the closet, and, in the next scene, the powerful, pre-genital, oral mother to whom the boy wants to return.

None of this is meant to suggest that *Blue Velvet* is confused, but rather that it is intriguingly complex and contradictory. It offers no single, logical system of understanding its dark imagery; rather, it taps into fascinating structures of sexual development and behavior that can be richly explored from differing and even conflicting perspectives, and perhaps still remain unexplained. The Hardy Boys–go-to-Hell level of the narrative is clearly a perverted Oedipal drama bordering on comedy. Jeffrey is called home because his father suffers a strange attack that totally incapacitates him. The father is not only weak, but voiceless. When Jeffrey goes to visit him in the hospital, the man is hooked up to an elaborate life-support system. He desperately tries to say a word to his son. Walking home from the hospital, Jeffrey discovers the severed ear that leads him to Detective Williams. Williams combines in one figure the Law and the Father. He simultaneously attempts to control and regulate Jeffrey's involvement with both his daughter Sandy and the case. He fails at both. Jeffrey deceives him about the extent of Sandy's activities and when Jeffrey solves the case, the ineffectual detective arrives too late to help. In one of the great comic moments of the film, Williams stands dramatically with his gun drawn and says, "It's all over, Jeffrey." All the father and law figures treated so seriously within the Hardy Boys model prove to be impotent.

The ending of the movie is a send-up of the restoration of the normal patriarchal family order. Everything is stupidly back in place. The father, miraculously recovered, is in the backyard with Detective Williams. Jeffrey is with Sandy, whom he has won in the process of completing his traditional Oedipal trajectory, and the women are all in the house. The imagery has a silly, unbelievable veneer to it. As Jeffrey and Sandy watch a robin on the windowsill, they speak of its relationship to the robins of her dreams. Earlier, she has told Jeffrey about a dream in which the world is shrouded in darkness because there are no robins. Robins, she says, represent love and bring light. But as they stand looking at the robin, Lynch shows a ludicrous close-up of the robin eating a bug. Jeffrey's aunt, looking on in disgust, says, "I don't see how they could ever do that. I could never eat a bug." In addition to undermining Sandy's view of the robin as symbolizing love and light, the moment recalls the opening shots of the film and reemphasizes the shallowness and futility of the characters' attempt to separate themselves from the bizarre and the repulsive. If the robin could talk, it might reply to the aunt, "You're just like me."

The scene also points to the importance of dream imagery in the film, and I want to conclude this discussion by linking that imagery to the use of music. *Blue Velvet* is a movie of startling brilliance in its use of sound and music. The manner in which Lynch works the title song into the plot of the film is a significant departure from the usual way in which pop music is used simply as aural backdrop in Hollywood films. The most extraordinary use of this technique, however, occurs during the sequence structured around Roy Orbison's "In Dreams."

Frank has forced Jeffrey and Dorothy to accompany him and his friends on a wild joy ride. They stop first at Ben's place, a whorehouse called "This is it." Ben (Dean Stockwell) is a sort of sadistic gay pimp whose women are all hugely overweight, recalling Frank's desire for the mother (they are reminiscent of the fat woman who dances for the boys on the beach in Fellini's *8½*). Ben punches Jeffrey in the stomach and then asks Frank to follow him into another room. He gives Frank drugs and immediately Frank starts talking about "a candy-colored clown they call the sandman." After repeating it several times, he walks over to a cassette player, drops in a tape, and "In Dreams" begins playing with the same line. Everything comes to a standstill; this is clearly a moment of near-religious intensity for Frank. Ben picks up a trouble light and, with the light shining in his face, lip-synchs the Orbison song.

After we hear most of the song, Frank forces everyone back into the car (Dorothy has been in a back room where her husband and son are kept hostage) and they ride into the countryside, where they stop the car. Frank takes drugs and abuses Dorothy; Jeffrey intervenes by punching Frank. Frank orders them out of the car, once again says, "a candy-colored clown they call the sandman," and the tape is played again.

Frank puts lipstick thickly over his mouth and kisses Jeffery repeatedly. Then he goes into a state of rapture, as he recites the lyrics of the song in counterpoint to Orbison's singing. Finally, he punches Jeffrey brutally while his friends hold him. All of this is highlighted by the spectacle of one of the fat women from Ben's, who dances next to the cassette player on top of the car.

These two scenes are unusually intense, even by the standards of this film, and they defy easy explanation. Who is Ben, and what is his relationship to Frank? Exactly what kind of establishment does Ben run? Why does Ben lip-synch "In Dreams," and why does he shine a light in his face while doing so? Does Frank's act of smearing lipstick on his mouth and kissing Jeffrey link him to homosexuality and to Ben? If so, what is the connection between his blue velvet fetish and homosexuality? Why does the fat woman dance as if nothing were happening? And, finally, what is the connection between all of this and Roy Orbison's "In Dreams"? A partial answer to the last question may explain the difficulty in answering the others. At this point, the film itself seems closer to dream logic than it does to any sort of waking or conscious rationality; the imagery is powerful, concentrated, disturbing, and exceedingly strange. As with so many dreams, we feel that it means something, but we are left wondering what.

The term "candyman" has long been linked to drugs, and no doubt one can read the candy-colored clown of "In Dreams" in this way, which is what Frank seems to do. One can imagine what is meant by "stardust." It would be a mistake, however, to tie either the song or its use in the film to drugs. Everything is not all right in the song, no matter how one reads it. Whether or not it is about a drug-induced sense of well-being, it begins by welcoming the "magic night" and the dreams that come with it and ends in anguish over their falsity: "It's too bad that all these things can only happen in my dreams." Frank's obsession with the song has to do with more than his drug addiction. The loneliness and sadness of which Orbison sings go well beyond teenage heartbreak; he evokes an image of a man sitting alone in the dark, looking out on a dark world, full of a sorrow that he faces directly. This is an extremely isolating and alienating form of loneliness. It is no coincidence that Orbison's rock legend, most associated with personal tragedy, dressing in black, wearing dark glasses, and being reclusive, is linked with Frank, who wears a black leather jacket, revels in darkness, and has become maniacally obsessed with "In Dreams." The song characterizes his very being and the world in which he lives.

The "In Dreams" sequence ends with a cut to a flickering flame, an image used several times in the film after its introduction in Dorothy's apartment. A loud noise is heard over it, almost as if the sound of the flickering was magnified a thousandfold. Then we hear a fading, eerie, electronically distorted echo of Orbison singing "can only happen in my dreams." The moment epitomizes much of what this film is about. After witnessing events so bizarre that we hardly know what to make of them, we are left to wonder what the relationship is between dreams and reality in the entire film. Can the puzzling events we have just witnessed happen only in dreams? If so, whose dreams?

Dreams are spoken about several times in the film and, at least once, part of a dream is shown but not immediately identified as such. A series of brief images we have already seen are repeated; they culminate with the shot of Frank "roaring" after sexually attacking Dorothy. Then, suddenly, we cut to Jeffery waking up from a dream. Lynch's earlier films (*Eraserhead* [1978] and *The Elephant Man* [1980]) also involved dream imagery. Although one dream is clearly marked in *Eraserhead*, much of the film is so bizarre that it is impossible to establish any clear line between dream and reality. In *The Elephant Man*, at the film's climax, we enter into the title character's dreams. Both of those films share another important feature with *Blue Velvet*—they erode comfortable distinctions between such polarities as beautiful/ugly, normal/perverse, and waking world/dream world. In David Lynch's dreams, our smug ways of judging and responding to these polarities are overturned. To dismiss Frank simply as a pervert is like dismissing the Elephant Man as a physical freak or the characters in *Eraserhead* as ugly. Lynch questions the very standards by which we make such judgments. *Blue Velvet* is not just David Lynch's dream, and Jeffrey is not the only voyeur hiding in the closet. We are in the closet with him.

Blue Velvet is shaped by some of the same cultural forces that shaped the late-1980s psychoanalytic debates in academic film theory—for example, Laura Mulvey's Freudian/Lacanian account of childhood development and Gaylyn Studlar's 1984 challenge to it (see Chapter 5). The film itself contains a similar tension; what is most notable about its obvious replay of psychoanalytic scenarios is that they make no sense with reference to Freud alone. Nearly all of the film's reviewers refer to the unusual ambiguity in the film in ways that I think are strongly linked to the use of "In Dreams." Kenneth Kaleta writes of the sequence, "It is narratively ambiguous" (Kaleta 1995, 125). Of the film in general, Michael Atkinson asks, "Indeed, isn't the rare film capable of fulfilling so many diagnoses best served by allowing them all to stand?" (Atkinson 1997, 11). And of the "In Dreams" sequence, Atkinson notes of Ben's "polymorphous perversity" that "we still have no clue as to what that perversity *is*" (57). Michel Chion remarks, "there is something in the fascination generated by *Blue Velvet* which resists the usual psychological keys or, rather, which opens so easily with them that it is disconcerting" (Chion 1995, 93). Martha Nochimson states bluntly, "Lynch is not a Freudian," and notes that "Franks's crime suggests a very different sexual pathology than the one in Freud's narrative" (Nochimson 1997, 102).

Although none of these critics notes it, one reason why Freudian psychology is inadequate to explain the film is that Lynch offers conflicting and unresolved accounts of psychoanalytic development. Lynch's challenge to easy Freudianism in film is similar to Studlar's challenge to such Freudianism in film theory. And the way that Lynch thwarts a simple Freudian reading corresponds to Studlar's emphasis on the powerful pre-Oedipal mother of the oral stage. Insofar as one can decipher their motivation, the characters in *Blue Velvet* alternate between seemingly classical Freudian accounts of psychoanalytical development, family relations, and sexual perversion centered around the father, and castration and challenges to that account centered around powerful bonding with the mother. Atkinson observes that "Frank can't make out if he's the Daddy, the Mommy, or the Baby anymore" (Atkinson 1997, 61), and this is precisely because Lynch does not create the character within a single, comprehensible psychoanalytical model. Indeed, Atkinson's insightful comment echoes his equally perceptive characterization of Ben as polymorphously perverse in a manner we cannot understand. Ben is somehow effeminate and somehow homosexual, but in a way that is difficult to explain or understand. And these characters who don't know whether they are father, mother, or baby, whether they are man or woman or straight or gay, are strongly linked not just to "In Dreams" but also, I would argue, to Roy Orbison's dark, dreaming, mysterious persona.

My reading of the "In Dreams" sequence emphasizes a series of unanswerable questions about the characters' motivations and relationships, and asserts that the sequence is rationally impenetrable and governed by a dream logic. In his own way, Lynch is as obsessed with dreams as Orbison is, and not just in his films. Speaking of the attraction of the continuing story in *Twin Peaks*, he remarks, "The problem is the continuing story is in my head and in Mark's head. . . . I visit it in my mind, *Twin Peaks*. It's frustrating in a way because there are many clues and many threads that have yet to be followed. But it's kind of nice having them out there, because they have not been solved, and because there's threads to dream on" (Patterson and Jenson 2000, 102). In the same interview Lynch discusses the notion of the continuing story in yet another manner, one equally tied to Orbison: "A continuing story is a beautiful thing to me, and mystery is a beautiful thing to me, so if you have a continuing mystery, it's so beautiful" (96). Both Roy Orbison's music and his persona also involve strong components of mystery; clearly there are deep connections between Lynch and Orbison, two mysterious dreamers. Indeed, Lynch claims that after writing the fourth draft of *Blue Velvet*, "I suddenly remembered this dream that I'd had the night before. And the dream was the ending to *Blue Velvet*" (Rodley 1997, 136). Roy Orbison had similarly claimed that he had a dream about a song, woke up and wrote it down, and, the next day, finished the song—"In Dreams."

It is instructive to look not just at the connection between Orbison and Lynch but also at the link between Orbison and the character of Frank. Robin Wood, in an otherwise scathing critique of *Blue Velvet*, praises the manner in which Lynch accesses his unconscious in the creative process: "the sequences involving Frank are the most impressive part of the film; they have a brutal intensity that might certainly be read as betokening a strong personal involvement" (Wood 1986, 47). I see precisely such a link between Frank and not only Lynch but Jeffrey, and ultimately the viewer. Perhaps Lynch himself best summed up Frank when he related an anecdote about casting Dennis Hopper for the role. Hopper had contacted Lynch, saying that he was perfect for the part because he *was* Frank. Lynch had reservations about casting Hopper because Frank was someone he never wanted to meet. Some critics have gone so far as to characterize Frank as the most repulsive character in the history of movies. This seems quite a contrast to Roy Orbison, who is nearly always characterized as the one of the nicest guys in the history of rock 'n' roll. Lynch certainly shares that assessment, saying, "I just loved the guy. He had the greatest aura about him, so humble, so kind, just a great guy—and so talented" (Lynch 2002). As Orbison himself put it, "In Dreams" is such a "pretty" song. In some ways, however, Frank is a version of Roy Orbison gone bad, and his love of "In Dreams" speaks to that. In Dave Marsh's terms, "Frank is somewhere in Roy Orbison's dreams, too; he is part of the cost of dreaming" (Marsh 1987a, 8).

Atkinson hits the nail on the head when he writes, "Frank's impulses lurk in controllable form within Jeffrey, and Jeffrey's state of equilibrium is something Frank has lost" (Atkinson 1997, 60). There are many different kinds of dreamers, and, indeed, dreamers of the Lynch and Orbison variety are all at times disturbing, because their dreams take them into dark places. I have twice played the entire recording of Orbison's "You May Feel Me Crying" at academic conferences, and both times a woman in the audience responded by characterizing the Orbison persona as a "stalker," what one of them termed "creepy." I had a similar response to "I Drove All Night," another posthumously released song. As we saw in Chapter 5, the singer literally sneaks into a woman's room without her knowledge to make love to her. Wim Wenders's quite literal use of "You May Feel Me Crying" in *The End of Violence* conjures up the stalker quality of that song. The main character returns home to confront his estranged wife. Her nude lover appears from the bedroom and the husband retreats into the darkness outside, where he stands watching the two lovers within.[3]

Most of Orbison's music is, of course, not so explicitly "creepy." Both songs are from the late period, and perhaps it is no coincidence that neither had been finished or planned for *Mystery Girl*. One can only conjecture that Orbison himself may have felt uncomfortable with such explicit lyrics, though they are characteristic of his late period insofar as they comment on the early work. And that is my point here. There is something potentially disturbing in the Orbison persona's sexuality as I have drawn it in this book. His intense dreams and daydreams, which at times appear totally delusional, border on a form of unauthorized "possession." Kaleta observes that there is a "violent sexual attraction between singer and listener" in "In Dreams" (Kaleta 1995, 125). Obviously, of course, there is a world of difference between possessing another person in dreams or daydreams and actual stalking. "I Drove All Night" is the only song in which he crosses the line; in the others, to use Atkinson's words, the stalking impulse lurks within him in controllable form. Frank, of course, lives on the other side of the line, where every perverse desire is acted upon. Like Orbison's persona, Frank constantly invokes the darkness, several times repeating the phrase, "Now it's dark." The crucial difference between them is that Frank "drives all night" every night.

It is somewhat surprising that, after *Blue Velvet*, another film would title itself after "In Dreams" and use the song in a central manner. If the song seemed shocking when Lynch first used it in a dark context in the mid-1980s, by the late 1990s the discourse of darkness in Orbison's music was so well established that Neil Jordan was acting within a tradition. I want to conclude with a consideration of that tradition. As we have seen, many critics regarded Lynch's use of "In Dreams" as so startling that they had to comment on it. Indeed, the consensus is that Lynch's use of the song imbued it with a different meaning than it previously had. How many critics made similar claims about Stanley Kubrick's use of Richard Strauss's *Also Sprach Zarathustra* in *2001: A Space Odyssey*, or Blake Edwards's use of Maurice Ravel's *Bolero* in *10*? What would such a claim mean? The use of those works in those films most probably changed the music for those who saw the films. How could it be otherwise, once a piece of music is memorably embedded in a narrative? But these uses of music, at times shockingly unexpected, tell us nothing about the aesthetic worth or "meaning" of the music. Critics seem to understand this when they respond to the use of classical music in film, and this is probably due to their deference for high art or "serious" music. That the great Stanley Kubrick might be drawn to a philosophical tone poem based on the writings of Nietzsche seems fitting. Only condescension toward popular music, however, can account for some of the response to David Lynch's use of Roy Orbison's music. A serious film that uses a pop song is assumed somehow to "change" the original meaning of the song, as if its original meaning were so deficient and inconsequential that there is no other explanation for its use. Recall that not a film critic but a music critic, Robert Hilburn, notes that the *song*, not the scene, is "tension-filled." The film does not add tension to the song but exploits something already present in the recording. Atkinson's remark that after seeing *Blue Velvet* no one could listen to "In Dreams" calmly again misses the fact that few listeners listened to it calmly *before* seeing the film. It contains its own "tension" and "violence," though apparently in an effective well-dressed-man disguise.

In the next chapter, I turn to a related "change" perceived in the meaning of Roy Orbison's music—the infamous 2 Live Crew cover of "Oh, Pretty Woman." For if Lynch's use of "In Dreams" somehow made the song darker than it was seen to be before, 2 Live Crew's version of "Oh, Pretty Woman" made that song "whiter" than it had been seen to be. In so doing, 2 Live Crew drew attention to an unusual discourse of race surrounding Orbison's music.

1

"The Finest White Pop Singer on the Planet"

"Oh, Pretty Woman," 2 Live Crew, and Discourses of Race

When, at the time of Roy Orbison's death, U2's lead singer Bono called him "the finest white pop singer on the planet," I interpreted the reference to race as a sign of Bono's sensitivity to racial matters. I assumed, that is, that he did not want to privilege this white singer over singers of color by elevating him above all others. While I still believe that that was Bono's intention (Bono, as is shown in the documentary film *Rattle and Hum*, has great knowledge of and affection for black music), I want to inflect his racial reference somewhat differently here. If many of the originators of rock 'n' roll can be fairly characterized as white "black" singers, Mike Jarrett has suggested to me that Orbison might more accurately be characterized as a white "white" singer. Krin Gabbard has similarly stressed to me the unusual whiteness of Orbison's singing style. And Craig Morrison writes that Orbison's "voice shows no strong black inflections" (Morrison 1996, 101). While these observations have some validity, the situation is more complex.

Like all of the earliest rock 'n' roll, Orbison's music was in the beginning deeply indebted to black music. Orbison performed numerous covers of black songs with his group the

Teen Kings, and Sam Phillips insisted that his white singers at Sun Records copy the styles of such black blues singers as Arthur Crudup. Although songs like "Chicken Hearted" and "The Clown" bear the seeds of Orbison's later persona, which departed radically from dominant forms of masculinity, nearly all of the Sun recordings and the newly discovered Teen King recordings present a conventional rock 'n' roll singer. Sam Phillips maintains, "I felt that he had the potential to be one of the really great rockers. . . . Also, Roy had probably the best ear for a beat of anybody I recorded outside of Jerry Lee Lewis" (Hawkins 1986, 2). Phillips also remarked that Orbison was such an excellent guitar player that "I would kid him about it. I said 'Roy, what you're trying to do is get rid of everybody else and do it all yourself'" (Hawkins 1986, 2–3).

Levon Helm's account of this phase of Orbison's career fits with Phillips's. Seeing Roy Orbison and the Teen Kings perform motivated his own career: "I loved that band because it was a country-R&B hybrid: electric mandolin, drums, doghouse bass, Roy playing electric guitar and another Martin flat picker. They made a country sound, with a lot of good bottom to it. I saw that band and wanted to be up there with it" (Helm 1993, 46).

Orbison would claim, however, that he wanted to do a different kind of music from the very beginning. Jack Clement, who worked with Orbison on many of the Sun sessions, recalls, "Musically, Roy was ahead of his time. . . . He wanted to do things in the studio that were a little bit over our heads production-wise. Memphis wasn't quite ready for that. We didn't have organized vocal groups and strings. He was thinking orchestrally. He was wanting to cut what he ultimately did cut. I told him, and he never let me forget it, that he would never make it as a ballad singer" (Dickerson 1996, 103–4). As early as the Sun days, then, Orbison wanted to be a singer of orchestral ballads, a form far removed from the black music that inspired rock 'n' roll.

There is no evidence that Orbison's desire to move away from singing like black musicians and doing cover versions of their songs had a racist dimension. It is important to remember that, like the evolution of jazz, the history of rock 'n' roll has involved very extensive interaction between whites and blacks. At its worst, that interaction took the form of white singers in effect stealing black songs, doing cover versions that became hugely popular with white audiences and greatly diminished the market for the black originals. Pat Boone's cover of Little Richard's "Good Golly Miss Molly" was a notable example, but there were many, many others; even Ricky Nelson's cover of Fats Domino's "My Bucket's Got a Hole in It" fits the pattern. Because the contracts black singers were offered were often highly exploitive, they realized no benefit at all when their compositions made stars of other performers.

The influence of black music on rock 'n' roll was not limited to the kind of blues Sam Phillips wanted his white singers to copy. Among the many traditions of black music, at least two influenced Orbison's ballads. The Platters sang ballads that employed the common Bolero-style rhythm and powerful vocals that would become so central in Orbison's style. The near-operatic outbursts at the end of such songs as "Smoke Gets in Your Eyes" and "My Prayer" prefigure Orbison's "Running Scared" and "Crying." Even the lyrics of some of their songs—"The Great Pretender," for example, which Orbison covered on his *Crying* LP—fit in strongly with his own motifs of theatricality. Orbison also recorded a cover of "My Prayer" on his *In Dreams* LP and of "Only You" on *The Big O*.

When Orbison was inducted into the Rock 'n' Roll Hall of Fame, he said that he was moved by his awareness that Jackie Wilson, who had passed away, would not be there (*VH1: A Tribute to Roy Orbison*, 1988). Although Wilson's first big hit, "Lonely Teardrops," was recorded in 1958, many of his songs were recorded during the early 1960s, contemporaneously with Orbison's Monument hits. While it is difficult to trace direct influence among contemporaries, there are some crucial similarities between the two men's music. Wilson was using strong string arrangements in the late fifties. In 1960, the year Orbison recorded "Only the Lonely," Wilson released "Night," a song derived from an operatic aria that he sang in an operatic manner. The song's lyrics are highly reminiscent of Orbison's: Wilson sings of how every night he experiences in dreams the love of a woman he has lost. Almost uncannily, Wilson's "Lonely Life," which uses Orbison's trademark Bolero-style rhythm, appeared in 1961, the same year that Orbison recorded "Running Scared," the song that would make that rhythm so central and dominant in his music. Both artists varied their styles. Roy Orbison mixed his operatic ballads with rockers like "Mean Woman Blues" and more conventional up-tempo songs like "Dream Baby" and "Candy Man," while Wilson mixed his operatic ballads with R&B songs. Perhaps the clearest connection between the two artists is that in 1965 Wilson released an orchestrated version of "Danny Boy" that ran four minutes sixteen seconds; seven years later Orbison recorded the same song in a heavily orchestrated version that ran just under six minutes.

If not a clear-cut, direct influence, Wilson was at least a musical soul mate whom Orbison admired. But, as with Johnnie Ray (see Chapter 4), the musical bond between Orbison and Wilson did not extend to performance style or persona. Wilson's nickname ("Mr. Excitement") would never apply to Orbison. Robert Pruter, the R&B editor of *Goldmine*, recalls Wilson's performance style: "No one could forget the way Wilson floated across the stage. Without missing a beat or note, he would perform elegant steps, classy spins, and at a high point do a crowd-pleasing split, slowly lowering himself to the stage" (Pruter 1994, 1).

This difference extended to appearance and backstage behavior as well. Pruter describes Wilson as "a beautiful physical specimen of strong lean physique, chiseled handsomeness, and smoldering sexuality, and in his resplendent sharkskin suit, tight at the thighs, he cut a simply magnificent figure under the spotlight" (1). Pruter asks, "And who among the young men next to their dates would not have wanted to be Jackie?" (Imagine asking such a question of men at an Orbison concert.) Characterizing Wilson's performance style as "sweat-drenched sexuality" (4), and quoting from Raynoma Gordy Singleton's autobiography, Pruter recounts how Wilson would come out of his dressing room in a "modest towel" to greet and kiss a line of waiting women, who would "scream and moan and faint" (5). Wilson's extreme masculine sexuality also stands in stark contrast to Orbison's subdued masculinity.

Another important distinction is that Wilson's work lacks the personal aspect of Orbison's music. Wilson primarily recorded songs written by others, while most of Orbison's music was his own. In this respect Orbison had more in common with Chuck Berry, another black artist he admired. Although Orbison recorded a cover version of Berry's "Memphis" for his album of the same name, and as yet unreleased 1973 versions of "Maybelline" and "Roll Over Beethoven," the two had little in common musically. Berry was important to Orbison chiefly as a model of the singer-songwriter who recorded distinctive songs of his own. Not until after the Beatles did the model of the singer-writer become common in rock 'n' roll: Buddy Holly, Chuck Berry, and Roy Orbison were pioneers.

In addition to the Chuck Berry covers, Orbison covered black songs on a number of his albums. During his Monument period he covered Ray Charles's "What'd I Say," and on *Milestones* (1974), his last MGM album, he recorded Otis Redding's "I've Been Loving You Too Long" and Dobie Gray's "Drift Away."

Orbison played a major role in promoting the Velvets, a black doo-wop group he first encountered in West Texas.[1] After he became successful at Monument, Orbison called Virgil Johnson, the lead singer of the Velvets and a junior high school teacher in Odessa. According to Johnson, Orbison said, "'How would you like to come to Nashville and record?' And I said, 'You're kidding,' and he said, 'I've got someone I want you to talk to,' and it was Fred Foster, the president of Monument records.... And that's how we came in to the recording business, we never forgot him for that" (*Complete Velvets*, liner notes, 1996). The Velvets recorded four Orbison songs: "Time and Again" (Roy Orbison–Joe Melson, 1960), "Spring Fever" (Roy Orbison, 1960), "Laugh" (Roy Orbison–Joe Melson, 1960), and "Lana" (Roy Orbison–Joe Melson, 1960). Of these four songs, "Lana" is the only one Orbison recorded himself. Johnson speaks of Orbison with the deepest respect: "he had to think a lot of The Velvets. And we appreciate that because we never would have been heard of if it hadn't been for Roy Orbison. And I tell everybody that, I don't care who's asking" (*Complete Velvets*, liner notes, 1996).

Thus Orbison cannot be seen as completely outside the black influence on rock 'n' roll. From his appropriation of dark glasses, to some of the songs he covered, to some of his musical influences, Orbison was indebted to African American culture and music, but in ways different from other rock 'n' roll singers.

Simon Frith's analysis of the white appropriation of black music helps to explain the unusual manner in which Orbison related to black music. In a remarkable passage Frith claims that

> The racism endemic to rock 'n' roll, in other words, was not that white musicians stole from black culture but that they burlesqued it. The issue is not how "raw" and "earthy" and "authentic" African-American sounds were "diluted" or "whitened" for mass consumption, but the opposite process: how gospel and r&b and doo-wop were *blacked-up*. Thanks to rock 'n' roll, black performers now reached a white audience, but only if they met "the tests" of "blackness"—that they embody sensuality, spontaneity, and gritty soulfulness. (Frith 1996, 131)

Bernard Grendon makes a similar point:

> The black pioneers of rock and roll were also driven to produce caricatures of *singing-black*. Chuck Berry, Little Richard, and Ray Charles ... quite radically changed their styles as their audience shifted from predominantly black to largely white. Though all three began their careers by singing the blues in a rather sedate manner (at least by rock and roll standards), they later accelerated their singing speed, resorted to raspy-voiced shrieks and cries, and dressed up their stage acts with manic piano pounding or guitar acrobatics. According to rock and roll mythology, they went from singing less black (like Nat King Cole or the Mills Brothers) to singing more black. In my judgement, it would be better to say that they adopted a more caricaturized version of singing black wildly, thus paving the way for soul music and the British invasion." (Quoted in Frith 1996, 131)

James Miller makes a similar argument, showing how Presley's initial approach to performing "That's All Right" was a "joke" and "tongue in cheek" (Miller 1999, 82). He also characterizes Presley's initial interpretation of "Hound Dog" as "ridiculous" and a "good-natured practical joke" (132), and he quotes Scotty Moore as calling it "comic relief" on stage (135). Miller also calls Chuck Berry's "Maybelline" a form of parody. Little Richard is particularly interesting within this context. "As the crowd grew whiter, his shows grew wilder," Miller observes (112). "Richard discovered that 'Tutti Frutti' worked best in the whites-only clubs: 'He only did "Tutti Frutti" in white clubs,' one old friend recalled, 'cause you see, blacks were a little more sensitive than whites.' Richard, too, remembers a difference in the crowd's reaction: 'White people, it always cracked 'em up, but black people didn't like it that much. They liked the blues'" (110–11).

Frith notes that common rock 'n' roll notions of the relationship between rhythm and sex are both racist and confused: "The assumption that a musical 'beat' is equivalent to a bodily beat . . . doesn't stand up to much examination. . . . There is equally little evidence that Western readings of African rhythmic patterns as 'sexual' have anything at all to do with their actual use, musical or otherwise" (131).

According to Frith, then, white rock 'n' roll has drastically misread black music, in the process forcing black musicians away from their musical heritage in favor of a burlesque of those very traditions. When one hears about manic piano pounding, black acts with shrieks and dressed-up stage shows, one might easily think of Orbison's Sun colleague, Jerry Lee Lewis, to take one example. Lewis's music can be read as a distortion of black music, as "blacking up."

Much of what characterized Orbison's best and most personal music had little to do with this dominant tradition of "white black" music and in this sense he was indeed a "white white" singer—one who was not deeply involved in the white appropriation of black blues, R&B, and rock 'n' roll. He clearly loved black music and was influenced by it, but he did not burlesque it. For Orbison, rock 'n' roll was never primarily about sexuality as conventionally constructed and displayed. It was not about body, rhythm, or even dancing. Frith notes that within the Western tradition of separating mind from body, "A good classical performance is measured by the stillness it commands. . . . A good rock concert, by contrast, is measured by the audience's physical response, by how quickly people get out of their seats, onto the dance floor, by how loudly they shout and scream" (124). In this respect Orbison must be considered a failure within the world of rock 'n' roll; the audiences at his concerts typically sat in silent, rapt attention—no dancing, no shrieking. Indeed, in a 1980s recording of a live concert in Alabama, Orbison shushes the audience at the beginning of "Running Scared," when an outburst of recognition occurs. Orbison tells the enthusiastic audience that he can't hear the quiet introduction to the song. Imagine such a moment during a Jerry Lee Lewis or Beatles concert. Orbison's audiences more closely resemble the classical music audience Frith describes than the typical rock audience. Something of this emerges in *People* magazine's review of Orbison's Cinemax special, *Roy Orbison and*

Friends: A Black and White Night. Rating the concert a D+, the reviewer complains that it does not conform to the spirit of such concerts: "He doesn't chat with the audience or his fellow stars," and the show has no "chummy charm" (Jarvis 1988, 9). Orbison's concerts were never fun in the dominant rock 'n' roll tradition of dancing and screaming. Orbison appeared in a 1965 live television show in Holland called "Combo." The host began the program with the announcement that "Things are a little different tonight. First of all, there will be no dancing this evening as we are used to having during other 'Combo' shows . . . we did not come here to dance. We only came to look and to listen." True to form, Orbison's performance made no concessions to the presence of the television camera. He stood almost perfectly still while performing; he, like the audience, did not come there to dance. Something of the racial implications of this became clear when Orbison performed a cover version of Ray Charles's "What'd I Say?" He performed this well-known blues rocker with the same restraint that he brought to his ballads—with no manic piano pounding, no guitar acrobatics, no flashy stage moves—nothing but the music. He used the same low-key style when he sang "Mean Woman Blues," one of his hits that falls within the dominant white rock 'n' roll tradition. Throughout the concert, the camera showed a perfectly quiet, still audience, many of whom had looks of intense concentration on their faces.

Orbison's performances of "What'd I Say" and "Mean Woman Blues" present something of a contradiction. Including them in the concert as well as on his recordings shows that he belongs in this dominant rock 'n' roll tradition, but the restrained manner in which he performs them does not fit the burlesque pattern of black music and culture that Frith and Grendon describe. Of course, songs of this sort enabled him to vary the pace in concerts. In the 1970s, "Land of a Thousand Dances," and in the 1980s such Sun songs such as "Oobie Doobie" and "Down the Line," gave rhythmic and lyrical variety to these performances. Such songs also provided a kind of smokescreen for the unusual nature of both Orbison's more typical songs and of his persona. As I have noted, the smokescreen may very well have been as important for Orbison creatively as for his fans; both probably needed to have one foot rooted in the norm in order to obscure the strange, dark music that lay at the center of the *oeuvre,* both on the recordings and in concert.

Despite the black influences on Orbison's music and persona, then, it was Orbison's "white white" persona that received new inflection within a legal and media discourse that emerged from three trials between 2 Live Crew and Acuff-Rose over the former's "unauthorized" recording of "Oh, Pretty Woman." A simple chronology of the events follows, even though, as we shall see, chronology itself became an issue in the legal proceedings.

On July 5, 1989, the rap group 2 Live Crew requested permission from Acuff-Rose to record a parody of "Oh, Pretty Woman," written in 1964 by Roy Orbison and Bill Dees. The request included new lyrics by Luther Campbell (a.k.a. Luke Skywalker) and an offer to pay for the rights. Acuff-Rose refused permission, but 2 Live Crew had already released their album, *As Clean as They Wanna Be*, which included "Oh, Pretty Woman" with altered lyrics. Acuff-Rose filed suit in federal district court in Nashville, charging that the lyrics were "disparaging and therefore not consistent with maintaining the value of the copyright in 'Oh, Pretty Woman'" (quoted in Greenhouse 1993). The court ruled in 1991 that the song was a parody and, as such, was "fair use" of the song within the meaning of copyright law—meaning that the portions of the original words and music could be copied without permission from the copyright holder.

The United States Court of Appeals for the Sixth Circuit in Cincinnati, however, overturned the ruling in 1992, ruling that a parody that sought only to make a profit rather than supply critical commentary was not protected by the fair-use doctrine. Attorneys for 2 Live Crew appealed the ruling to the U.S. Supreme Court; the Court agreed in March 1993 to hear the case and determine the status of parody under copyright law (Greenhouse 1993). On March 7, 1994, the Court ruled unanimously in favor of 2 Live Crew, with Justice Souter writing the opinion for the unanimous Court and Justice Kennedy writing a concurring opinion.

The case attracted major media coverage, as it shaped up as the one that would determine the extent to which parody was protected under the constitutional right of free speech. The case also revealed a great deal of legal confusion as to what parody is and what is protected as fair use. As they have done with pornography, the courts have tried to draw clear-cut distinctions between two different categories of representations (art vs. pornography and parody vs. copying), in cases where such distinctions may be difficult if not impossible to maintain. I am not so much interested in the legal issues as in the discourses that emerged around Orbison's song as a result of this trial. In a different sense from what Bono meant when he called Orbison a "white pop singer," and in a different sense from what I mean when I call him a "white white" singer, Orbison's whiteness once again became central. The courts considered a number of issues relevant to the 2 Live Crew version of the song, such as whether it would limit the market for the Orbison original and whether it borrowed more of the original than was necessary to hold it up for parodic purposes. The legal discourse most directly intersected musical discourse in those portions of the trials that attempted to determine what constitutes parody. The progress of the case through the courts affected the interpretation of Orbison's song and created a racial identity for it as well as for the 2 Live Crew song. And the songs ultimately became associated with racial and sexual identities.

The district court ruled that "2 Live Crew's lyrics provide the strongest evidence of its attempt to parody 'Oh, Pretty Woman.' Although the parody starts out with the same lyrics as the original, it quickly degenerates into a play on words, substituting predictable lyrics with shocking ones. . . . In sum, 2 Live Crew is an anti-establishment rap group and this song derisively demonstrates how bland and banal the Orbison song seems to them" (U.S. District Court 1991, 1155). The court notes that the nature of the parody centers on the manner in which 2 Live Crew transforms the physical beauty of Orbison's pretty woman into something repulsive.

The district court concluded that

> having applied . . . four factors, the Court finds that they weigh in favor of the defendants. 2 Live Crew's "Pretty Woman" is a parody. Its purpose is to poke fun at the original version of "Oh, Pretty Woman." In so doing, the parody copies from the original. Notwithstanding the copying needed to conjure up the original song, for the foregoing reasons the Court concludes that 2 Live Crew's use of the original copyrighted song is protected fair use. (U.S. District Court 1991, 1158–59)

Although 2 Live Crew was characterized as an "anti-establishment rap group," racial issues were muted in the district court's ruling but emerged more fully in the court of appeals. The chronology also became an issue there, as it related to determining parody. The defendants claimed that Campbell wrote the song as a parody and requested permission from Acuff-Rose prior to the song's release, but the court noted that this claim contradicted Campbell's affidavit. Furthermore, the court noted that the defendants had deposited $13,867.56 in a bank account for the purpose of paying Acuff-Rose the royalties owed them for the use of the song and added:

> Our review of the record reveals confusion over the status of "Pretty Woman" as either "comic" effort, such as those created by comic musician Weird Al Yankovic, or a "parody," which purports to deliver social commentary within a humorous framework. Yankovic's works are licensed uses, not "fair uses" for which a license is not required. This confusion on the part of 2 Live Crew adds weight to Acuff-Rose's assertion that Campbell's intent to create a parody was only formed after "Pretty Woman" was released. (U.S. Court of Appeals 1992, 1433)

The appeals court, in other words, did not share the district court's opinion about the clear-cut nature of the parody.

It is, however, during the consideration of the parody issue that the race issue emerges most directly. The appeals court decision devotes substantial attention to an affidavit that had been presented by Oscar Brand to the district court. "African-American rap music, Brand stated, uses parody as a form of protest, and often substitutes new words to 'make fun of the "white-bread" originals and the establishment. . . .' In 'Pretty Woman,' Brand concluded, 'this anti-establishment singing group is trying to show how bland and banal the Orbison song seems to them. It's just one of many examples of their derisive approach to "white-centered" popular music'" (U.S. Court of Appeals 1992, 1433). Brand's use of the terms "bland and banal" to describe 2 Live Crew's perceptions of Orbison's song was obviously persuasive to the district court, because the same words appear in that decision. Also, the terms "white-bread" and "white-centered" are now introduced to characterize Orbison's song.

The appeals court judges distinguished between popular notions of parody, which they felt the district court relied upon, and legal definitions of parody. Although they accepted the legal definition of parody for the 2 Live Crew song, they noted, "In our opinion, this is not a new work which makes ridiculous the style and expression of the original, although there is plainly an element of the ridiculous to the new work. We cannot see any thematic relationship between the copyrighted song and the alleged parody. The mere fact that both songs have a woman as their central theme is too tenuous a connection to be viewed as critical commentary on the original" (U.S. Court of Appeals 1992, 1436). The court concluded in regard to the parody issue, "It is the blatantly commercial purpose of the derivative work that prevents this parody from being a fair use" (1439).

All of these issues were further complicated by Judge David A. Nelson's dissenting opinion, an opinion that once again brought racial issues to the fore. Contradicting his colleagues, Nelson wrote, "Under anyone's definition it seems to me the 2 Live Crew Song is a quintessential parody" (1441). Nelson, adopting Brand's language as his own, went on, "The parody (done in an African-American dialect) was clearly intended to ridicule the white-bread original. . . . The District Court accepted Brand's explanation. . . . So do I" (1442).

Nelson's description of Orbison's song and 2 Live Crew's version of it get to the center of Nelson's notion of race issues and Orbison's aesthetics:

> Consider the plot, if one may call it that, of the original work. A lonely man with a strangely nasal voice sees a pretty woman (name unknown) walking down the street. The man speculates on whether the woman is lonely too. Apostrophizing her in his mind, he urges her to stop and talk and give him a smile and say she will stay with him and be his that night. The woman walks on by, and the man resigns himself to going home alone. Before he leaves, however, he sees the woman walking back to him. End of story.
>   This little vignette is intended, I think, to be sweet. While it is certainly suggestive, it is also, by the standards of its time "romantic" rather than indelicate. The singer evokes a sexual theme in his soliloquy, but then leaves the realization of his desire to the listener's imagination.
>   The parody by 2 Live Crew is much more explicit, and it reminds us that sexual congress with nameless streetwalkers is not necessarily the stuff of romance and it is not necessarily without its consequences. The singers (there are several) have the same thing on their minds as the lonely man with the nasal voice, but there is no hint of wine and roses. The 2 Live Crew singers—randy misogynists, not lonely Sir Lancelots—raucously

address a "big hairy woman" and her "bald-headed friend," one or both of whom are urged to "let the boys jump in." One singer chides a woman (the big hairy one, I think) for having cheated on him ("Two timin' woman / You's out with my boy last night"). In the end, this cloud proves to have what the singer sees as a silver lining: "Two timin' woman / That takes a load off my mind / Two timin' woman / Now I know the baby ain't mine."

This, I should say, is "criticism" with a vengeance—and the thematic relationship to the original is obvious. (U.S. Court of Appeals 1992, 1442)

Nelson's interpretation of the song is the fullest reading offered within the legal proceedings up to that point, though I will argue that it is a somewhat bizarre, contradictory interpretation that misses much of importance.

Once again, Nelson claims that Brand is on firm ground when he describes the audience for the Orbison song. "There is no question in my mind that the song 'Oh, Pretty Woman' by Roy Orbison and William Dees was intended for Mr. Orbison's country music audience and middle-America" (1145). Brand is off base here. In 1964, when Orbison released "Oh, Pretty Woman," it was clearly intended for his Top 40 rock 'n' roll audience, where it became his biggest hit ever. Orbison had no country audience at that time, the song did not place on the country charts, and his records were not stocked in the country racks of music stores. Brand seems to link Orbison with the 1980s discourse of country music that includes the hit duet of "That Lovin' You Feeling Again" with Emmylou Harris and "Crying" with k. d. lang. Orbison's limited success within country music was confined to the 1980s, and even then was a minor part of his musical output. In 1964 Orbison was a pop-rock singer, and within that context the term "middle America" is partly accurate. His audience for "Oh, Pretty Woman" was primarily a teenage audience, and rock 'n' roll functioned in some ways at the time as a point of resistance to the values and mores of middle America. The middle America to which Roy Orbison's song appealed was composed of white, middle-class teenagers.

Declaring that 2 Live Crew's version was "hopelessly vulgar," Nelson concluded, "The original may not seem vulgar, at first blush, but the 2 Live Crew group are telling us, knowingly or unknowingly, that vulgar is precisely what 'Oh, Pretty Woman' is. Whether we agree or disagree, this perception is not one we ought to suppress" (1446).

Two important elements are added to the district court's opinion in Nelson's dissenting appellate opinion. One is racial: Orbison's version is described as "whitebread," a term with explicit negative connotations. His vision is also characterized as "wine and roses," a phrase implying a romantic vision that falsely colors gritty reality.

I want to reiterate that my purposes here are limited to understanding how Orbison's song was interpreted within these legal discourses, particularly with reference to racial issues. It is not my primary intention to analyze the wisdom of any of the courts' rulings on what constitutes parody and whether or not the commercial nature of material affects whether it is covered by "fair use." Nor am I interested in judging either the value of 2 Live Crew's version or its nature (i.e., is it or isn't it a parody?). My interest lies in how the 2 Live Crew/Orbison conflict affected interpretations of Orbison's song and how it created a racial opposition between the two versions, the original of which became synonymous with white, while the other became synonymous with black. (I will return later to the fact that, as this racial discourse developed, no one in any of the courts bothered to point out that two major black artists had already recorded cover versions of "Oh, Pretty Woman": the Count Basie Orchestra recorded it with vocals by Leon Thomas in 1965 and Al Green recorded the song in 1972.)

I do, of course, have an opinion about this case. I believe that the Supreme Court made the right decision, though I agree with Justice Kennedy's concurring opinion regarding the parody issue, and here, as we shall see, the issues of parody and race overlap. I for one do not want to live in a society where Acuff-Rose has the right to block any version of a song to which they hold the copyright regardless of whether or not it is a parody and regardless of whether or not it is of a commercial nature. At the same time, I believe that all three courts engaged in naïve and erroneous aesthetic judgments even when, as in the case of the Supreme Court, they wisely counseled against just such a danger. Souter wrote, "As Justice Holmes explained, 'it would be a dangerous undertaking for persons trained only to the law to constitute themselves final judges of the worth of [a work], outside of the narrowest and most obvious limits'" (U.S. Supreme Court 1993, 1173). Yet in my view this is precisely what the Supreme Court did.

The Supreme Court decision quotes from the district court's ruling that "2 Live Crew's version was a parody which 'quickly degenerates into a play on words, substituting predictable lyrics with shocking ones' to show 'how bland and banal the Orbison song is'" (U.S. Supreme Court 1993, 1168). Souter then refers to Judge Nelson's dissenting appellate opinion: "Judge Nelson . . . came to the same conclusion, that the 2 Live Crew song 'was clearly intended to ridicule the whitebread original' and 'reminds us that sexual congress with streetwalkers is not necessarily the stuff of romance and is not necessarily without its consequences. The singers (there are several) have the same thing on their minds as did the lonely man with the nasal voice, but there is no hint of wine and roses.' . . . Although the majority below had difficulty discerning any criticism of the original in 2 Live Crew's song, it assumed for purposes of its opinion that there was some" (1173). The Supreme Court's response is brief and to the point: "We have less difficulty in finding . . . [a] critical element than the Court of Appeals did, although having found it we will not take the further step of evaluating its quality" (1173). At this point, the Court seems wisely to heed its own advice and sidestep the aesthetic quality issue.

Yet the Justices then set themselves up as competent aestheticians and make judgments about quality. Aesthetics, of course, involves much more than judgments about how good or bad works are; it involves assumptions about such things as progress in the arts, realism, and so on—weighty issues that "those trained only to the law" apparently know as little about as judgments of good and bad. The Supreme Court offers close readings of both versions of "Oh, Pretty Woman":

> While we might not assign a high rank to the parodic element here, we think it fair to say that 2 Live Crew's song reasonably could be perceived as commenting on the original or criticizing it, to some degree. 2 Live Crew juxtaposes the romantic musings of a man whose fantasy comes true, with degrading taunts, a bawdy demand for sex, and a sigh of relief from paternal responsibility. The later words can be taken as a comment on the naivete of the original of an earlier day, as a rejection of its sentiment that ignores the ugliness of street life and the debasement that it signifies. (1173)

The Supreme Court notes that the district court interpreted 2 Live Crew's version as a "derisive" demonstration of Orbison's "bland and banal" original. The district court obviously rushed to aesthetic judgment; declaring the original bland and banal is not a neutral account of the song but an evaluation. The district court's characterization seems to give more credit to the parody than to the original composition. Critics and musicians in both rock 'n' roll and rap might well take issue with such an assessment. My point, however, is not to declare the court wrong but to note that it makes inappropriate aesthetic judgments. The district court's aesthetic judgment implicitly assumes that current views are inherently more progressive ("shocking") than those of an earlier era ("predictable").

In addition to being inappropriate, this judgment is simply "presentist," because whatever one thinks of the Orbison original, it was anything but "predictable" in 1964. Its opening, for example, with a pounding drum beat before the statement of the main guitar riff or the entrance of the singer, was quite innovative and would affect such later songs as "Paint It Black" by the Rolling Stones. Even the lyrics—for those who, like the district court judges, make the serious mistake of separating form from content—were quite daring for a 1964 Top 40 radio single.

The appeals court supplies variations on some of these discourses and introduces new ones. Judge Nelson, for example, derisively refers to the original as "whitebread." He thus makes explicit the racial component of the case, which is only implicit in the district court's opinion. He implies that the woman of the title is a prostitute, a "nameless streetwalker" with whom the singer wants to have "sexual congress." He is here referring to the Orbison original as well as the 2 Live Crew version, as he says, "The singers . . . have the same thing on their minds as did the lonely man with the nasal voice." Moreover, he is arguing that the 2 Live crew version is ridiculing the original's romantic notion about "sexual congress with streetwalkers." Yet nothing in Orbison's song suggests that it is about prostitution. The entire song is structured around the man's desire for an unattainable woman. Far from being able to buy her, he gives up, and then is held in suspense wondering whether she will indeed approach him. The only plausible explanation for Judge Nelson's reading is the new cultural discourse that developed around the song with the release of the hit film *Pretty Woman* (1990). In that film, the pretty woman of the title is indeed a prostitute, and Julia Roberts's star image embodies the woman of the title specifically as a certain kind of white beauty, and one who becomes identified with fashion. The song, by contrast, says nothing about the woman's appearance in body or clothing. Indeed, 2 Live Crew's repeated ridicule of the "big hairy woman" and the "bald headed woman," specifies a body type that is totally lacking in the original. Orbison's song is not about the woman but about a passive form of male desire for her.

Judge Nelson's "wine and roses" reference implies that Orbison looks at the world through rose-colored glasses (he has probably never seen a picture of Orbison in his dark glasses). Thus, the "whitebread" world view is rose-colored, unrealistic, and apparently indifferent to social problems. Again an aesthetic judgment is made, this time with explicit racial and social dimensions: "Responsible" art, it seems, is realistically aware of the "consequences" of "the stuff of romance."

The Supreme Court Justices make many of these same assumptions, despite paying lip service to the notion that judges are not qualified aestheticians. They credit 2 Live Crew with commenting on the "naivete of the original of an earlier day" that "ignores the ugliness of street life." The naïveté here lies in the Court's assumption about an "earlier day." The Court's progressive ideology is inescapable: the current wisdom is more sophisticated than what came before. The "whitebread," bland, banal, naïve, establishment original is pitted against the shocking, black, realistic, socially aware, gritty anti-establishment parody by 2 Live Crew. The Justices' caution about their proper role is meaningless rhetoric; they are mired in aesthetic assumptions.

Only Justice Kennedy was bothered by any of this, and his objection was to the way the other Justices were willing to assume that the 2 Live Crew version was a parody within the context of social commentary described above. In his concurring opinion, Kennedy wrote that he was "not so assured that 2 Live Crew's song is a legitimate parody" (U.S. Supreme Court, 1181). Observing that it would be easy for musicians to "exploit existing works" by claiming that their version was "valuable commentary on the original," Kennedy got to the heart of the matter. "Almost any revamped modern version of a familiar composition," he wrote, "can be construed as a 'commentary on the naivete of the original,' . . . because of the difference in style and because it will be amusing to hear how the old tune sounds in the new genre" (1181). He went on to conjure up rap versions of Beethoven's Fifth Symphony and the then-current country hit "Achy Breaky Heart."

Kennedy recognized that a work as critically esteemed as Beethoven's Fifth Symphony could easily be treated in the same way that 2 Live Crew had treated Orbison's "Oh, Pretty Woman." At the other end of the spectrum, a song widely regarded as trivial, such as "Achy Breaky Heart," could be similarly treated. Although he stopped short of raising many important issues, Kennedy at least acknowledged that the easy manner in which the other Justices accepted the notion of naïveté in the original was inadequate. Although the majority opinion granted that "we might not assign a high rank to the parodic element here," Kennedy pointed out that the entire notion of parody is at stake by such a dodge, since, by definition, any modern version will contain an element of commentary on the original.

Kennedy concurred with the majority because the Court had to decide on a definition of parody as well as three other issues, including the question of whether commercial use prevents parody from being covered by fair use. In other words, given that 2 Live Crew recorded the song to make money, could it also be protected as parodic critical commentary? Quoting Samuel Johnson's pronouncement that "No man but a blockhead ever wrote, except for money," the Court showed much more aesthetic judgment in this area by acknowledging that no line should be drawn between art and money. Commercial purpose is implicit in all forms of art and thus all forms of parody. A related question concerned the claim by Acuff-Rose that such commercial parody would hurt the market for the original. The Court wisely determined that if the market value of the original was hurt, the damage would result from criticism of it comparable to a bad theater review. Such parodic criticism "suppresses demand" of the original whereas copyright infringement "usurps it" (1178).

The Court's decision reversed the appellate court ruling and the case was remanded to the district court. Kennedy's concurring opinion concluded, "While I am not so assured that 2 Live Crew's song is a legitimate parody, the Court's treatment of the remaining factors leaves room for the District Court to determine on remand that the song is not fair use. As future courts apply our fair use analysis, they must take care to ensure that not just any commercial take-off is rationalized *post hoc* as a parody" (1182).

That the press gave little attention to Kennedy's concurring opinion points to the significance of the press discourses surrounding the case. For my immediate purposes, the importance of the legal discourse on parody lay in the manner in which it was related to the racial discourse: the argument for parody rested on assumptions of how the black, grittily realistic remake of the song commented on the white, naïve fantasy of the original.

Once the Supreme Court announced that it would hear the case, there was heavy media coverage. In addition to the bewildering number of discourses surrounding Orbison and "Oh, Pretty Woman" in the trials, a number of other, at times related, discourses appeared in the press. One involved Orbison's newfound stature as a major figure in the history of American popular music. From the mid-1960s to the mid-1980s, as I have demonstrated, Orbison's career was in various stages of decline. Some regarded him as an overlooked and forgotten minor figure, others as a bad joke. Yet the press gave much attention during this trial to the fact that Michael Jackson, as well as the estates of Leonard Bernstein, George and Ira Gershwin, Rodgers and Hammerstein, Lerner and Lowe, and Cole Porter filed briefs on behalf of Acuff-Rose (Diebel 1993; *Arizona Daily Star* 1993). Nearly ten years earlier it would have been nearly unimaginable that Orbison would have been in such company. Imagine that years earlier had Orbison offered a brief on behalf of Leonard Bernstein; the lawyers would not even have bothered to use it. Now Orbison belonged to a number of super groups: the Traveling Wilburys, the megastars who played with him on *Roy Orbison and Friends: A Black and White Night* (among them Bruce Springsteen, Tom Waits, Elvis Costello, and Bonnie Raitt), and now some of the legendary all-time greats of American music.

This discourse also intersected with a race discourse. Apart from Michael Jackson, the tradition of American popular music invoked by the above names is a white tradition. *Rolling Stone* reported of the case:

For the rap community, there's more at stake than legal issues. The justices' presumed lack of familiarity with rap genre conventions has led rap artists to fear a court bias against rap music. "A parody of 'Oh, Pretty Woman' done in a country version would have a much better chance," claims Gregory Hutchinson aka 187 um, producer and lead rapper for the gangsta group Above the Law. Says Chris Schwarz, chief executive officer of Ruffhouse records whose acts include Cypress Hill, "Roy Orbison is a staple of the American musical heritage. The only times the justices probably hear about rap, on the other hand, is when its problems are reported in news stories." (Soocher 1993, 13)

While such concerns have much validity, I want to underscore that the characterization of Orbison as a prominent figure in the history of American music was a new phenomenon, the product of his recognition by David Lynch, Bruce Springsteen, Bob Dylan, George Harrison, and others. It must not be forgotten that Orbison spent much of his career relatively unknown or forgotten. He lost his recording contracts and even sued Wesley Rose, his longtime friend and manager, for millions of dollars in damages. His rockabilly recordings during his Sun days suffered in comparison to those of Elvis Presley and the other Sun rockers; even his hits between 1960 and 1964 were quickly lost because that time period was characterized as a rock 'n' roll wasteland, between Elvis's induction into the army and the arrival of the Beatles, the saviors of rock 'n' roll.

Even the whiteness of the privileged tradition in which Orbison is now included has its contradictions. The mainstream tradition of white music has always owed a great deal to African American music, always influenced by it, often borrowing from it, and not infrequently even shamelessly copying it. (Gershwin and Bernstein come readily to mind, among others.) Much of Orbison's music shows an extreme refusal to copy black music. Orbison bluntly voiced his displeasure with Sam Phillips's orders that Sun artists copy black music. In contrast to Presley, Jerry Lee Lewis, Carl Perkins, and others, Orbison felt oppressed and sought other paths. In this sense, rock singers like Presley can be termed white black singers and Orbison can be termed a white white singer, even though he does not fit in well with much of the white tradition of which he is now a part. Curiously, if this earned him the contempt of 2 Live Crew, it earned him the respect of many black musicians, including B. B. King, John Lee Hooker, and Booker T. Jones, all of whom paid tribute to him at the 1989 Los Angeles Tribute Concert. Furthermore, the Al Green and Count Basie versions of "Oh, Pretty Woman" are not only further evidence of respect for Orbison within a part of the African American musical community, but also evidence that the song is not tied to a peculiarly white notion of female beauty.

Unlike the various judges involved in the 2 Live Crew case, I want to confront the aesthetics of Orbison's "Oh, Pretty Woman," head on and place the song in to the context of the masochist discourse detailed in Chapter 5. I noted there that Orbison's music employs a number of formal devices (to which, in their form/content split, none of the courts paid any attention), such as temporal delays that draw out moments of unbearable suspense, and a passive persona, only dreaming of action that is always deferred to the future. As we have seen, Orbison's persona is also frequently responsible for his own suffering. Even "Oh, Pretty Woman," a somewhat uncharacteristic Orbison song, conforms to this aesthetic. John Morthland, a former associate editor of *Rolling Stone*, has characterized Orbison's best songs as a form of "thinking out loud," and this is an apt description of "Oh, Pretty Woman." Here the Orbison persona does little more than express a feverish, dreamlike desire for a passing woman, and then resigns himself to going home alone. In the original version of the song, as I noted, he doesn't get the girl; only Fred Foster's intervention changed the outcome. I have already described the heightened moment of suspense that occurs before the final resolution. Like "Running Scared," another song where he waits passively to see if his dreams will be fulfilled, the song is about unfulfilled desire and delayed gratification, about longing rather than fulfillment. In his own poetic way, Tom Waits acknowledged this when he remarked, "Roy Orbison's songs were not so much about dreams but more like dreams themselves" (Goldberg 1989, 33). What Waits, himself a highly regarded composer and musician, recognizes here is the unique form of the songs. Those who devalue "fantasy" or "dreams" in relationship to realism and social commentary are fated to misunderstand and undervalue the Orbison aesthetic. As we have seen, Orbison's brief flirtation with late-1960s songs of social criticism were of limited success; in some ways they contradicted the "fantasy" melodramas that lay at the center of his greatest aesthetic accomplishments.

Orbison's music, even when it is about such matters as war and poverty, has little or nothing to do with social reality, racial or otherwise. "Oh, Pretty Woman" is much less about a white view of female beauty and the ugliness of the realities of street life than it is about a male form of masochistic desire. Compare Orbison's 1966 song, "Harlem Woman." Arguably it is "Harlem Woman," not "Oh, Pretty Woman," that should be criticized for its reduction of black poverty to a background for masochistically pleasurable white male suffering. In this song the Orbison persona falls in love with a black prostitute, excusing her occupation on account of her impoverished circumstances (see Chapter 5). This song *is* in fact about sexual congress with a streetwalker, but one far removed from the social realities Judge Nelson imagines such a song is or should be about.

Eric Lott sheds some light on how Orbison's "white white" masochist aesthetic relates to his distance from black music. Lott has argued that in the nineteenth century the white working class adopted black masculinity (as whites understood or misunderstood it) as an ideal, and that even in the twentieth century that ideal persists in much popular culture, including rock 'n' roll. The stereotypical white perception of black masculinity is, as many have pointed out, one of hyper-masculinity; it is active, powerful, phallic, sexual, aggressive. Lott goes so far as to characterize Mick Jagger as being a blackface performer without the blackface. Orbison's masochist aesthetic, by contrast, rejects this stereotypical notion of powerful, phallic maleness for a passive, fearful, dreaming/suffering position. The dominant, white-appropriated model of black sexuality offered no such possibilities, even though certain black musicians, such as the Platters and Jackie Wilson, did. Orbison's masochist aesthetic was inconsistent with the white working-class model of black male sexuality, and in this light his alignment with various white discourses, including that of classical music, can be seen as having nothing to with racism. Consciously or not, Orbison devised a form of rock 'n' roll that was at odds with the model of black masculinity that lay at the very center of the genre.

According to Frantz Fanon, that model has a masochistic element: "In the United States, as we can see, the Negro makes stories in which it becomes possible for him to work his aggression; the white man's unconscious justifies this aggression and gives it worth by turning it on himself, thus reproducing the classic schema of masochism" (Fanon 1967, 176). Fanon relates this to cultural production:

> It is usual to be told in the United States, when one calls for the real free-dom of the Negro: "That's all they're waiting for, to jump our women." Since the white man behaves in an offensive manner toward the Negro, he recognizes that in the Negro's place he would have no mercy on his oppres-sors. Therefore it is not surprising to see that he identifies himself with the Negro: white "hot jazz" orchestras, white blues and spiritual singers, white authors writing novels in which the Negro proclaims his grievances, whites in blackface. (176–77)

Fanon's point offers an explanation for a central paradox of rock 'n' roll: If, for whites, the black man stands for a particularly virile, phallic sex-uality, why would the white man chose a model that he cannot fully fit? The answer involves a form of what Fanon calls "self-castration" (177). Much as the white man attributes a large penis to black men, thereby marking his own as inadequate, he attributes an excess of mas-culinity to black men, thereby marking his as, once again, lesser. This model of masochism, significant as it might be in relation to rock 'n' roll, differs from the one that I am identifying in Orbison's music. Whereas Fanon's white men embrace the hyper-masculine black ideal, albeit in a self-punishing way, Orbison rejects it; whereas they eagerly attempt to perform it, Orbison turns away from it or only regards it as an unavoidable and anxiety-producing cultural mandate: "Gotta stay, be a man, if I can."[2]

Count Basie's cover of "Oh, Pretty Woman" shows how the domi-nant cultural model of black masculinity differed from Orbison's mas-culinity. In Orbison's music, a masochistic sense of time finds expres-sion via a number of classic masochist temporalities, including bad timing, missed opportunities, delay, and drawn-out moments of height-ened suspense and anguish. At the climax of "Oh, Pretty Woman," the masochistic sense of timing finds formal expression when the Orbison persona cries out, "But wait, what do I see?" The opening guitar riff, itself structured around a disruption of time, is repeated, freezing time as the Orbison persona passively waits to see what action the desired woman will take.

The Orbison version of the song is entirely about this climax, but it is absent from the Count Basie version, in which vocalist Leon Thomas actively talks to the woman in a hip manner. Leonard Feather, in the original liner notes, observes of Thomas: "His sound is blues-edged; the concluding recitative is an attractive flourish." Indeed, the moment that comes closest to the Orbison use of the word "wait" is its use in the aggressive command, "Hey, wait a minute." But this is followed immediately by the closing exclamation "Pretty Woman." In this version, although the man seems to lose the woman, he acts in a conventionally masculine manner, and one marked through language as black. Within this context, the main formal trope of the opening guitar riff makes no sense, and indeed the Basie version lacks a big-band equivalent of it at the beginning as well.

Feather is clearly correct in describing Thomas's singing as "blues-edged," and this is nowhere more evident than in what he calls the "attractive recitative." What interests me here, however, is the connection between the black vocal style and the masculine posturing that contrasts so sharply with Orbison's white vocal style and passive submissiveness to his fate; he simply cannot adopt such a version of black masculinity because that notion is highly sexualized and active, even aggressive.

Orbison's career was bracketed by race issues: its beginning was highlighted by his rejection of Sam Phillips's edict that all his singers copy black R&B, and the end by the 2 Live Crew court case. His early rejection of the white appropriation of black music, and his posthumous condemnation by 2 Live Crew as a racist purveyor of a white norm of female beauty, may seem to indicate that Orbison had little relation to black culture, other than one of racist rejection. The reality, as we have seen, is much more complex.[3] The reverse may be closer to the truth, with Orbison rejecting the burlesque version of black culture and 2 Live crew embracing it.

Black performers as diverse as John Lee Hooker, B. B. King, Al Green, Booker T. Jones, and Don Byron have paid tribute to Orbison and respectfully and even lovingly have sung and recorded his songs, including "Oh, Pretty Woman."

Ultimately, a monstrous stereotype of black masculinity reduces it to one thing. That Orbison's departure from dominant models of masculinity should be attractive to some blacks should surprise no one. Nor should we be surprised that for 2 Live Crew, he came to stand for an offensive form of whiteness. Such are the vagaries of the unusual, indeed unique, position in which Orbison placed himself. In the next chapter, we will see that his legacy is full of such baffling contradictions.

Beyond the End

*Roy Orbison's Posthumous Career
and Legacy*

R oy Orbison frequently mentioned that his earliest association with music was death: as a little boy, he remembered
singing at home as part of farewell parties for young men
going off to fight in World War II.[1] As we have seen, death
played an unusually prominent role in his music, and the
untimely deaths of Claudette and his two children preceded
his at the age of fifty-two, when he was on the brink of a
major comeback.

But did his death really end his career? In some ways
Orbison's posthumous career has been as unusual as—and
more successful than—his career while he was alive. Perhaps fittingly, in 1985 he contributed a remarkable vocal
track to Jimmy Buffet's song about crossing over after death,
"Beyond the End." Orbison is heard at the end of the song,
and his eerie voice represents within the song's narrative a
voice singing to us mortals from the beyond. And Orbison
has, as it were, been singing to us from the beyond since his
death. I do not mean simply that *Mystery Girl* (1989) was his
most successful album. The cliché that some artists are
appreciated more after their death aside, Orbison's case is
unmatched within the annals of rock 'n' roll. How can it be
that a man now sometimes called the greatest singer in the

world, a man whose music has permeated popular consciousness through movies and radio and television commercials, was so overlooked and underestimated during his own lifetime? Although the Presley estate makes more annual income now than Presley did at the time of his death, Presley was recognized as a figure of overwhelming importance during his lifetime. Elvis was the first rock 'n' roll superstar, and so his posthumous career is hardly surprising. Orbison, by contrast, even at the height of his career, was never perceived as important (in fact, was hardly perceived at all) and, after his brief four-year period of fame, fell into virtual oblivion.

In the December 4, 1998, issue of *Entertainment Weekly*, the article entitled "Orbison's Last Dream" concludes, "In the end it's that goose-bump-inducing voice that endures. Does anyone who's heard it need to ask why Elvis Presley once called Orbison the greatest singer in the world?" (Fong and Sinclair 1998, 120). The authors simply assert that for anyone who will listen, it is self-evident that Orbison is the greatest singer in the world. When Presley made the statement, nearly twenty years before Orbison died, no one paid any attention. When Bruce Springsteen burst on the scene in the mid-1970s, despite his direct homage to Orbison on *Born to Run*, the critics talked endlessly about the Dylan influence on Springsteen, overlooking or minimizing the Orbison influence—as if they couldn't conceive of it. By 2000, in part thanks to Springsteen, things had changed. A critic covering the final concert of Springsteen's world tour with the E Street Band, noted, "He clearly wanted to put this Cadillac of bands—with its roots reaching to Chuck Berry, James Brown, Roy Orbison and Bob Dylan—into drive one more time" (Rodgers 2000). It is no longer surprising to find Orbison in such exalted company.

Of Orbison's rescue from obscurity, the *Entertainment Weekly* article notes, "Fortunately, those singular tunes had made a lasting impact on some influential folks" (Fong and Sinclair, 120). During his lifetime Orbison was never fully discovered or embraced by either the critics or the public: his resuscitation was thanks entirely to other artists. These "influential folks," including film director David Lynch and a virtual who's who of musicians, barraged the culture in the year before Orbison's death, and their message began to sink in. His membership in the

Traveling Wilburys may have been the turning point. If Bob Dylan and George Harrison could accept Orbison into their group, there must have been something more to him than the critics had realized. The members of the group were honored by his presence. According to Tom Petty, "'we just went crazy.' . . . All the way home we were going, 'Roy Orbison's in our band!' I don't think we ever got over it" (Goldberg 1989, 32). Only after Orbison's death did it become commonly known that Dylan had long admired him and had written "Don't Think Twice" for him, recording the song himself only after Orbison decided not to record it. Beginning with Elvis Presley, the greats of rock 'n' roll did not consider Orbison their equal but their superior. Such "influential folks" must be credited with creating and maintaining Orbison's posthumous career in a manner quite different from those of Jim Morrison, John Lennon, Buddy Holly, Elvis Presley, Jimi Hendrix, and Janis Joplin, all of whom were famous in their lifetimes as well as in their deaths.

But Orbison's posthumous career is unusual in a more significant way. A number of influential musicians have made music with him *after* his death, raising interesting authorship issues related to those discussed in Chapter 1. Let me begin at the intersection of film and music. As we have seen, Wim Wenders's 1998 film *The End of Violence* includes a "new" Roy Orbison song on its soundtrack: "You May Feel Me Crying." Of all the Orbison songs left unfinished at the time of his death that have been released to date, this one may be the most unfinished of them all. Orbison had recorded only a vocal track with guitar accompaniment into a boom box. Barbara Orbison reportedly approached Peter Gabriel, who was too busy to work on the project; Gabriel played it for Brian Eno, who then finished it.

Eno, of course, is a rock 'n' roll great in his own right. In what sense, then, is this song Orbison's? He neither wrote it (though it was written for him by Will Jennings, his cowriter at the time of his death) nor produced it nor had any say over its production. And of course he had no control over whether or how it would be used in Wenders's film. Furthermore, the skeleton form in which he left it shows that he was far from finished working out even the preliminary vocals. Yet the song seems to me to be an important *Orbison* song. Among other well-respected producers who have worked with Orbison's music since his death are Robbie Robertson, Don Was, and T. Bone Burnett. And the musicians are equally illustrious, including, for example, k. d. lang, Max Weinberg, and Clarence Clemmons, the latter two from Springsteen's E Street Band.

As we have seen, even when a singer is alive, the issue of authorship is often complex. Recall Simon Frith's statement: "Voices, not songs, hold the key to our pop pleasures: musicologists may analyze the art of the Gershwins or Cole Porter, but we hear Bryan Ferry or Peggy Lee" (Frith 1996, 201). Or, as *Entertainment Weekly* put it, "In the end it's the goose-bump-inducing voice that endures." If these critics are right, how much does it matter whether that enduring voice is part of a record made after the death of the singer? To take the point to its logical extreme, why should we even privilege the original recording, made during the singer's life, over endless possible other recordings made after his or her death? This question challenges the most fundamental assumptions about authorship and integrity. But the recorded pop voice is a complex aesthetic text, and *it* is what should be compared to the dense notational text of classical music, or the dense aesthetic language of a Shakespeare play. Why can't it endure limitless productions/interpretations and still retain its identity and integrity? It can.

To "update" an old recording has until very recently been viewed as crass commercialism. The exceptions prove the rule: Natalie Cole's duets with Nat King Cole and Hank Williams Junior's duet with Hank Williams were respected because of the cultural privileging of the bond between parent and child, a bond that overrode the usual presumptions of exploitation or crass commercialism. When, years earlier, Hank Williams's songs had been reissued with strings added to make them more mainstream, the new recordings were ignored in favor of the authenticity of the originals. Very recently, however, a few recordings have indicated a new awareness for an expanded approach to reusing the pop voice in a new production. Think, for example, of Kenny G using Louis Armstrong's "What a Wonderful World," or a tribute album to Bob Marley composed of new duets recorded by current singers with Marley's vocal tracks. In other variations, Charlie Hayden's Quartet West's *Haunted Heart* CD places songs by Jo Stafford, Joni Southern, and Billie Holiday in the midst of his new recordings, thus recontextualizing the old songs, though not "reproducing" them. And much was made of the fact that Frank Sinatra's last album of duets was recorded without any of the other singers being present in the studio with Sinatra; they recorded their vocal tracks separately. And the many dance mixes, re-mixes, and hip-hop samplings all contribute to a related aesthetic—music is made and remade in the studio, reusing vocal tracks or parts of them by well-known pop voices and recombining them with other voices.

There is no reason why we shouldn't think of producing a new recording using an old vocal track as equivalent to a theater director's staging a new production of a Shakespeare play. If it is the voice that endures and causes the goosebumps, then why shouldn't that enduring voice be reinterpreted? The 2001 remix of Elvis Presley's "A Little Less Conversation" is the most commercially successful example of this to date. Even if Orbison—or any other artist—wanted things done a certain way, there is no reason not to do them differently. We know, for example, how Leonard Bernstein wanted his works conducted (though even he changed his mind quite a bit), but that need not privilege his wishes over other conductors' interpretations.

If, as is generally agreed, Orbison's work declined during the MGM years due to poor production, why shouldn't Brian Eno go back and reproduce those songs? Why, for that matter, shouldn't he go back and reproduce the highly regarded Monument hits? Why would this be cheap "updating?" Why shouldn't the concept of an Orbison for the twenty-first century make as much sense as the same concept of a Hamlet?

A producer working with a dead artist's unfinished tracks is obviously in a more limited position than one working with a living artist—there can be no interaction between the two concerning tempo, phrasing, and so on, and, obviously, the original artist can have no input into trying new arrangements. (Though it is worth noting that Jeff Lynne electronically sped up Orbison's vocal track on "I Drove All Night" and then electronically corrected for pitch.)

A brief consideration of Robbie Robertson's production of "Love in Time" and Eno's production of "You May Feel Me Crying" is illuminating. Typically, the songs Orbison wrote and those written for him did not have instrumental breaks. Yet "Love in Time" has such a break. At the height of the emotional and formal climax of the song, Robertson plays a beautiful guitar solo that seems to take over from Orbison's voice in a manner that brings to mind Eric Clapton's homage that Orbison could do things with his voice that Clapton couldn't do with his guitar. Robertson does try to do with his guitar what Orbison might attempt with his voice, were he alive. Of course the song is not what it might have been had Orbison been present to collaborate. Had he been present, he would almost certainly have used his voice instead of the guitar, or at least combined his vocal pyrotechnics with the instruments, as he did on such other late-period songs as "You Got It" and "A Love So Beautiful." In those songs, the high point occurs when Orbison's voice sails away from language to become a pure musical instrument. (It is common for musicians who cover Orbison songs to replace such vocal pyrotechnics with instrumentals. Bonnie Raitt, for example, plays guitar in "You Got It," and Levon Helm uses the harmonica in "Mean Woman Blues.")

"You May Feel Me Crying" contains something even more shocking than an instrumental break. Bruce Springsteen, among many others, has observed that Orbison's songs abandoned the typical verse-bridge-chorus structure so common in pop at the time. But "You May Feel Me Crying" comes dangerously close to repeating that structure. Indeed, the chorus is repeated three times, the first two times identically. Only on the third chorus do we get a nuanced variation, when Orbison accents the word "me." Considering the crudely unfinished form in which the song was left, it is highly likely that Eno had to repeat the chorus three times; there was virtually nothing to work with. Orbison probably would have worked out a different structure, or at least a set of variations on the chorus. The extended instrumental fadeout is an equally unusual way to end an Orbison song.

In spite of these limitations, the song, as I argued in Chapter 5, is one of the most important of Orbison's career. To fully grasp the recorded voice as the complex aesthetic text of pop, we have to stop privileging the moment when the record was made or even finished. Orbison's posthumous career may help focus attention on the full theoretical implications of both Frith's and *Entertainment Weekly's* claim that in pop, in the end and beyond the end, it is the voice that matters.

One of Roy Orbison's legacies, then, may be that, out of apparent necessity, the possibilities for accomplished musicians of integrity returning to and reproducing recordings are now expanded. I am unaware of another instance of such highly regarded producers and musicians wanting to work with a "dead" artist. Here again the exception proves the rule: the remaining Beatles "reunited" with John Lennon when they took an unfinished, previously unreleased Lennon vocal track and made a new record in 1995. The new recording, "Free as a Bird" was, notably, produced by Jeff Lynne, who produced several posthumous Orbison tracks for the *King of Hearts* CD. Once again an extreme logic was needed: this was the *only* way a "new" Beatles song could be recorded and released. In contrast to the weak and minor Beatles effort, however, Orbison's *King of Hearts*, combined with "You May Feel Me Crying," have demonstrated that major music can be made and remade after the death of a pop vocalist. As of this writing, a number of Orbison's previously unreleased MGM songs that already circulate as bootleg tracks have been newly produced for possible release. As previously mentioned, one is a duet of "Bridge over Troubled Water" with Raul Malo. It is conceivable that in time we will have the release of the original MGM Orbison track, a newly produced version of that song using only Orbison's vocal from the MGM original, and the Malo duet. Orbison has left a huge catalogue of unreleased material (the number of unreleased songs is probably greater than the number of released songs) that in one form or another may continue to be part of his legacy.

Of course, Orbison left more conventional legacies as well. Interestingly, most of the singers who profess to have been influenced by Orbison sound nothing like him, write songs nothing like his, look and/or dress nothing like him, and perform nothing like he did. Indeed, they frequently seem to be nearly the opposite—flamboyant, charismatic, attractive, sexy performers with elaborate stage shows in which they move around a great deal and talk to their audiences. There are few if any overt clues to their love and admiration for Orbison. Part 1 of Dave Marsh's book on Bruce Springsteen is entitled "Only the Lonely" and begins with a quotation from the Orbison song. But Orbison is mentioned again only once, near the end of the book, when Marsh notes the reference to Orbison in the lyrics of "Thunder Road." If Springsteen did not actually sing about Orbison by name, who would ever associate him with Springsteen's music, with "Thunder Road" or any other Springsteen song? Springsteen's love for Orbison is not in doubt. He had the honor of inducting Orbison into the Rock 'n' Roll Hall of Fame, and made an impassioned and poetic speech on the occasion; he expressed a reverence bordering on awe in the videotaped concert *Roy Orbison and Friends: A Black and White Night*. But listen to Springsteen's music till the end of time, and you will never hear Roy Orbison in it. Mick Jagger has remarked, "From watching Roy, I learned how to sing a dramatic ballad," but no one is likely to think of Orbison while listening to Jagger sing (Goldberg 1989). And who would recognize Orbison's influence in the work of Leonard Cohen? Yet, according to Cohen's biographer, Orbison was the musical signature for Cohen's 1988 tour. "In rehearsal Cohen would tell the band to 'make it like Roy Orbison would do it,' which led to an onstage joke, 'Orbisize this song.' The musicians had a picture of Orbison pasted into their chart folder" (Nadel 1996, 251).

There are several possible reasons for this unusual state of affairs. Many of Orbison's songs are notoriously difficult to sing, at least to sing the way Orbison sang them. They require a more powerful voice, with a greater octave range, than most pop singers possess. Recall Jeff Lynne's remark that he had learned a great deal from working with Orbison, all of it useless, as the other singers he worked with lacked Orbison's vocal skills. There are bootleg recordings of Bruce Springsteen's live version of "Crying," a song he performed during one of his tours for sound checks prior to the concerts. Although his rendition is heartfelt, Springsteen was wise not to add it to his concert repertoire; he simply doesn't have the range or power that he reaches for in the performance.

The same is undoubtedly true for performance styles as well. The quality of the singing and the songs has to be extremely high to focus a rock audience's attention without the aid of any stage show or entertaining interaction between performer and audience. Nik Cohen has captured beautifully the paradox of Orbison's successful but unusual performance style:

> The last time I saw him was the 1966 New Musical Express poll winner's concert and he shared the bill with the Beatles, the Rolling Stones, the Walker Brothers, Cliff Richard, the Shadows, Dusty Springfield, the Who,

and umpteen others, the full flower of British pop. With hardly any exceptions, he cut them to pieces ... his puff-pastry face and those impenetrable tinted glasses. All the time he was on stage he didn't move an inch, didn't even nod his head. He just stamped his foot, stood his ground, and belted ... he banged it out so solid, so impossibly confident, that he made everything that had gone before seem panicky. (Cohen 1969, 68–69)

After the sixties, as rock 'n' roll "grew up," stage shows became ever more complex, with elaborate lighting, professional choreography, special effects, large-screen video, and so on. Orbison's direct influence as a performer has been as minimal as his influence as a singer—one does not hear or see him in the work of others. But there are exceptions. One can, for example, hear Orbison's vocal influence in some of the work of Chris Isaak and Raul Malo. Indeed, one of the few daring covers of an Orbison song is Isaak's version of "Only the Lonely" on his *Baja Sessions* CD. Although Isaak did not attempt to reproduce the famous Orbison trademark "operatic" production, his range and style are extremely nuanced, and he deliberately sings sophisticated variations on Orbison's phrasings.[2]

Cover versions are, of course, another means of gauging an artist's influence. Isaak is not the only singer to cover Orbison's songs since his death. The covers worth mentioning are Bonnie Raitt's rendition of "You Got It" on the *Boys on the Side* soundtrack (a single of the song was a modest hit on the adult contemporary charts); Dwight Yoakam's cover of "Claudette" on *Under the Covers;* the Cox Family's cover of "Blue Bayou" on *Beyond the City;* and Don Byron's cover of "It's Over" on *A Fine Line: Arias and Lieder.* In addition, several songs that Orbison was writing and planning to record at the time of his death have been finished and recorded by others. Notably, Rodney Crowell recorded "What Kind of Love" (Rodney Crowell, Will Jennings, Roy Orbison) on *Life is Messy,* and k. d. lang included "Till the Heart Caves In" (T-Bone Burnett, Bob Neuwirth, Roy Orbison) on *Drag.* It is also worth noting that these covers are performed in a wide range of styles—country, bluegrass, R&B, pop, rock, and jazz. Still, if one were to measure Orbison's influence by the covers of his songs or the recording by others of songs he wrote but never recorded himself, it would be nearly as slight as his direct influence on anyone's vocal style.

Orbison's influence as a songwriter, while not much greater, has been more complex. Dave Marsh has claimed that "Orbison's way of describing archetypal psychological predicaments ... certainly was the inspiration for all of Bruce Springsteen's songs of restless, troubled hearts" (Marsh 1989b, 28). Undoubtedly, the "darkness" in *Darkness at the Edge of Town*, for example, can also be linked to the darkness of Orbison's songs, but nothing about Springsteen's recording of "Darkness at the Edge of Town" recalls Orbison. Albert Goldman claims that "Please Please Me" was "inspired primarily by Roy Orbison" (Goldman 1988, 131). While Lennon himself confirmed that he and McCartney used Orbison as a model for the song, George Martin claimed that he changed the song in such a manner as to minimize the comparison with Orbison, and the released version certainly bears Martin out. Critics have also noted that Lennon's "Imagine" is indebted to Orbison's dream ballads, and while this claim is credible, nothing in the song resembles Orbison's work. Bernie Taupin has said that "Don't Let the Sun Go Down on Me" was his and Elton John's effort to approximate an Orbison song, but it stands as a single moment in large body of work that is nothing like Orbison's. Mick Jagger has acknowledged Orbison's influence on "Satisfaction," but there is little if anything in the song that sounds like Orbison. In short, none of these songs recalls Orbison in any direct way.

Diane Warren credited Orbison as cowriter of a song she composed after his death, but the circumstances are revealing. She originally worked with Orbison on *Mystery Girl*. When the two first met, she started to play Orbison a song she had begun writing, but he quickly took over and her idea was dropped. Although she is credited as a cowriter on "Careless Heart," she later returned to her initial idea and finished the song in the way she thought he would have done it. While a touching tribute, and possibly the first time an artist was credited on a song written after his death, this was an isolated moment in the career of a highly successful songwriter whose music generally does not call Orbison to mind.

The Bee Gees have also acknowledged Orbison's influence. According to Maurice Gibb, "Roy was part of the biggest influence we ever had on our ballads because of the orchestrations, the build-up, the emotions that they applied to every record he made." Gibb called Orbison's talent "unbeatable. And I know everybody in the business feels that way about Roy. Every person I spoke to from songwriters, to up and coming songwriters to people who've been writing for years and years have all said the same thing, how Roy was such an influence on their writing" (*Roy Orbison: The Anthology* 1999).

It seems beyond question that Orbison's influence extended far and wide, yet it is difficult to identify a single band or artist whose work clearly and consistently shows that influence. This was not the case with other influential rock artists, whose influence can be clearly identified in the work of others. Take the Beatles. As soon as they achieved success, they had a clearly traceable impact on other groups. The Dave Clark 5, who appeared shortly thereafter, showed the Beatles' influence in everything from their fashions in clothing and hair styles to their songwriting and harmonies. And key moments in the evolution of the Beatles' style—such as the *Sergeant Pepper's Lonely Hearts Club Band* album—had an immediate impact on others. Partly as a result of this LP, albums began to be more integrated, unified wholes rather than more or less random collections of songs.

Orbison had no such immediate, direct effect. There was no Dave Clark 5 equivalent; indeed, there was no one who looked or sounded even remotely like him. Pop rockers did not develop an operatic style in the wake of "Running Scared," nor did they abandon the typical verse-chorus-verse structure of rock at the time. Bob Dylan, Elvis Presley, and Bruce Springsteen have all had direct major influences on rock 'n' roll in a manner that Orbison has not had and probably never will have. Orbison went his way, and rock 'n' roll continued on its parallel path.

In Chapter 1 I quoted Robert Hilburn's observation about the wide variety of artists who paid tribute to Orbison at the 1990 tribute concert in Los Angeles. Anyone attending that concert must have been struck by the diverse array of musical styles and musicians, from traditional country to blues to the wildest extremes of rock 'n' roll. The presence of such country musicians as Dwight Yoakam, Ricky Skaggs, Radney Foster, and Larry Gatlin points to the unusual relationship Orbison bore to country music. On the one hand, there is a strand of his career that places him within country rather than rock or pop, or that at least puts him on the line between the two. After his rockabilly career at Sun, Orbison recorded nearly all of his Monument work in Nashville, and he lived in Hendersonville, Tennessee. Indeed, he was often characterized as a favorite son in Nashville. At MGM he recorded albums covering the songs of Hank Williams and Don Gibson. In the 1980s his career revived with his duet of "That Lovin' You Feeling" with Emmylou Harris, a song that made it onto the Top 10 country charts. *The Class of '55*, while not a big hit, had a strong mid-level presence on the country album charts. His duet of "Crying" with k. d. lang, who was at the time considered a country artist, further anchored his association with country music, and by the time of his death "You Got It" was a crossover hit, charting in pop, adult contemporary, and country music.

On the other hand, as I have noted, Orbison enjoyed no success on the country charts with either his 1960s hits (Presley, by contrast, had many crossover hits) or his MGM covers. Other Sun artists, such as Conway Twitty and Jerry Lee Lewis, had immensely successful country careers during the 1970s, after falling from the pop charts. For all of his affinities with country music, Orbison was never popular with country music audiences, though he has plenty of admirers in the field, just as he does within many other musical genres. Dwight Yoakam calls Orbison "completely unique" and says, "If a lesson is to be learned for any singer/songwriter it's to follow Roy's lead in allowing your vocal instrument to lead you on your journey" (*Roy Orbison: The Anthology* 1999). Vince Gill has remarked, "Roy's ability to write songs with melodies to perfectly match his glorious voice were what to me made him stand out way above the rest. His abilities to write and sing were effortless and forever inspiring" (*Very Best of Roy Orbison*, liner notes 1996).

Several interesting patterns do emerge from the variety of artists who admired, worked with, and paid tribute to Orbison. As Gill indicates, the combination of the writing and the voice was special and highly personal. Klaus Meine of the Scorpions agrees: "Roy had a very unique voice. When I heard, 'Oh, Pretty Woman' the first time it was inspiring." It is probably fair to say that Orbison was more an inspiration to other artists than an influence on them. Brian Eno has called Orbison "one of the truly original songwriters and genuine soul singer[s]." Gill, Eno, Yoakam, and Meine are worlds apart musically, but all value the combination of Orbison's songwriting and voice as "unique" and "truly original." In another hyperbolic tribute, Bono called Orbison "an original of the species" (*Roy Orbison: The Anthology* 1999).

Many of Orbison's admirers speak of the intimacy and emotional intensity that distinguished Orbison's music from much rock of the time. Barry Gibb says, "He made emotion fashionable—that it was alright to talk and sing about very emotional things. For men to sing about very emotional things that counted . . . things in life" (*Roy Orbison: The Anthology* 1999). Bono has similarly emphasized the gender aspects of Orbison's music: "There is something very powerful to hear a male, especially, you know, someone as male as Roy, to sing in falsetto . . . it leaves you wide open as a man" (*Roy Orbison: The Anthology* 1999). Orbison opened rock 'n' roll to a wide range of emotions and intensity for these artists, far removed from the dominant macho posturing of the time. There were, to be sure, some elements of vulnerability in Elvis Presley, to take one example, but nothing comparable to Orbison. The combination of the intense songwriting and singing with the range of emotions made his music seem more personal. In this way it paved the way for, encouraged, and even inspired other artists to find their own voices and styles rather than copy his. This may indeed be where his greatest influence lies.

Once again, however, I would caution against seeing Orbison's emotionally charged music as somehow more "authentic" than the macho posturing that characterized other rock singers. Rock criticism frequently falls into the "authenticity" trap, a variation of the "roots" aesthetic. Many critics praise as "best" rock that they think is true to its roots and therefore more authentic than other rock music. This approach is similar to that of movie critics who praise certain Hollywood movies as more "realistic" than others. But the notion of authenticity in music is as misguided as the notion of realism in movies, and it is critical to remember that Orbison's music and persona were carefully constructed. He may have opened rock up to the expression of intense masculine vulnerability and fear, but those emotions are no more "authentic" than, say, Jerry Lee Lewis's macho carryings on—just different. The difference itself, of course, is of great importance, and in it lies a major part of Orbison's legacy. He was to white rock what Little Richard was to black rock—a figure of startling gender difference. Orbison was the first important white rock singer to be a true oddball, and this is another of his legacies.

In his autobiography, *Take It Like a Man*, Boy George writes of his album *Tense Nervous Headache*, "I didn't know if I wanted to be Prince, Bowie, or Roy Orbison, who I convincingly impersonated on 'Don't Cry,' a rumbling string-driven ballad" (Boy George 1995, 447). Boy George, of course, was another of rock's "weird" gender figures, both during his time as lead singer of Culture Club and his later, much publicized coming out as a homosexual. David Bowie, another of Boy George's models, is himself an Orbison fan and a rock star who epitomized androgyny and made much of his bisexuality early in his career. When k. d. lang recorded her duet of "Crying" with Roy Orbison, she had not yet come out as a lesbian, but her image was one of gender disruption and she, like Boy George, later acknowledged her sexual orientation publicly. Lang has spoken repeatedly of how important Orbison's music—and her collaboration with him—is to her. In her concerts, she routinely pays tribute to him before singing "Crying." That homosexuals, lesbians, and bisexuals should be drawn to Orbison's music is not surprising, although, to the best of my knowledge, it has never been rumored that Orbison was anything but heterosexual. Given his troubled, unconventional masculinity and his perverse masochist aesthetic, it makes perfect sense that artists who felt alienated by conventional gender categories would be drawn to him. During the early 1960s, a period of strict gender conformity, Orbison's music was already crying out in spirit with what would not be openly articulated until the posthumously released plaintive cry, "There are stronger men than me." Orbison had the courage to be different as a singer, a songwriter, a performer, and a star persona at a crucial moment in the evolution of rock 'n' roll. There are no stronger or more inspiring men than that.

Appendix

Analysis of Songs and Recordings

or the sake of brevity and familiarity, I am focusing in this
analysis on a comparatively small number of Roy Orbison
recordings, most them from the Monument period. All of
the Monument recordings are credited as produced by Fred
Foster, though Foster later claimed that Wesley Rose produced "Goodnight" and "(Say) You're My Girl" (see Chapter 1). "Crawling Back," the sole MGM song, credits Bill
McElhiney as arranging the orchestra and chorus and Val
Valentin as director of engineering; no producer is credited.
All of these songs were written by Orbison or cowritten with
Joe Melson and Bill Dees, his two major songwriting col-
laborators. All were initially released between 1961 and 1965
and are currently available on CD, including the box set
Orbison 1955–1965. I am deeply indebted in the following
analyses to Brandt Sleeper, who served as a music consultant,
helping me find a clear and musically accurate way of writing about these songs without becoming bogged down in
overly technical language accessible only to those with formal training in music.[1]

I want to stress at the outset that part of what makes this
task so challenging is that Orbison not only departed from
many of the norms of his time but went beyond simply
replacing one formula with another. Although his songs have

some common characteristics, they are, with a few exceptions, remarkably different from each other. "Running Scared," for example, builds with a near maniacal intensity toward its climax, while "It's Over" builds toward two climaxes, the second more dramatic than the first. Other songs, like "Goodnight" and "In Dreams," offer diverse melodic material that could be the basis of many songs rather than be unified in one. "Crawling Back" has a crashing climax, but rather than ending there it concludes with an unexpectedly soft, quiet section. None of these songs follows the pattern of any of the others, except in the most general manner (e.g., they build toward a climax that is either remarkably powerful and/or sung in an eerily high falsetto).

Perhaps the simplest way to begin is by tracing the patterns of musical development in a number of Orbison songs. Each section of new material is simply identified with a letter. Song form is generally binary, such as A B (verse-chorus), ternary, such as A B A, or based on combinations such as A A B A. Since some of Orbison's songs begin with an introduction, those will be identified as an "Intro" rather than the first section of the song proper. Thus, for example, "In Dreams" (1963) can be described as follows: Intro-A-B-C-D-E-F. In this song, lyrics and music written by Orbison, nothing repeats. Counting the "Intro," there are seven sections of changing, developing material in a period of two minutes and forty-eight seconds! The "Intro" is performed in an eight-bar "songsprecht," or speech-song, style like that used in some operas, musicals, and song cycles. Sometimes referred to as "sprechgesang" or "Sprechstimme," such techniques blur the line between speaking and singing—the singer hints at the melodic line without delivering the notes at precise pitches. Each of the following six sections is characterized by independent melodies and different chord progressions. The A section repeats an eight-bar progression. The B section is also sixteen bars, but the C, D, E, and F sections are all eight-bar melodies.

Like "In Dreams," "It's Over" (Orbison-Dees, 1964) begins with an "Intro," followed by a repeated A section. The rhythm of this section is very unusual, however, in that it adds two beats after two of the lines (a point to which I shall return). At this point, we are introduced to the C section in a very shortened form with the lyric "It's over," here stated only one time! It initially seems like an add-on to the A section, but it returns in its full form as the C section. Orbison then jumps into a new melodic twelve-bar B section. At the end of the B section we get another two-beat delay, followed by the full four-bar C section with the lyric repeated. In extending the phrase through repetition, we get a sense of completeness of the previously heard fragment. We then return to the A section and a final C section. Thus, this two-minute-forty-six-second song can be described as follows: Intro-A-C-B-C-A-C. This brief schematic, however, doesn't hint at the variety and complexity that result from the building intensity of the C sections, first briefly stated, then fully stated, then fully restated with a growing intensity due to changes in pitch and rhythm that will be discussed below.

"(They Call You) Gigolette" (Orbison-Melson, 1963) follows an Intro-A-B-A-C-D-E pattern. The A material stands in sharp contrast to the Intro. The B section may initially be interpreted as a chorus within the verse-chorus format so common in pop music, but the song never returns to either the melody or the lyric. The song then returns to the A section and the listener anticipates the expected B section to return as a chorus, but instead the song moves in an entirely different melodic and harmonic progression. Rather than returning to any recognizable material, this in turn leads into new melodic content that makes up a D section, which leads to a finale of yet more new material that ends the song on an unresolved climax.

By contrast, "Running Scared" (Orbison-Melson, 1961) departs from the normal verse-chorus form by introducing material that will repeat melodically, rhythmically, and with regard to chord progression. Yet the repetitions are varied in terms of pitch and orchestration. After four A sections building the same melody, rhythm, and chord progressions, Orbison moves into a new melody with the lyric "Then all at once." The lyric is also appropriate to describing the form of the music, as the new melody also appears all at once and is emphasized even more heavily by a modulation up a fourth to a C in the chord structure, this being the first appearance of the C major chord in the song. Thus, the form of the song is: A-A-A-A-B.

In contrast to "Running Scared, "Crying" (Orbison-Melson, 1961) introduces much new material and then repeats it in a modified form: A-B-C-D-E-A-B mod.-C mod.-D mod.-E mod. Unlike some of his songs that follow such a format, Orbison does not use an Intro section in "Crying." The repetition of the A section is very close to the first passage, the repetition of the B section changes only at the end. From the C section on, the song is sung about an octave higher in pitch, with additional variation. The song further complicates expectations with a B section that has an unusual length of seven bars rather than the more normative eight. In a related manner, "Goodnight" begins with an Intro that is followed by five different sections: Intro-A-B-C-D-E. The only consistent element is the key, and each of the various sections could have been the thematic material for five independent songs.[2]

With "Crawling Back" (Orbison-Dees, 1965) we have an entirely different form from any of the songs described above. It begins with an A section ("Only you . . .") that is repeated ("You know . . .") before introducing the B section ("After all . . ."), which initially resembles a chorus. This "chorus," however, begins a typical Orbison-style non-repeating chain of segments: B-C-D-E-F. Taking this "chorus" apart, we have after the B section a C section with a distinctly different melodic and harmonic content ("You know I would die . . .") followed by another complete departure ("People stop . . ."), leading to a climactic E section ("That you're lonely . . ."), which is contrasted with a soft, emotional F section ("When the world . . ."). Here the listener anticipates a recap or coda of the E or even E-F section, but instead, in a manner atypical for Orbison, it returns to the melodic content of the A section. Thus what sounds like a repeat of what would traditionally be called the chorus section is actually a repeat of the initial verse, but this time sung an octave higher. Thus the song can be described as follows: A-A-B-C-D-E-F-A-A. Ending a song with a verse is highly irregular in rock and roll. Even if we collapsed the B section down into a traditional chorus we would have the equally unusual form of A-A-B-A-A.

"(Say) You're My Girl" (Orbison-Dees, 1965) shares some characteristics with "Crawling Back," though it too is unique in the Orbison *oeuvre*. On the surface it seems to conform more closely to the pop music verse-chorus structure. The song begins with a typical Orbison "Intro," this time sung with a jazz-waltz musical accompaniment. We do not expect the Intro to be repeated, especially since the following A section is drastically different in melody, rhythm, and tone. The A section ("How have you . . .") switches from the jazzy waltz rhythm to a bouncy Calypso rhythm. This section is repeated with, "Oh no it won't be repeated." This leads to the B or "chorus" section on the lyric "Be my girl . . . ," which seems like a classic A-A-B or A-A-B-A-B form. But we quickly learn otherwise when the B section, rather than serving as a simple, unified chorus, develops into a complex A-B-C form within itself. "Be my girl . . ." begins the "chorus" and can be seen as the A section of the B section. With "I still don't," we progress into a new melodic and harmonic section, the B section within the B section. Next we enter the C section of the "chorus" with the lyric "With your big eyes." In a highly sophisticated manner, Orbison reintroduces the melody presented in the Intro. First he expands the note length of the original line ("Hello, may I . . .") on the new lyric "big eyes, full lips." Then he returns to the same notes and rhythm of the Intro line ("have this dance with you") on the lyric "high cheek bones and." "Personality girl" begins the Bd section, which then leads into the solo section, which is a shortened instrumental version of the A section. Then the song concludes with the B section, repeated with variation on the melody and ending with a tag of new material ("you're my girl," with harmony ending with cha-cha-cha).

Part of what makes "You're My Girl" so unusual is the extreme brevity of the various sections within the B section. They are almost too short to be identified. Indeed, the above schematic is somewhat simplified. Within Bb, for example, there is new material that could easily be classified as Bc. The important point is that what at first resembles a conventional chorus section turns into a richly shifting section of diverse new material. Indeed, this is an intensification of a technique that characterizes much of Orbison's songwriting and singing. I have listed the running times of these songs in order to stress how much new material is introduced in a very brief period of time. Orbison frequently compresses what sounds like half a dozen songs into the running time of one song! Part of their extraordinary dramatic power and complexity results from this strict coherence to Top 40 radio format. Ironically, had he used the longer free form that logic might dictate and that radio and album formats allowed and even encouraged in the late 1960s, his songs would (and in "Southbound Jericho Parkway" did) actually lose some of their power. "You're My Girl" reaches an extreme condensation in the B section that points to the heart of Orbison's creative departure from writing and singing repetitively.

"Oh, Pretty Woman" (Orbison-Dees, 1964) begins with a driving drum beat almost unheard of at the time. A guitar motif is then introduced and becomes the thread that holds the song together. The motif is unusual in that we first hear a five-note fragment of the full motif stated twice before then hearing the complete eight-note melody. The song itself is filled with asymmetrical sections. The opening lyric, "Pretty Woman walking down the street," introduces the A section. Then we have a two-beat extension bar as we begin the B section with "I don't believe." The extension is almost a foreshadowing of the extended B section that appears at the finale. This entire stanza is then repeated after the guitar motif is heard again. With the exception of the B sections, the entire song is harmonized. This helps set this section of the song, which will reappear in exaggerated form at the end, apart from the rest. The C section follows the repeated A-B section, beginning with the lyric, "Pretty woman stop a while." This is accentuated by both a modulation and new melodic material encompassing eight bars. The C section is repeated, beginning with "Pretty woman, yeah, yeah, yeah." The lyric "Cause I need you" introduces yet a new direction melodically and in terms of chord progression. At this point we return to the A-B section, but with a variation. The A section is modified with "Pretty woman, don't walk ..." and the song seems to stall on the B section, beginning with the lyric, "Don't walk away." Not only does the melody become suspended but we remain on the same chord and rhythm for twelve bars, until the lyric "But wait." Then we hear the five-note guitar motif stated twice again before the full eight-note motif, which is followed by the question, "Is she walking back to me?" Again, we are teased by the guitar motif, this time finally followed by the answer and the guitar motif fully stated. The form can be summarized as A-B-A-B-C-C-D-A-B extended.

It may be useful simply to summarize the variety of form in these Orbison songs:

"In Dreams": Intro, A, B, C, D, E, F
"It's Over": Intro, A, C, B, C, A, C
"(They Call You) Gigolette": Intro, A, B, A, C, D, E
"Running Scared": A, A, A, A, B
"Crying": A, B, C, D, E, F, A, B slightly mod., C mod., D mod.,
    E mod., F mod.
"Goodnight": Intro, A, B, C, D, E
"Crawling Back": A, A, B, C, D, E, F, A, A
"(Say) You're My Girl": Intro, A, A, Ba, Bb, Bc, Bd, A mod. (instr.
    solo), Ba, Bb, Bc, Bd, Concluding Tag
"Oh, Pretty Woman": A, B, A, B, C, C, D, A, B ext.

Of course, a schematic summary of the forms of the songs only hints at the total picture of the recordings. I want to try now to fill in these formal structures with some analysis of how the songs were produced and sung, using the same order of songs used above. "In Dreams" is comprised of eight-bar sections that, when chained together, total sixty-four (not including the Intro), which is not unusual. Each of the sections has a melody that fits within a five- to eight-note range. In addition to the unusual amount of melodic material, the various melodies combine to create a span of a two-octave range, well outside the range of most singers. Orbison sings in a falsetto and near contra-tenor range. Further complexity arises from the manner in which the song uses violins that play a countermelody in what amounts to a singing style of their own.

"It's Over" highlights several of Orbison's and Foster's singing and production techniques with respect to rhythm. The rhythm in the A section is unusual in that Orbison adds two beats after the lines "Whisper secrets to the wind" and "send falling stars that seem to cry." The song is in 4/4 time. When we count out the A section, we find that after four bars of four beats each Orbison pauses for two beats before he sings the next line. This occurs again at the end of the B section, when we get another two-beat delay and Orbison then hits us with the true, full-length C section. When we return to the familiar A section with "All the rainbows," we once again get the two-beat delay. Another two-beat delay occurs before the finale, which Orbison sings in full voice two octaves above the beginning of the song. When we finally get to the lyric "It's over," it is thrust upon us in rapid succession. Rhythmically, the melody is sung in half the time of the first or second versions, a technique of diminished meter referred to as "cut time." In other words, Orbison soars in full voice to the apex of pitch within the song, and he does so at twice the speed of the earlier two versions.

"It's Over" is unusual in that it builds toward two climaxes in two minutes and forty-six seconds. It accomplishes this through a systematic intensification of the C section. The first, abbreviated C section has a high note of G3, the second a high note of A5 (G4 is one note lower than A5, which makes the pitch difference about an octave higher than the first), and the last has a high note of B-flat 5, which is the highest note of the song. The song moves from D3 to B-flat 5 in full voice! This is an octave plus a fifth, or a thirteen diatonic note range in full voice (twelve chromatic notes make one octave, whereas eight diatonic notes make one octave). B-flat 5 is an octave above the full voice of a baritone, a fourth above the full voice of a tenor, and it is beyond the range of the full voice of an alto. Suffice it to say that few performers can do this.

"Only the Lonely," a song I have not analyzed above, has an even greater range. Here Orbison sings from B-flat 3 to C5, the C5 in falsetto. This represents two octaves plus a note, or a total of a seventeen-note range. Listening to the low note, Orbison sounds very much like a baritone, while the C5 has a tenor falsetto quality. The range he exhibits transcends even that of a classically trained vocalist in the baritone or tenor range. "(They Call you) Gigolette" moves from a gentle melodic introduction to a climax without resolution. Both the melody and the musical intensity progress from the beginning of the song to the end. If we look at the song in graphic waveform on a software system such as ProTools, "Gigolette" appears as a continuous amplitude crescendo from beginning to end. Within this structure we encounter Orbison's sophisticated use of shifting rhythms. The tempo of the song (beats per minute) is constant throughout, but the rhythm shifts in each section. During the "Intro" the rhythm is ambiguous, and by the latter part of the song we have a march-type pattern emphasized by the snare drum. It is precisely these constantly switching rhythms that make dancing to Orbison's songs so difficult.

"Running Scared" builds through repetition in a number of ways. We begin with the guitar alone. Next, snare drum and bass are added to the same progression. The third time, strings are added, while on the fourth pass background vocals are present. When we finally get to the B section, the orchestration becomes very elaborate, with the addition of strings and horns.

In "Running Scared," Orbison employs a rubato singing style, playing around the beat. Orbison maintains the tempo (beats per minute) but slows the singing down in one section and speeds it up in a later section to catch up to the tempo, which ticks along unaltered. He elongates certain notes such as those on the italicized words: "Just *running* scared ... each *place* we go ... so *afraid* ... that *he* might show." The tempo never changes, and he always ends on the correct beat. Underneath we hear the Bolero-like pattern around which he is singing and which defines the downbeat. At the lyric, "Then all at once" Orbison actually begins to sing with the Bolero-like pattern that he had previously been singing around. Basically, he locks into the rhythm that he had been ignoring. He is, however, always singing in tempo. If we tap our foot to the beat, it never changes. Nevertheless, what seemed to be a slow song now seems faster. This is further accentuated by the prominence of horns, accentuating the Bolero-like pattern. Added to this, the backup vocals become prominent and a high-hat rhythm of eighth notes is introduced from what sounds like a cymbal. Everything suddenly seems different and it catches our attention.

In effect, the rhythmic pattern of the singing changes and the other elements emphasize the new pattern. Initially, the lyrics sound as if they are in slow motion and "then all at once" we are thrust into the prevailing rhythmic pattern. The first part sounds almost dreamy, as the lyrics move around the guitar pattern. The singing, the writing, and the producing all combine here in a complex and indistinguishable manner.

Before continuing, it may be helpful to address the oft-noted connection between "Running Scared" and Ravel's *Bolero*. It is particularly important to clarify this, since many critics refer in general to *Bolero* when discussing Orbison's ballads (see Chapter 3). "Running Scared" does indeed share three specific connections to the Ravel composition. First, its rhythm is strongly reminiscent of that used by Ravel and can be schematized as follows (bold indicates accented notes):

bum
ba, ba, ba, **bum**
ba, ba, ba-**ba,** ba, ba-**ba,** ba, ba
bum
ba, ba, ba, **bum**
ba, ba, ba, **bum**
ba, ba, ba-**ba,** ba, ba,-**ba,** ba, ba
bum

Second, like *Bolero*, "Running Scared" starts softly and builds in intensity by adding instrumentation and volume as it progresses. Third, it is a string of A sections with a sudden, unexpected B section at the climax. Indeed, Fred Foster had asked Orbison to write a song around the rhythm in Ravel's *Bolero*. As I noted in Chapter 3, according to Foster, Orbison misread the 3/4 time signature as 4/4 (Escott 2001, 40).

The connection between "Running Scared" and *Bolero* has been generalized across Orbison's career, as if all his ballads followed the same form. A number of unfortunate consequences have resulted from this that may obscure critical understanding of Orbison's music. When reviewing the Cinemax cablecast of *Roy Orbison and Friends: A Black and White Night*, the *New York Times* noted that with the ballads, it sometimes sounded as if Orbison "may have overdosed at some point on Ravel's 'Bolero'" (O'Connor 1988).

In fact, however, "Running Scared" is Orbison's only major song with all three of the connections with Ravel's *Bolero* outlined above: it begins quietly with a *Bolero*-style rhythm, repeats its A section by continually adding instrumentation and volume to the series of repetitions, and ends with an unexpected B section. Indeed, most of Orbison's songs share none of the three characteristics. "It's Over," for example, begins with a crashingly loud drum introduction of its central rhythmic motif, immediately following Orbison's single vocal line of the Intro. The song then builds toward two climaxes and does not incessantly repeat its A section along the way. Nor does the rhythm in the song closely resemble that of *Bolero*. A song like "Gigolette" shares part of one of the three characteristics: it builds in one sonic wave of increasing sound from beginning to climax. But, unlike *Bolero*, it doesn't start softly. Indeed, immediately after Orbison sings the opening line, there is a loud orchestral punctuation. In bold contrast to "Running Scared," "Gigolette" constantly develops new melodic material rather than repeat its A section, which in fact never reappears. Furthermore, "Gigolette" never once employs a *Bolero*-like rhythm.

Indeed, when people generalize about the *Bolero*-like quality of Orbison's music, they can have only two things in mind: the manner in which his songs build to a crashing climax, and the rhythm they employ along the way. Yet neither of these things really distinguishes *Bolero*. It is the near maniacal focus on repetition, with varying orchestration and building intensity and volume followed by the brief, unexpected B section, that characterizes *Bolero*. Most of Orbison's songs in fact use a nearly opposite strategy: far from maniacal repetition, they contain enough melodic material for as many as five or six songs in less than three minutes. In fact, a lack of repetition is what best characterizes Orbison's songs.

It is true that Orbison is attracted to the rhythm of *Bolero* and that at times he employs it in his compositions and even the compositions of others. But that rhythm has been present in many popular songs. Orbison did not bring that rhythm into popular music; he merely gave it structural prominence in some of his work. Nor is that rhythm of particular aesthetic significance in itself. In many songs, it is little more than a cliché. What makes it unique in *Bolero* is the manner in which it is subjected to endless repetition as the work builds and intensifies its orchestrations. Of all of Orbison's major hits, "Running Scared" is the only one to follow that pattern.

The *Bolero*-like rhythm, however, points to a related aspect of Orbison's music: the frequent use of march-like rhythms. The rhythm in *Bolero* and Orbison's appropriation of it has a march-like feel to it. Of the songs analyzed here, both "Gigolette" and "The Crowd" also rely on march-like rhythms. Marches are generally of either a military or ceremonial nature, and it is perhaps no coincidence that Orbison recorded two military songs that use marches: "Distant Drums," during the

Monument period, and "There Won't Be Many Coming Home," during the MGM period. In the former he sings, "I hear the sound of distant drums," and the march of the soldiers, quiet at first, builds in volume and intensity throughout the song.

Consider for a moment two very popular works by Tchaikovsky: *Capricio Italien* and *Marche Slav*. Both works are so popular and accessible that they have entered the domain of light classical music. *Capricio Italien* uses a portion of the same rhythm that Ravel uses in Bolero:

> ba, ba, ba, **bum**
>
> ba, ba, ba, **bum**

Furthermore, it begins softly and is intensified during the first portion of the work. And, as the title suggests, *Marche Slav* uses a march-like rhythm that becomes very prominent in places that sound not unlike moments in songs like "The Crowd" and "Gigolette." It is useful also to remember that Orbison played in his high school marching band.

Finally, none of the characteristics of Ravel's *Bolero* define the Bolero romantico popular song form. While there are notable differences between the Cuban Bolero and the Mexican Bolero, neither is defined by Ravel's *Bolero* beat, building in intensity toward a crashing climax. Insofar as Orbison's music can be described as *Bolero*-like, the adjective only makes sense in regard to Ravel's composition, not the popular song form. The reference to Ravel is of limited value.

"Gigolette" is similar to "Running Scared" in that the tempo never changes but the rhythmic patterns within the sections do. Again, we have a march-type pattern that is emphasized by the snare drum in the latter part of the song. The main difference, of course, is that whereas only one such rhythmic shift occurs in "Running Scared," several occur in "Gigolette." In "The Crowd," however, Orbison uses a *fermata* technique whereby he actually disrupts the tempo. In a *fermata*, the performer holds the note longer than usual, intentionally arresting the music's tempo and causing a slight pause in the performance. On the lyric "steal," Orbison pauses the tempo before proceeding with the tune. This is a true *fermata* as opposed to the *rubato* technique in "Running Scared." Orbison similarly uses a *fermata* in "Only the Lonely," on the lyric *"You've ... got ... to ... take ... if you're lonely."*

In "Crying," Orbison once again uses a delay. In the D section, we not only have new melodic content; the harmonic progression also seems to stall as it is repeated on the line "left me standing." The subtle delay increases the anticipation of the lyric "crying," which is then sung four times over the now familiar harmonic progression of the previous B section. As the song develops, the melody becomes more intense both in vocal range and orchestration. The rhythm is initially introduced only with rhythm guitar, but by the return of the C section it becomes pronounced when the drums slowly bang it out. Orbison sings this section in a falsetto an octave above the previous version. He finishes the song, however, in full voice rather than falsetto. Technically, he could easily have sung the falsetto in full voice. Or he could have ended the song in falsetto rather than the powerful full voice he employs. His technique here, in other words, strongly varies the vocal style of the song in a manner that is consistent with the variety in the songwriting style and the instrumental production style. Nothing is repeated in such a way that it sounds the same twice. At the finale of "Crying," the initial rhythm returns, full of bravado and heavy orchestration.

In "Goodnight," Orbison once again employs the *fermata* technique both in the Intro and once again at the song's conclusion. In the following, the italicized words are the ones on which he holds the notes. From the "Intro" and the beginning of the A section: "My Lovely woman *child*, / I found you *out* running wild with someone *new* / You've been *untrue*, and everybody *knows* we're *through*. / But I can't *say good*-bye to you." The last two words of the song are similarly emphasized.

In "Crawling Back," Orbison varies his vocal styling in yet another unexpected way. He sings the climactic-sounding E section in a powerful full voice that is then contrasted with the quiet F section. At this point we anticipate a recap or coda of the E or even E-F section, but this does not occur. Although stylistically similar to these sections, Orbison uses the melodic content of the A verse section, though this time in a powerful vocal style an octave above the original. But, as in the E and F sections, rather then ending in the powerful style, the final phrase is sung in contrasting quiet softness. What sounds like a repeat with variation of the chorus section is actually a repeat of the verse.

In "(Say) You're My Girl," Orbison uses yet another technique for varying the music. Unlike his other songs, here the melody of the Intro returns in the C section. Orbison reintroduces the melody by expanding the note length of the original line ("Hello, may I . . .") on the new lyrics ("big eyes, full lips"). He then uses the same notes and rhythm of the introductory line ("have this dance with you") on the lyric "high cheek bones."

In "Oh, Pretty Woman," with the exception of the B section ("I don't believe you") and its extended reprise at the end (Don't walk away"), the entire song is harmonized by a countermelody. When we first hear Orbison singing without the harmony in the B section, it sets the section apart from the rest of the song. His voice has a liquid purity that the harmonies cover up. This difference in singing and recording technique helps set up the extended return of the B section in the song's finale, where once again Orbison's voice seems to soar to the foreground when the harmony disappears.

While I hope the above analyses outline some important distinguishing features of Orbison's songs, singing style, and the production style, they cannot, of course, capture the quality of heard music. I hope that they may be of some value to the new listener who turns to (or the familiar listener who returns to) the songs with these points in mind. I am mindful of Simon Frith's insight that we do not really hear and respond to what musicology analyzes in these songs; we respond rather to the voice that sings them—in this case a voice so beyond comparison that description is impossible. I have kept this Appendix brief; it is at best a roadmap to be used while listening to the music. Although it is much easier to talk about lyrics than singing style, there is a connection between the unique songwriting, singing, and production styles of Orbison's recordings outlined here and the formal and ideological analyses of the music that constitute much of this study.

Notes

Chapter One

1. All of these recordings are now available, many for the first time, in the box set *Orbison: 1956–1965* (Bear Records).

2. Although never released, those songs are now also available on *Orbison 1956–1965* and form a significant part of understanding Orbison's development at the beginning of his recording career. Of equal importance is the 1995 release of *Are You Ready?* by the Teen Kings, a CD included in the box set *Orbison 1956–1965*, comprising a live 1956 performance by Orbison's band at that time.

3. Although they went unreleased at the time, they are also included in the Orbison box set.

4. Fortunately, bootleg recordings of these concerts exist and a few have been remastered and were released in 1999 on Orbison Records as *The Official Bootleg Series, Vol. 1*.

Chapter Two

1. My account of Orbison's persona describes its development in the United States. There are significant variations in Europe and elsewhere in the world. During part of his career, for example, he had a much greater presence on radio and television in England than he had in the United States. The cover art for his singles and albums abroad also varied. Further study is needed of how differing receptions inflected Orbison's music and persona in different ways. The element of mystery, for example, may have been less extreme in England than it was in the United States.

Chapter Four

1. Dreams frequently have a sexual component, and Orbison's dreams are no exception. In a list entitled "Onan's Greatest Hits: The Twenty-Five Greatest Songs about Masturbation," Dave Marsh and Kevin Stein include "Only the

189

Lonely" as one of the great rock masturbation songs (March and Stein 1984, 465–66). Though the song is not literally about masturbation, the opening line— "Only the lonely know the way I feel tonight"—invokes masturbation, the night-time activity of the lonely. The song "Darkness" is even more explicit in the manner in which it intertwines images of a lonely man hallucinating voices and images in a feverish desire: "I long to hold you, thrill to your charms." Within this context, "thrill" has strong sexual connotations. Orbison was actually more explicit in "Pantomime," from the MGM period. After singing about his lonely exclusion from partying, he sings, "Get set for lonely fun time." Although the line literally seems to refer to being lonely during a loud party, the phrase "lonely fun time" has sexual connotations.

2. Although Orbison was the most successful, several other singers of the time explored melodramatic excess, Johnny Ray foremost among them. Orbison recorded a cover version of his hit "Cry." Johnnie Ray's "Cry" is less extreme than many of Orbison's melodramatic songs, as the male persona in the song sings to a woman whom he urges to cry. Nevertheless, *The Rolling Stone Encyclopedia of Rock & Roll* notes that "Ray is frequently cited as the first popular singer to break with the cool, professional stance of such early crooners like Perry Como" (1983, 461). Arnold Shaw, in his book *The Rockin' '50s*, subtitles his section on Ray "The Anatomy of Self-Pity" and notes that "no one seemed prepared for the emotive singing Ray represented" (Shaw 1988, 52). Ray adopted a near-hysterical performance style when he sang the song in concert. The *New York Times* review wrote, "Ray sings like a man in an agony of suffering. Drenched in tears. . . . His hair falls over his face. He clutches at the microphone and behaves as if he were about to tear it apart. His arms shoot out in wild gesticulations and his outstretched fingers are clenched and unclenched" (quoted in Shaw 1988, 52). The review concludes, "This young man's style speaks for young people beset by fears and doubts in a difficult time" (53). *Rock of Ages: The Rolling Stone History of Rock & Roll* sums it all up much more succinctly in describing Johnnie Ray as a "fragile, almost effeminate boy . . . who took his own advice every time he performed his smash hit 'Cry'" (Ward, Stokes, and Tucker 1986, 86). From one perspective, then, Orbison stands in stark contrast to Ray, singing motionless on the stage while Ray used his body most expressively. Yet, as I have argued, Orbison's motionlessness was like a paralysis of fright. When he wasn't crying, he was running scared. Like Ray, he also had a fragile body that departed from the rock 'n' roll norm.

3. It is worth noting that several of Orbison's more conventionally restrained songs, such as "Dream Baby" and "Candy Man," were not written by him, whereas all of the characteristic hits of melodramatic excess were. Much as Foster understood the need to have rockers break up the potential monotony of the ballads, he seems also to have grasped the need to rein in Orbison's melodramatic excess by having him record songs written for him by others. This middle-period strategy is quite different from the late-period strategy best seen on *Mystery Girl*, where all the songs written for Orbison by others refer to his unique songwriting style.

Chapter Five

1. Ambiguity surrounds the deaths of both Fuller and Ace. Fuller was found dead in his car and Ace shot himself (see Rees and Crampton 1996; Clayson 1997; Salem 1999). Regardless, Orbison may have been drawn to these songs in part by their extra-textual associations with the deaths of the artists who first recorded them.

Chapter Six

1. In 1987 I wrote an essay entitled "'You're Like Me': In David Lynch's Dreams." It was published in *SPOT/A Publication of the Houston Center for Photography* under the title "'You're Like Me': Reading *Blue Velvet*." Lew Thomas, *SPOT*'s editor, made the change, fearing that my title might be obscure to his readership. He wanted to stress the film title, while I wanted to stress the connection between Roy Orbison's "In Dreams" and the role of dreams in Lynch's vision. I mention this for two reasons. First, at the time of the film's release, the use of Orbison's song seemed central to me, and in fact Frank's somewhat startling assertion to Jeffrey ("You're like me") was linked to its use. Second, I refer to several aspects of the context of the 1986 reception of the film in my discussion here, which is a minimally revised version of my 1987 essay.

2. Martha Nochimson points out that the line originally was "You like me" but that Lynch misheard it in editing as "You're like me." He liked what he heard better than what he had written and changed it (Nochimson 1997, 239). That Lynch changed the line testifies to how important this theme was to him.

3. This description of the film is based on the U.S. VHS videotape. The scene that appears on the DVD version is quite different, and "You May Feel Me Crying" is in fact used in a related but different scene. Regardless of the circumstances surrounding the two versions, the VHS version more fully foregrounds the disturbing sexual nature of the Orbison song.

Chapter Seven

1. Interestingly, Bill Millar's liner notes for the *Complete Velvets CD* begins, "The Velvets didn't conform to any of doo wop's norms." Millar goes on to note that, "like their mentor Roy Orbison, they sang songs which straddled that increasingly invisible line between country and pop." I would simply add that not conforming to the norms of doo-wop also connect them to Orbison, who did not conform to the pop-rock norms of his time.

2. This is not, of course, to say that there is not or cannot be a black masochist aesthetic. It is simply to say that the dominant cultural model of black masculinity was far removed from Orbison's passive, suffering dreamer. Some black men can and do occupy such a position, but the white appropriation of black masculinity in the 1950s allowed no such option.

3. The reception of Orbison's records among African Americans is puzzling. During the initial period of his Monument hits, between 1960 and 1964, Orbison

had five crossover hits on the R&B charts: "Only the Lonely" (which reached number fourteen and remained on the charts seven weeks), "Blue Angel," "In Dreams," "Mean Woman Blues" (which peaked at number eight and was on the charts for six weeks), and "Blue Bayou" (Whitburn 2000). Except for "Mean Woman Blues," it is hard to understand why these songs would appeal to an R&B audience, but in the same period several white pop singers whose music bore little or no relation to black music crossed over, including Frankie Avalon, Neil Sedaka, and the Beach Boys.

Chapter Eight

1. He knew then that some of them would never return home, and later cowrote and recorded a song about war entitled "There Won't Be Many Coming Home."

2. Chris Isaac paid elaborate homage to Orbison on the opening episode of the 2001 season of his Showtime series *The Chris Isaac Show*. The episode, entitled "In the Name of Love," deals with a reporter (Bridget Fonda) who wants to interview Isaac for a book she is writing on Orbison. Isaac, who calls Orbison a "musical genius," is reluctant to participate in what he fears will be a sensationalistic "tell-all" account of Orbison's life. When he meets the reporter however, he falls in love with her and makes up stories about Orbison simply to prolong the interview and begin a personal relationship with her.

Appendix

1. Brandt Sleeper has a bachelor's degree in musicology and a master's degree in film, with a minor in recording studio production, from the University of Arizona. He is a classically trained pianist with an extensive jazz background. As a professional musician, Sleeper has performed rock, pop, jazz, country, reggae, and salsa for twenty-five years, and has scored music for film and video.

2. This analysis has since been confirmed by Colin Escott, who claims that "Goodnight," "according to Bill Dees . . . was three or four songs cobbled into one" (Escott 2001, 63).

Works Cited

Amburn, Ellis. 1990. *Dark Star: The Roy Orbison Story.* New York: Lyle Stuart.

Atkinson, Michael. 1997. *Blue Velvet.* London: British Film Institute.

Arizona Daily Star. 1993. "High Court to Decide if Rappers Made Fair Use of Orbison Song." Nov. 10.

Barthes, Roland. 1977. *Image—Music—Text.* Trans. Stephen Heath. New York: Hill and Wang.

Bingham, Dennis. 1994. *Acting Male: Masculinities in the Films of James Stewart, Jack Nicholson, and Clint Eastwood.* New Brunswick, N.J.: Rutgers University Press.

Boy George, with Spencer Bright. 1995. *Take It Like a Man.* New York: Harper Collins.

Byron, Don. 2000. *A Fine Line: Arias and Lieder,* liner notes. Hollywood: Capitol Records.

Campbell, Bob. 1986. Review of *Blue Velvet. Arizona Daily Star,* Oct. 10, 1D.

Chion, Michel. 1995. *David Lynch.* Trans. Robert Julian. London: British Film Institute.

Clark, Mike. 1991. "John Candy Sweetens 'Lonely'." *USA Today,* May 24, 7D.

Clayson, Alan. 1989. *Only the Lonely: Roy Orbison's Life and Legacy.* New York: St. Martin's Press.

———. 1997. *Death Discs: An Account of Fatality in the Popular Song.* London: Sanctuary Publishing.

Cohn, Nik. 1969. *Rock from the Beginning.* New York: Pocket Books.

Complete Velvets, liner notes. 1996. Ace Records.

Dickerson, James. 1996. *Goin' Back to Memphis: A Century of Blues, Rock 'n' Roll, and Glorious Soul.* New York: Schirmer Books.

Diebel, Mary. 1993. "Court to Decide if Rap Song Is Parody, Copyright Violation." *Arizona Daily Star,* Nov. 7, A3.

Down Beat. 1989. March 13.

Dyer, Richard. 1982. "Don't Look Now: The Male Pin-Up." *Screen* 23 (3–4): 61–73.

Eisenberg, Evan. 1987. *The Recording Angel: Explorations in Phonography.* New York: McGraw-Hill.

Ellis, John. 1982. *Visible Fictions: Cinema, Television, Video.* London: Routledge & Kegan Paul.

Escott, Colin. 2001. *Orbison.* Book with *Orbison 1955–1965* box set. Hambergen, Germany: Bear Family Records.

Escott, Collin, with Martin Hawkins. 1991. *Good Rockin' Tonight: Sun Records and the Birth of Rock 'n' Roll.* New York: St. Martin's Press.

Fanon, Frantz. 1967. *Black Skin, White Masks.* Trans. Charles Lam Markmann. New York: Grove Press.

Feather, Leonard. 1965. *Pop Goes Basie,* liner notes. Reprise Records.

Frith, Simon. 1996. *Performing Rites: On the Value of Popular Music.* Cambridge: Harvard University Press.

Gates, David. 1988. "The Voice That Sang in the Dark: Rock and Roll's Mr. Lonely." *Newsweek,* Dec. 19, 73.

Goldberg, Michael, with Jeffrey Resner and Steven Pond, comp. 1989. "Tributes." *Rolling Stone.* Jan., 32–33.

Goldman, Albert. 1988. *The Lives of John Lennon.* New York: William Morrow.

Greenhouse, Linda. 1993. "Court Enters New Era in Rap Copyright Case." *New York Times,* March 30, A16.

Harvey, John. 1995. *Men in Black.* Chicago: University of Chicago Press.

Hawkins, Martin. 1986. *Go Go Go,* liner notes. Charly Records.

Helm, Levon, with Stephen Davis. 1993. *This Wheel's on Fire: Levon Helm and the Story of the Band.* New York: William Morrow.

Hilburn, Robert. 1989. "The Big Surprise at Orbison Tribute." *Los Angeles Times,* Feb. 26, F1, F7.

———. 2000. "'High Fidelity' Right Up There with All-time Greatest Rock Films." *Arizona Republic,* April 21, 6.

Hinckley, David. 1988. "Farewell to 'One of Those 50s Kids.'" *New York Daily News,* Dec. 9, D20.

Holden, Stephen. 1991. "The Pop Life." *New York Times,* April 17.

Internet Movie Database. 1999. User Comments on *Little Voice.* Accessed at <www.u.s.imdb.com/Title?0147004> (Jan. 19).

Jarrett, Michael. 1998. *Sound Tracks: A Musical ABC.* Vols. 1–3. Philadelphia: Temple University Press.

Jarvis, Jeff. 1988. Review of *Roy Orbison and Friends: A Black and White Night. People,* Jan. 11, 9.

Kaleta, Kenneth C. 1995. *David Lynch.* New York: Twayne.

Kennedy, Rick, and Randy McNutt. 1999. *Little Labels—Big Sound: Small Record Companies and the Rise of American Music.* Indianapolis: Indiana University Press.

Kent, Nick. 1994. *The Dark Stuff.* New York: DaCapo Press.

Lehman, Peter. 1978. "Script/Performance/Text: Performance Theory and Auteur Theory." *Film Reader* 3: 197–206.

———. 1987. "'You're Like Me': Reading *Blue Velvet.*" *Spot: A Publication of the Houston Center for Photography* 5 (spring): 4–5.

———, ed. 1990. "Texas 1868/America 1956: *The Searchers.*" *Close Viewings: An Anthology of New Film Criticism.* Tallahassee: Florida State University Press.

———. 1993. *Running Scared: Masculinity and the Representation of the Male Body.* Philadelphia: Temple University Press.

Lott, Eric. 1995. *Love and Theft: Blackface Minstrelsy and the American Working Class.* New York: Oxford University Press.

Luhr, William, and Peter Lehman. 1989. *Returning to the Scene: Blake Edwards.* Vol. 2. Athens: Ohio University Press.

Lynch, David. 2002. Unpublished interview by Peter Lehman. April 19.

Maltin, Leonard. 1996. *1997 Movie and Video Guide.* New York: Signet.

Marsh, Dave. 1987a. "All That You Dream." *Rock & Roll Confidential* 49 (Aug.): 7–8.

———. 1987b. *Glory Days: Bruce Springsteen in the 1980s.* New York: Pantheon Books.

———. 1989a. "Crying." *Rock & Roll Confidential* 69 (Jan.): 1–2.

———. 1989b. "Music." *Playboy*, April 28.

Marsh, Dave, and Kevin Stein. 1984. *The Book of Rock Lists.* New York: Dell.

Meyer, Leonard B. 1967. *Music, the Arts, and Ideas: Patterns and Predictions in Twentieth-Century Culture.* Chicago: University of Chicago Press.

Miller, James. 1999. *Flowers in the Dustbin: The Rise of Rock and Roll, 1947–1977.* New York: Simon and Schuster.

Morrison, Craig. 1996. *Go Cat Go!: Rockabilly Music and Its Makers.* Urbana: University of Illinois.

Morthland, John. 1990. Booklet for the Time-Life Music box set *Roy Orbison: 1960–1965.*

Mulvey, Laura. 1975. "Visual Pleasure and Narrative Cinema." *Screen* 13 (autumn): 6–18.

Nadel, Ira B. 1996. *Various Positions: A Life of Leonard Cohen.* New York: Pantheon.

Nochimson, Martha P. 1997. *The Passion of David Lynch: Wild at Heart in Hollywood.* Austin: University of Texas Press.

O'Connor, John J. 1988. "Orbison Is Still Around and Rocking." *New York Times*, March 8, C18.

O'Donnell, Red. 1966. Liner notes for the MGM LP *The Orbison Way.*

Orbison, Roy. 1965. Liner Notes for the MGM LP *There Is Only One Roy Orbison.*

Pareles, Jon, ed. 1983. *The Rolling Stone Encyclopedia of Rock & Roll.* New York: Simon & Schuster.

Patterson, Troy, and Jeff Jenson. 2000. "Our Town." *Entertainment Weekly, Our First Decade: A Special Collector's Issue* (spring): 92–102.

People. 1987. "The Boss Is Just One of the Guys as an All-Star Band Salutes Rock 'n' Roll Great Roy Orbison." Oct. 19, 44–45.

———. 1988. "The Haunted Life of Rock Legend Roy Orbison, 1936–1988." Dec. 19, cover.

Perkins, Carl, and David McGee. 1996. *Go, Cat, Go!: The Life and Times of Carl Perkins.* New York: Hyperion.

Perry, Mick. 1995. Booklet for the Rollercoaster Records CD *Are You Ready?*

Pruter, Robert. 1994. Booklet for the Rhino CD *The Very Best of Jackie Wilson.*

Rees, Dafydd, and Luke Crampton. 1996. *Encyclopedia of Rock Stars.* New York: DK Publishing.

Rodgers, Larry. 2000. "Boss' Tour Ends on a Glorious Note." *Arizona Republic*, July 9, E3.

Rodley, Chris. *Lynch on Lynch.* Boston: Faber and Faber.

Roy Orbison: In Dreams. 1999. White Star Video.

Roy Orbison International Fan Club Newsletter. 2000. "Virgil Johnson of the Velvets: An Exclusive Interview." June, 3–6.

Roy Orbison: The Anthology. 1999. White Star DVD.

Sacher-Masoch, Leopold von. 1989 [1870]. *Venus in Furs.* New York: Zone Books.

Salem, James. 1999. *The Late Great Johnny Ace and the Transition from R&B to Rock 'n' Roll.* Urbana: University of Illinois Press.

Shaw, Arnold. 1988. *The Rockin' 50s: The Decade That Transformed the Pop Music Scene.* New York: DeCapo.

Silverman, Kaja. 1992. *Male Subjectivity at the Margins.* New York: Routledge.

Smith, Jacob. 2000. "Rough Mix." Paper presented at the International Association for the Study of Popular Music Conference, Toronto, Nov. 3.

Soocher, Stan. 1993. "Supreme Justice: Rap's Day in Court." *Rolling Stone,* Nov. 11, 13.

Springsteen, Bruce. 1987. Reprinted in the liner notes to *Roy Orbison, In Dreams: The Greatest Hits.* Virgin.

Studlar, Gaylyn. 1984. "Masochism and the Perverse Pleasures of the Cinema." *Quarterly Review of Film Studies* (fall): 267–82.

———. 1988. *In the Realm of Pleasure: Von Sternberg, Dietrich, and the Masochist Aesthetic.* Urbana: University of Illinois Press.

Tichi, Cecilia. 1994. *High Lonesome: The American Culture of Country Music.* Chapel Hill: University of North Carolina.

Tucson Citizen. 1988. "Voice of an Angel: Rock 'n' Rollers Recall Roy Orbison." Dec. 8, 1C.

U.S. Court of Appeals, Sixth Circuit. 1992. *972 Federal Reporter,* 2d Series: 1429–46.

U.S. District Court, M.D. Tennessee. 1991. *754 Federal Supplement:* 1150–60.

U.S. Supreme Court. 1993. *114 Supreme Court Reporter,* Interim Edition: 1164–82.

Very Best of Roy Orbison. 1996. Liner Notes. Virgin Records America.

VH1: A Tribute to Roy Orbison. 1988.

Ward, Ed, Geoffrey Stokes, and Ken Tucker. 1986. *Rock of Ages: The Rolling Stone History of Rock & Roll.* New York: Rolling Stone Press/Summit Books.

Watrous, Peter. 1988. "Roy Orbison Mines Some Gold." *New York Times,* July 30, 48.

Whitburn, Joel. 2000. *Joel Whitburn Presents Top R&B Singles, 1942–1999.* Milwaukee: Hal Leonard.

Wolff, Daniel. 1999. "Elvis in the Dark, Review of *Careless Love: The Unmaking of Elvis Presley.*" *ThreePenny Review* (fall 1999). Accessed at <www.threepennyreview.com/samples/wolff_f99.html> (Nov. 7, 2000).

Wong, Fan, and Tom Sinclair. 1998. "Orbison's Last Dream." *Entertainment Weekly,* Dec. 4, 120.

Wood, Robin. 1981. *Howard Hawks.* London: British Film Institute.

———. 1986. *Hollywood from Vietnam to Reagan.* New York: Columbia University Press.

———. 1989. *Hitchcock's Films Revisited.* New York: Columbia University Press.

Zimmerman, David. 1988. "His Voice Haunted a Generation." *USA Today,* Dec. 8, 1D–2D.

Song Acknowledgments

All I Need Is Time: B. Reneau © Chess Music, Inc.

A Love So Beautiful: Jeff Lynne–Roy Orbison © SONY/ATV Acuff-Rose Music, Inc.

Bad Cat: Roy Orbison–Joe Melson © SONY/ATV Acuff-Rose Music, Inc. / Barbara Orbison Music Company / Roy Orbison Music Company

Best Friend: Roy Orbison–Bill Dees © 1967 SONY/ATV Acuff-Rose Music, Inc. / Orbi-Lee Music / R-Key Darkus Music / Barbara Orbison Music Company

Blue Angel: Roy Orbison–Joe Melson © 1960 (renewed 1988) Roy Orbison Music Company / Barbara Orbison Music Company / SONY/ATV Acuff-Rose Music, Inc.

Blue Bayou: Roy Orbison–Joe Melson © 1961 (renewed 1989) Barbara Orbison Music Company / Orbi-Lee Music /R-Key Darkus Music / SONY/ATV Acuff-Rose Music, Inc.

Careless Heart: Roy Orbison–Diane Warren–Albert Hammond © 1989 Realsongs / Albert Hammond Music / Warner Bros. Music Corp. / Orbisongs / SONY/ATV Acuff-Rose Music, Inc.

Come Back to Me (My Love): Roy Orbison–Joe Melson © 1960 (renewed 1989) SONY/ATV Acuff-Rose Music, Inc. / Roy Orbison Music Company / Barbara Orbison Music Company

Comedians: Elvis Costello © 1984 (renewed 1989) Plangent Visions Music, Ltd.

Comin' Home: Roy Orbison–Will Jennings–J. D. Souther, Orbisongs / Blue Sky Rider Songs, Irving Music

Crawling Back: Roy Orbison–Bill Dees © 1966 (renewed 1994) Barbara Orbison Music Company / Orbi-Lee Music / R-Key Darkus / SONY/ATV Acuff-Rose Music, Inc.

Cry Softly Lonely One: Joe Melson–Don Gant © SONY/ATV Acuff-Rose Music, Inc. / Just Good Music

Darkness: Gene Pitney © Super Songs Unlimited / Unichappell Music Inc.

Defeated: Roy Orbison © Barbara Orbison Music Company / Roy Orbison Music Company

Dream Baby: Cindy Walker © 1962 (renewed 1990) TEMI Combine Inc. (administered EMI Blackwood Music Inc.)

Harlem Woman: Roy Orbison–Joe Melson © 1972 (renewed 2000) SONY/ATV Acuff-Rose Music, Inc. / Orbi-Lee Music / R-Key Darkus Music / Barbara Orbison Music Company

Heartache: Roy Orbison–Bill Dees © 1968 (renewed 1997) Acuff Rose Music, Inc. / Orbi-Lee Music / R-Key Darkus Music / Barbara Orbison Music Company

How Are Things In Paradise?: Roy Orbison–Joe Melson © 1965 (renewed 1994) SONY/ATV Acuff-Rose Music, Inc. / Orbi-Lee Music / R-Key Darkus / Barbara Orbison Music Company

I Can't Stop Loving You: Don Gibson © SONY/ATV Acuff-Rose Music, Inc.

I Drove All Night: Billy Steinberg–Tom Kelly © 1989 Billy Steinberg Music / Sony Tunes, Inc.

I'll Say It's My fault: Roy Orbison–Fred Foster © SONY/ATV Acuff-Rose Music, Inc. / Barbara Orbison Music Company / Roy Orbison Music Company

I'm Hurtin': Roy Orbison–Joe Melson © SONY/ATV Acuff-Rose Music, Inc. / Barbara Orbison Music Company / Roy Orbison Music Company

I'm in a Blue, Blue Mood: Roy Orbison–Joe Melson © 1961 Roy Orbison Music Company / Barbara Orbison Music Company / SONY/ATV Acuff-Rose Publications

Indian Summer: Larry Gatlin–Barry Gibb © Gibb Brothers Music and Songs of Universal, Inc.

In Dreams: Roy Orbison © 1963 (renewed 1991) Barbara Orbison Music Company / Orbi-Lee Music / R-Key Darkus Music / SONY/ATV Acuff-Rose Music, Inc.

In the Real World: Will Jennings–Richard Kerr © Blue Sky Rider Songs / Careers BMG Music Publishing / Irving Music

Last Night: Roy Orbison–Bob Dylan–George Harrison–Jeff Lynne–Tom Petty © 1988 Gone Gator Music /Jane Ann Music

Leah: Roy Orbison © 1962 (renewed 1990) Barbara Orbison Music Company / Orbi-Lee Music / R-Key Darkus Music / SONY/ATV Acuff-Rose Music, Inc.

Life Fades Away: Glenn Danzing–Roy Orbison © SONY/ATV Acuff-Rose Music, Inc.

Love in Time: Roy Orbison–Will Jennings © Blue Sky Rider Songs / Irving Music

Mama: Roy Orbison–Joe Melson–Ray Rush © 1962 (renewed 1991) SONY/ATV Acuff-Rose Music, Inc. / Orbi-Lee Music / R-Key Darkus Music / Barbara Orbison Music Company

Mean Woman Blues: Claude DeMetruis © 1957 Gladys Music, Inc. (BMI), Copyright renewed and assigned to Gladys Music (administered by Williamson Music)

Mother: R. C. Price © Hott Bobb Music

Nightlife: Roy Orbison–Joe Melson © 1961 SONY/ATV Acuff-Rose Music, Inc.

Oh, Pretty Woman: Roy Orbison–Bill Dees © 1964 (renewed 1992) Barbara Orbison Music Company / Orbi-Lee Music / R-Key Darkus Music / SONY/ATV Acuff-Rose Music, Inc.

Only the Lonely: Roy Orbison–Joe Melson © 1960 (renewed 1988) Roy Orbison
Music Company / Barbara Orbison Music Company / SONY/ATV Acuff-Rose
Music, Inc.

Pantomime: Roy Orbison–Bill Dees © SONY/ATV Acuff-Rose Music, Inc. /
Orbi-lee Publishing / R-Key Darkus Publishing

Penny Arcade: Sammy King © 1969 USA/Canada: Milene Music, Inc. (ASCAP) /
Elsewhere: SONY/ATV Acuff-Rose Music, Ltd. (ASCAP)

Ride Away: Roy Orbison–Bill Dees © 1965 (renewed 1994) Barbara Orbison
Music Company / Orbi-Lee Music / R-Key Darkus Music / SONY/ATV
Acuff-Rose Music, Inc.

Running Scared: Roy Orbison–Joe Melson © 1961 (renewed 1980) Barbara
Orbison Music Company / Orbi-Lee Music / R-Key Darkus Music /
SONY/ATV Acuff-Rose Music, Inc.

(Say) You're My Girl: Roy Orbison–Bill Dees © 1965 (renewed 1994) Barbara
Orbison Music Company / Orbi-Lee Music / R-Key Darkus Music /
SONY/ATV Acuff-Rose Music, Inc.

She's A Mystery to Me: David Evans (The Edge)–Paul Huson (Bono) © U2 /
Chappell

So Young: Roy Orbison–Mike Curb–Roger Christian © 1970 (renewed 1999)
Hastings Music / SONY/ATV Acuff-Rose Music, Inc. / Orbi-Lee Music /
R-Key Darkus Music / Barbara Orbison Music Company

Sweet Mama Blue: Roy Orbison–Joe Melson © 1974 SONY/ATV Acuff-Rose
Music, Inc. / Roy Orbison Music Company / Barbara Orbison Music
Company

The Actress: Roy Orbison–Joe Melson © 1962 (renewed 1990) Barbara Orbison
Music Company / Orbi-Lee Music / R-Key Darkus Music / SONY/ATV
Acuff-Rose Music, Inc.

The Defector: Roy Orbison–Bill Dees–Angie Morrow © 1969 (renewed 1998)
SONY/ATV Acuff-Rose Music, Inc. / Orbi-Lee Music / R-Key Darkus Music /
Barbara Orbison Music Company

The Loner: Bill Dees–John Atkins © SONY/ATV Acuff-Rose Music, Inc.

(They Call You) Gigolette: Roy Orbison–Joe Melson © 1962 (renewed 1991)
SONY/ATV Acuff-Rose Music, Inc. /Orbi-Lee Music / R-Key Darkus Music /
Barbara Orbison Music Company

Time Changed Everything: John Adkins–Buie Perry © EMI / Unart / Catalogue Inc.

Too Soon to Know: Don Gibson © 1957 SONY/ATV Acuff-Rose Music, Inc.

Twinkle Toes: Roy Orbison–Bill Dees © 1965 (renewed 1994) Barbara Orbison
Music Company / Orbi-Lee Music / R-Key Darkus Music / SONY/ATV
Acuff-Rose Music, Inc.

Uptown: Roy Orbison–Joe Melson © 1959 (renewed 1987) Roy Orbison Music
Company / Barbara Orbison Music Company / SONY/ATV Acuff-Rose
Music, Inc.

Wait: Roy Orbison/Bill Dees © 1965 (renewed 1994) SONY/ATV Acuff-Rose
Music, Inc. / Orbi-Lee Music / R-Key Darkus Music / Barbara Orbison Music
Company

Index

Titles of albums, films, television programs, books, and magazines are shown in *italic* type; song titles are placed within quotation marks. Page numbers for photographs are shown in **bold**.